McGraw-Hill Education

MCAT

BIOLOGICAL AND BIOCHEMICAL
FOUNDATIONS OF LIVING SYSTEMS

2015

McGraw-Hill Education
MCAT
Test Preparation Series

- Biomolecules
- Molecules, Cells, and Organs
- Systems of Tissues and Organs

- Physical Foundations of Biological Systems
- Chemical Foundations of Biological Systems

- Perception and Response
- Behavior
- Self and Others
- Social Structure
- Social Strata
- Critical Analysis and Reasoning Skills

- Practice Test 1
  - Answers and Explanations
- Practice Test 2
  - Answers and Explanations

McGraw-Hill Education

MCAT

BIOLOGICAL AND BIOCHEMICAL FOUNDATIONS OF LIVING SYSTEMS

2015

George J. Hademenos, PhD

Candice McCloskey Campbell, PhD

Shaun Murphree, PhD

Amy B. Wachholtz, PhD

Jennifer M. Warner, PhD

Kathy A. Zahler, MS

Thomas A. Evangelist, MA   Contributor

Mc
Graw
Hill
Education

New York   Chicago   San Francisco   Athens   London   Madrid
Mexico City   Milan   New Delhi   Singapore   Sydney   Toronto

1 2 3 4 5 6 7 8 9 10 RHR/RHR 1 0 9 8 7 6 5 4

ISBN   978-0-07-182203-9
MHID   0-07-182203-8

e-ISBN   978-0-07-182160-5
e-MHID   0-07-182160-0

Library of Congress Control Number 2014947589

MCAT is a registered trademark of the Association of American Medical Colleges, which was not involved in the production of, and does not endorse, this product.

McGraw-Hill Education products are available at special quantity discounts to use as premiums and sales promotions or for use in corporate training programs. To contact a representative, please visit the Contact Us pages at www.mhprofessional.com.

This book is printed on acid-free paper.

Contents

MCAT Basics | The Computerized Test Format | Where and When to Take the MCAT | How to Register for the MCAT | Taking the MCAT More Than Once | Your MCAT Scores | How Medical Schools Use MCAT Scores | Reporting Scores to Medical Schools | For Further Information | The Format of the Test | What Is Tested in the Science Sections | What Is Tested in Critical Analysis | General Test-Taking Strategies

Unit I   Biomolecules

Amino Acids | Protein Structure | Functions of Proteins | Enzyme Structure and Function | Enzyme Kinetics

Nucleic Acid Structure and Function | DNA Replication | Mutations and DNA Repair | The Central Dogma | Ribonucleic Acid | Transcription | Translation | Chromosome Organization | Control of Gene Expression | Recombinant DNA and Biotechnology

DNA Is the Genetic Material | Basic Mendelian Concepts | Predicting Genotypes | Exceptions to Mendel's Laws | Pedigree Analysis | Environmental Influences on Genes and Epigenetics | Genetic Variability

About the Authors

George J. Hademenos, PhD, is a former Visiting Assistant Professor of Physics at the University of Dallas. He received his BS from Angelo State University, received his MS and PhD from the University of Texas at Dallas, and completed postdoctoral fellowships in nuclear medicine at the University of Massachusetts Medical Center and in radiological sciences/biomedical physics at UCLA Medical Center. His research interests have involved potential applications of physics to the biological and medical sciences, particularly with cerebrovascular diseases and stroke. He has published his work in journals such as *American Scientist, Physics Today, Neurosurgery,* and *Stroke.* In addition, he has written several books including *The Physics of Cerebrovascular Diseases: Biophysical Mechanisms of Development, Diagnosis and Therapy,* and *Schaum's Outline of Biology.* He currently teaches general and advanced physics courses.

Candice McCloskey Campbell, PhD, received her doctorate in organic chemistry from Georgia Tech in 1985. She has been teaching at the undergraduate level since 1987. She currently teaches at Georgia Perimeter College in Dunwoody, Georgia. Her professional work has been in synthetic organic chemistry and mechanistic organic chemistry. She has been active with the Two-Year College Chemistry Consortium to enhance the chemistry curriculum at the two-year college level.

Shaun Murphree, PhD, is Professor and Chair of Chemistry at Allegheny College in Meadville, Pennsylvania. He received a BA in chemistry from Colgate University (Hamilton, New York) and a PhD in organic chemistry from Emory University (Atlanta, Georgia), and he conducted a postdoctoral study at Wesleyan University (Middletown, Connecticut). His current research interests include microwave-assisted organic synthesis (MAOS), synthetic methodology, and heterocyclic synthesis. In addition to the present work, he has coauthored a monograph on microwave chemistry, several chapters and reviews on heterocyclic synthesis, and numerous articles in both the synthetic chemistry and chemistry education literature.

Amy B. Wachholtz, PhD, MDiv, MS, is an Assistant Professor of Psychiatry at the University of Massachusetts Medical School and the Director of Health Psychology at UMass Memorial Medical Center. Dr. Wachholtz graduated with a Master of Divinity degree from Boston University, where she specialized in Bioethics. She then continued her education to earn a Master's and PhD in Clinical Psychology from Bowling Green State University where she had a dual specialization in Behavioral Medicine and Psychology of Religion. She completed an internship through a fellowship at Duke University Medical Center, where she focused on medical psychology. She has also completed a postdoctoral Master's of Science degree in Psychopharmacology. Dr. Wachholtz has multiple funded research projects with her primary focus on (1) bio-psycho-social-spiritual model of chronic pain disorders and (2) the complexities of treating of comorbid pain and opioid addiction in both acute pain and chronic pain situations. She enjoys teaching students from a variety of health disciplines, both in the classroom and on the clinical floors of UMass Memorial Medical Center Hospitals.

Jennifer M. Warner, PhD, is the Director of the University Honors Program and a member of the faculty in the Department of Biological Sciences at the University of North Carolina at Charlotte. She received her BS in Biology from the University of North Carolina at Chapel Hill, her MS in Biology with a focus in microbiology from the University of North Carolina at Charlotte, and her PhD in Curriculum and Teaching from the University of North Carolina at Greensboro. Her current research interests revolve around variables that influence student success and retention in the sciences. She currently teaches a variety of courses including principles of biology, human biology, the nature of science, and pathogenic bacteriology.

Kathy A. Zahler, MS, is a widely published author and textbook writer. She has authored or coauthored numerous McGraw-Hill Education preparation guides for tests, including the GRE®, the Miller Analogies Test, the Test of Essential Academic Skills (TEAS®), and the Test Assessing Secondary Completion™ (TASC™).

How to Use the McGraw-Hill Education MCAT Preparation Series

Welcome to the McGraw-Hill Education MCAT Preparation series. You've made the decision to pursue a medical career, you've studied hard, you've taken and passed the most difficult science courses, and now you must succeed on this very tough exam. We're here to help you.

This series has been created by a dedicated team of scientists, teachers, and test-prep experts. Together, they have helped thousands of students to score high on all kinds of exams, from rigorous science tests to difficult essay-writing assignments. They have pooled their knowledge, experience, and test-taking expertise to make this the most effective self-study MCAT preparation program available.

The four books in this series contain a wealth of features to help you do your best. The four volumes are organized as follows:

MCAT Biological and Biochemical Foundations of Living Systems provides:

➤ **A general introduction to the MCAT,** including basic facts about the structure and format of the test and the kinds of questions you will encounter.

➤ **Important test-taking strategies** that can help you raise your score.

➤ **An in-depth review of all the topics tested in Part 1 of the exam: Biological and Biochemical Foundations of Living Systems.** This is the exam section that assesses your knowledge of foundational concepts in biology and biochemistry, and your understanding of how biological processes function both separately and together in living systems, including the human body.

➤ **Minitests modeled on Part 1 of the exam.** These practice exams are designed to simulate the actual MCAT in format and degree of difficulty. The questions ask you to use your scientific research and reasoning skills to solve problems demonstrating your mastery of the skills required for success in medical school.

MCAT Chemical and Physical Foundations of Biological Systems provides:

➤ **A general introduction to the MCAT,** including basic facts about the structure and format of the test and the kinds of questions you will encounter.

➤ **Important test-taking strategies** that can help you raise your score.

➤ **An in-depth review of all the topics tested in Part 2 of the exam: Chemical and Physical Foundations of Biological Systems.** This is the exam section that assesses your knowledge of foundational concepts in organic chemistry and physics, and your understanding of how chemical and physical processes function both separately and together in living systems, including the human body.

➤ **Minitests modeled on Part 2 of the exam.** These practice exams are designed to simulate the actual MCAT in format and degree of difficulty. The questions ask you to use your scientific research and reasoning skills to solve problems demonstrating your mastery of the skills required for success in medical school.

MCAT Behavioral and Social Sciences & Critical Analysis provides:

➤ **A general introduction to the MCAT,** including basic facts about the structure and format of the test and the kinds of questions you will encounter.

➤ **An in-depth review of all the topics tested in Parts 3 and 4 of the exam: Psychological, Social, and Biological Foundations of Behavior and Critical Analysis and Reasoning Skills.** Part 3 of the exam tests your knowledge of basic concepts in psychology and sociology that are important to understanding how behavioral and sociocultural factors affect health outcomes and the provision of healthcare. Part 4 of the exam tests your ability to analyze, evaluate, and apply information from reading passages in a wide range of social sciences and humanities areas.

➤ **Minitests modeled on Parts 3 and 4 of the exam.** These practice exams are designed to simulate the actual MCAT in format and degree of difficulty. The questions ask you to use your scientific research and reasoning skills to solve problems that demonstrate your mastery of the skills required for success in medical school.

MCAT 2 Full-Length Practice Tests provides:

➤ **A general introduction to the MCAT,** including basic facts about the structure and format of the test and the kinds of questions you will encounter.

➤ **Important test-taking strategies** that can help you raise your score.

➤ **Two full-length practice MCAT tests** designed to simulate the real exam in structure, format, and degree of difficulty. Of course, these practice tests can provide only an approximation of how well you will do on the actual MCAT. However, if you approach them as you would the real test, they should give you a very good idea of how well you are prepared.

➤ **Explanations for every question.** After you take each test, read carefully through these explanations, paying special attention to those you answered incorrectly or had to guess on. If necessary, go back and reread the corresponding subject review sections in the earlier volumes.

Different people have different ways of preparing for a test like the MCAT. You must find a preparation method that suits your schedule and your learning style. We have tried to make this series flexible enough for you to use in a way that works best for you, but to succeed on this extremely rigorous exam, there is no substitute for serious, intensive review and study. The more time and effort you devote to preparing, the better your chances of achieving your MCAT goals.

Introducing the MCAT

MCAT BASICS

The Medical College Admission Test (MCAT) is a standardized exam that is used to assess applicants to medical schools. The test is sponsored by the Association of American Medical Colleges (AAMC) in cooperation with its member schools. It is required as part of the admissions process by most US medical schools. The test is administered by Prometric, a private firm that is a leading provider of technology-based testing and assessment services.

The questions on the MCAT are basically designed to measure your problem-solving and critical-thinking skills. Two test sections assess your mastery of fundamental concepts in biology, biochemistry, general chemistry, organic chemistry, and physics. A third section tests your understanding of concepts in psychology, sociology, and biology that are important to understanding how behavioral and sociocultural factors affect health outcomes and the provision of health care. For most questions in these sections, choosing the correct answer requires more than just a rote response; you must calculate a solution, interpret and evaluate given data, or apply a particular scientific principle to a given situation. You will need to demonstrate that you can reason scientifically and employ the principles of research methodology and statistics. There is also a fourth section that tests your ability to analyze, evaluate, and apply information from reading passages on topics in ethics, philosophy, cross-cultural studies, and population health.

According to the AAMC, the skills tested on the MCAT are those identified by medical professionals and educators as essential for success in medical school and in a career as a physician. The importance of the biological, biochemical, and physical sciences is self-evident. Psychological and sociological concepts are included, according to the AAMC, because "knowledge of the behavioral and social determinants of health and wellness [is] becoming more important in medical education," and "tomorrow's doctors need to know [these concepts] in order to serve a more diverse population and to understand the impact of behavior on health and wellness."

THE COMPUTERIZED TEST FORMAT

You will take the MCAT on a computer. You will view the questions on the computer screen and indicate your answers by clicking on on-screen answer ovals. As you work through the on-screen questions, you will be able to highlight relevant portions of the reading passages for easy reference. You will also be able to strike out answer choices that you know are incorrect. This will help you use the process of elimination to pick the correct answer. You will also be allowed to make notes on scratch paper (although all of your notes will be collected at the end of the test). Within each test section, you will be able to go back, review questions that you have already answered, and change your answer if you decide to do so. However, once you have finished a test section, you cannot go back to it and make any changes.

Don't be concerned if you are not a whiz with computers; the skills required are minimal, and in any case, on test day you will have the opportunity to access a computer tutorial that will show you exactly what you need to do.

WHERE AND WHEN TO TAKE THE MCAT

The MCAT is offered at approximately 275 sites in the United States (including the US territories of Puerto Rico and the Virgin Islands) and at 12 sites in Canada. All of these sites are testing labs operated by Prometric. The test is also offered at numerous locations outside North America, including sites in Europe, Great Britain, the Middle East, Africa, Asia, and Australia.

There are 22 test dates every year. Two of the dates are in January, and the rest are in the period from April through early September. Most test dates are weekdays, but a few are Saturdays. On some dates, the test is given only in the morning; on others, it is given only in the afternoon. On a few dates, the test is given in both morning and afternoon sessions.

It is a good idea to take the MCAT in the spring or summer of the year before the fall in which you plan to enroll in medical school. That way, you have enough time to submit your scores to meet the schools' application deadlines.

For up-to-date lists of testing sites and also for upcoming test dates, make sure to check the official MCAT website at www.aamc.org/mcat.

HOW TO REGISTER FOR THE MCAT

You can register for the MCAT online at www.aamc.org/mcat. Online registration for each test date begins six months prior to that date. Registration is available until two weeks before the test date. It's a good idea to register early, because seating at the testing centers may be limited and you want to make sure you get a seat at the center of your choice. When you register, you are charged a fee, which you can pay by credit card. If you wish to change your test date, you can do so online.

TAKING THE MCAT MORE THAN ONCE

If your MCAT score is lower than expected, you may want to take the test again. You can take the MCAT up to three times in the same year. However, the AAMC recommends retesting only if you have a good reason to think that you will do better the next time. For example, you might do better if, when you first took the test, you were ill, or you made mistakes in keying in your answers, or your academic background in one or more of the test subjects was inadequate.

If you are considering retesting, you should also find out how your chosen medical schools evaluate multiple scores. Some schools give equal weight to all MCAT scores; others average scores together, and still others look only at the highest scores. Check with admissions officers before making a decision.

YOUR MCAT SCORES

When you take the MCAT, your work on each of the four test sections first receives a "raw score." The raw score is calculated based on the number of questions you answer correctly. No points are deducted for questions answered incorrectly. Each raw score is then converted into a scaled score. Using scaled scores helps make test-takers' scores comparable from one version of the MCAT to another. For each of the four sections, scaled scores range from 1 (lowest) to 15 (highest).

Your score report will be mailed to you approximately 30 days after you take the MCAT. You will also be able to view your scores on the online MCAT Testing History (THx) System as soon as they become available. (For details on the THx system, see the MCAT website.) MCAT score reports also include percentile rankings that show how well you did in comparison to others who took the same test.

HOW MEDICAL SCHOOLS USE MCAT SCORES

Medical college admission committees emphasize that MCAT scores are only one of several criteria that they consider when evaluating applicants. When making their decisions, they also consider students' college and university grades, recommendations, interviews, and involvement and participation in extracurricular or health care–related activities that, in the opinion of the admission committee, illustrate maturity, motivation, dedication, and other positive personality traits that are of value to a physician. If the committee is unfamiliar with the college you attend, they may pay more attention than usual to your MCAT scores.

There is no hard-and-fast rule about what schools consider to be an acceptable MCAT score. A few schools accept a score as low as 4, but many require scores of 10 or higher. To get into a top-ranked school, you generally need scores of 12 or higher. A high score on the Writing Sample may compensate for any weaknesses in communication skills noted on the application or at an interview.

Note that many medical schools do not accept MCAT scores that are more than three years old.

REPORTING SCORES TO MEDICAL SCHOOLS

Your MCAT scores are automatically reported to the American Medical College Application Service (AMCAS), the nonprofit application processing service used by nearly all U.S. medical schools. When you use this service, you complete and submit a single application, rather than separate applications to each of your chosen schools. Your scores are submitted to your designated schools along with your application. There is a fee for using AMCAS. If you wish to submit your scores to other application services or to programs that do not participate in AMCAS, you can do so through the online MCAT Testing History (THx) System.

FOR FURTHER INFORMATION

For further information about the MCAT, visit the official MCAT website at
www.aamc.org/mcat

For questions about registering for the test, reporting and interpreting scores, and similar issues, you may also contact:

Association of American Medical Colleges
Medical College Admission Test
655 K Street, NW, Suite 100
Washington, DC 20001-2399

THE FORMAT OF THE TEST

The MCAT consists of four separately timed sections as outlined in the following chart.

MCAT: Format of the Test		
Section	Number of Questions	Time Allowed (minutes)
1. Biological and Biochemical Foundations of Living Systems *Break: 10 minutes*	65	95
2. Chemical and Physical Foundations of Biological Systems *Break: 10 minutes*	65	95
3. Psychological, Social, and Biological Foundations of Behavior *Break: 10 minutes*	65	95
4. Critical Analysis and Reasoning Skills	60	90
Totals	255	375 (= 6 hours, 15 minutes)

WHAT IS TESTED IN THE SCIENCE SECTIONS

The natural sciences sections of the MCAT (sections 1 and 2) test your mastery of the concepts and principles of biology, biochemistry, general chemistry, organic chemistry, and physics as they apply to living systems, including the human body.

The behavioral and social sciences section of the MCAT (section 3) tests your understanding of the behavioral and sociocultural factors that play a role in health care.

These three sections have three main organizing principles:

1. **Foundational concepts:** what the AAMC calls the "big ideas" in the sciences that underlie the subjects taught in medical school
2. **Content categories:** the topics that support the foundational concepts
3. **Scientific inquiry and reasoning skills:** the skills needed to solve scientific problems

Foundational Concepts and Content Categories

According to the AAMS, the foundational concepts and categories for sections 1, 2, and 3 of the MCAT are as follows:

1. BIOLOGICAL AND BIOCHEMICAL FOUNDATIONS OF LIVING SYSTEMS

Foundational Concept 1: *Biomolecules have unique properties that determine how they contribute to the structure and function of cells and how they participate in the processes necessary to maintain life.*

Content categories:

➤ Structure and function of proteins and their constituent amino acids

➤ Transmission of genetic information from the gene to the protein

➤ Transmission of heritable information from generation to generation and the processes that increase genetic diversity

➤ Principles of bioenergetics and fuel molecule metabolism

Foundational Concept 2: *Highly organized assemblies of molecules, cells, and organs interact to carry out the functions of living organisms.*

Content categories:

➤ Assemblies of molecules, cells, and groups of cells within single cellular and multicellular organisms

➤ Structure, growth, physiology, and genetics of prokaryotes and viruses

➤ Processes of cell division, differentiation, and specialization

Foundational Concept 3: *Complex systems of tissues and organs sense the internal and external environments of multicellular organisms and, through integrated functioning, maintain a stable internal environment within an ever-changing external environment.*

Content categories:

➤ Structure and functions of the nervous and endocrine systems and ways in which these systems coordinate the organ systems

➤ Structure and integrative functions of the main organ systems

2. CHEMICAL AND PHYSICAL FOUNDATIONS OF BIOLOGICAL SYSTEMS

Foundational Concept 4: *Complex living organisms transport materials, sense their environment, process signals, and respond to changes using processes that can be understood in terms of physical principles.*

Content categories:

➤ Translational motion, forces, work, energy, and equilibrium in living systems

➤ Importance of fluids for the circulation of blood, gas movement, and gas exchange

➤ Electrochemistry and electrical circuits and their elements

➤ How light and sound interact with matter

➤ Atoms, nuclear decay, electronic structure, and atomic chemical behavior

Foundational Concept 5: *The principles that govern chemical interactions and reactions form the basis for a broader understanding of the molecular dynamics of living systems.*

Content categories:

➤ Unique nature of water and its solutions

➤ Nature of molecules and intermolecular interactions

➤ Separation and purification methods

➤ Structure, function, and reactivity of biologically relevant molecules

➤ Principles of chemical thermodynamics and kinetics

3. PSYCHOLOGICAL, SOCIAL, AND BIOLOGICAL FOUNDATIONS OF BEHAVIOR

Foundational Concept 6: *Biological, psychological, and sociocultural factors influence the ways that individuals perceive, think about, and react to the world.*

Content categories:

➤ Sensing the environment

➤ Making sense of the environment

➤ Responding to the world

Foundational Concept 7: *Biological, psychological, and sociocultural factors influence behavior and behavior change.*

Content categories:

➤ Individual influences on behavior

➤ Social processes that influence human behavior

➤ Attitude and behavior change

Foundational Concept 8: *Psychological, sociocultural, and biological factors influence the way we think about ourselves and others, as well as how we interact with others.*

Content categories:

➤ Self-identity

➤ Social thinking

➤ Social interactions

Foundational Concept 9: *Cultural and social differences influence well-being.*

Content categories:

➤ Understanding social structure

➤ Demographic characteristics and processes

Foundational Concept 10: *Social stratification and access to resources influence well-being.*

Content category:

➤ Social inequality

Scientific Inquiry and Reasoning Skills

The scientific inquiry and reasoning skills that are tested on Sections 1, 2, and 3 of the MCAT are as follows:

➤ **Skill 1:** Knowledge of Scientific Concepts and Principles
➤ **Skill 2:** Scientific Reasoning and Evidence-Based Problem Solving
➤ **Skill 3:** Reasoning About the Design and Execution of Research
➤ **Skill 4:** Data-Based and Statistical Reasoning

To demonstrate mastery of **Skill 1: Knowledge of Scientific Concepts and Principles,** you need to be able to recall and apply basic scientific concepts and principles to solve problems in science. In many cases, you will need to analyze and interpret information presented in diagrams, charts, graphs, and formulas.

To demonstrate mastery of **Skill 2: Scientific Reasoning and Evidence-Based Problem Solving,** you need to be able to understand and use scientific theories, to propose hypotheses, and to analyze scientific models or research studies in order to identify assumptions, make predictions, and draw conclusions.

To demonstrate mastery of **Skill 3: Reasoning About the Design and Execution of Research,** you need to be able to identify appropriate research designs for investigating specified research questions, to critique and evaluate those designs, to predict results, and to recognize ethical issues involved in research.

To demonstrate mastery of **Skill 4: Data-Based and Statistical Reasoning,** you need to be able to interpret data or to describe or evaluate the results of a research study using statistical concepts.

WHAT IS TESTED IN CRITICAL ANALYSIS

The Critical Analysis and Reasoning Skills section of the MCAT (Section 4) tests your ability to comprehend information in a reading passage, to analyze and evaluate arguments and supporting evidence, and to apply concepts and ideas to new situations. The passages in this section cover a wide range of topics in both the social sciences and the humanities. You may encounter readings in philosophy, ethics, cultural studies, and similar topics. All the information you need to answer the questions will be provided in the passage; no outside knowledge of the topics is required.

According to the AAMC, the questions in the Critical Analysis and Reasoning Skills section test the following four specific skills:

➤ **Comprehension:** the ability to understand new information or to view facts or ideas in a new light

➤ **Evaluation:** the ability to analyze ideas or arguments presented in a passage and to make judgments about their reasonableness, their credibility, and the soundness of supporting evidence

➤ **Application:** the ability to apply information in a passage to new conditions or situations and to predict possible outcomes

➤ **Incorporation of information:** the ability to consider how new information affects the ideas presented in a passage; for example, whether it strengthens or weakens an argument or a hypothesis

GENERAL TEST-TAKING STRATEGIES

The following sections present some general test-taking strategies that apply to the multiple-choice questions on the MCAT. These strategies can help you to gain valuable points when you take the actual test.

Take Advantage of the Multiple-Choice Format

All of the questions on the MCAT are in the multiple-choice format, which you have undoubtedly seen many times before. That means that for every question, the correct answer is right in front of you. All you have to do is pick it out from among three incorrect choices, called "distracters." Consequently, you can use the process of elimination to rule out incorrect answer choices. The more answers you rule out, the easier it is to make the right choice.

Answer Every Question

Recall that on the MCAT, there is no penalty for choosing a wrong answer. Therefore, if you do not know the answer to a question, you have nothing to lose by guessing. So make sure that you answer every question. If time is running out and you still have not answered some questions, make sure to enter an answer for the questions that you have not attempted. With luck, you may be able to pick up a few extra points, even if your guesses are totally random.

Make Educated Guesses

What differentiates great test takers from merely good ones is the ability to guess in such a way as to maximize the chance of guessing correctly. The way to do this is to use the process of elimination. Before you guess, try to eliminate one or more of the answer choices. That way, you can make an educated guess, and you have a better chance of picking the correct answer. Odds of one out of two or one out of three are better than one out of four!

Go with Your Gut

In those cases where you're not 100% sure of the answer you are choosing, it is often best to go with your gut feeling and stick with your first answer. If you decide to change that answer and pick another one, you may well pick the wrong answer because you have over-thought the problem. More often than not, if you know something about the subject, your first answer is likely to be the correct one.

Take Advantage of Helpful Computer Functions

On the MCAT, you have access to certain computer functions that can make your work easier. As you work through the on-screen questions, you are able to highlight relevant portions of the reading passages. This helps you save time when you need to find facts or details to support your answer choices. You are also able to cross out answer choices that you know are incorrect. This helps you use the process of elimination to pick the correct answer.

Use the Scratch Paper Provided

The MCAT is an all-computerized test, so there is no test booklet for you to write in. However, you are given scratch paper, so use it to your advantage. Jot down notes, make calculations, and write out an outline for each of your essays. Be aware, however, that you cannot remove the scratch paper from the test site. All papers are collected from you before you leave the room.

Because you cannot write on the actual MCAT, don't get into the habit of writing notes to yourself on the test pages of this book. Use separate scratch paper instead. Consider it an opportunity to learn to use scratch paper effectively.

Keep Track of the Time

Make sure that you're on track to answer all of the questions within the time allowed. With so many questions to answer in a short time period, you're not going to have a lot of time to spare. Keep an eye on your watch or on the computerized timer provided.

Do not spend too much time on any one question. If you find yourself stuck for more than a minute or two on a question, then you should make your best guess and move on. If you have time left over at the end of the section, you can return to the question and review your answer. However, if time runs out, don't give the question another thought. You need to save your focus for the rest of the test.

Don't Panic if Time Runs Out

If you pace yourself and keep track of your progress, you should not run out of time. If you do, however, run out of time, don't panic. Because there is no guessing penalty and you have nothing to lose by doing so, enter answers to all the remaining questions. If you are able to make educated guesses, you will probably be able to improve your score. However, even random guesses may help you pick up a few points. In order to know how to handle this situation if it happens to you on the test, make sure you observe the time limits when you take the practice tests. Guessing well is a skill that comes with practice, so incorporate it into your preparation program.

If Time Permits, Review Questions You Were Unsure Of

Within each test section, the computer allows you to return to questions you have already answered and change your answer if you decide to do so. (However, once you have completed an entire section, you cannot go back to it and make changes.) If time permits, you may want to take advantage of this function to review questions you were unsure of or to check for careless mistakes.

UNIT I
Biomolecules

Foundational Concept: Biomolecules have unique properties that determine how they contribute to the structure and function of cells and how they participate in the processes necessary to maintain life.

Structure and Function of Proteins and Their Constituent Amino Acids

AMINO ACIDS

Proteins are constructed from an ensemble of 20 or so naturally occurring amino acids. In contrast with the saccharides, which possess only carbonyl and hydroxyl functionality, the amino acids boast a wide array of functional groups, as shown in the following table. The properties of each amino acid residue are governed by the characteristics of the side chain. Thus the various amino acids can be classified as polar, nonpolar, neutral, acidic, or basic, as shown in Figure 1-1. As monomers at physiological pH, all amino acids exist as ionized species, as shown in Figure 1-2. The carboxylic acid is entirely deprotonated, and the amino group is completely protonated—so even though the molecule is ionized, there is a net coulombic charge of zero. Such a species is known as a zwitterion.

The Naturally Occurring Amino Acids					
Name	Abbreviation 3-Letter	1-Letter	Side Chain Structure	Side Chain Functionality	Side Chain pK_a
glycine	Gly	G	‑H	none	
alanine	Ala	A	‑Me	alkane	
valine	Val	V		branched alkane	
leucine	Leu	L		branched alkane	
isoleucine	Ile	I		branched alkane	
phenylalanine	Phe	F	‑Ph	phenyl ring	
tryptophan	Trp	W		indole	
histidine	His	H		imidazole	6.1
tyrosine	Tyr	Y	‑OH	phenol	10.1
serine	Ser	S	‑OH	1° alcohol	
threonine	Thr	T	‑OH	2° alcohol	
methionine	Met	M	‑SMe	dialkyl sulfide	
cysteine	Cys	C	‑SH	mercaptan	8.2
asparagine	Asn	N		amide	
glutamine	Gln	Q		amide	
aspartic acid	Asp	D		carboxylic acid	3.7

5

CHAPTER 1:
Structure and
Function of Proteins
and Their
Constituent
Amino Acids

Name	Abbreviation 3-Letter	1-Letter	Side Chain Structure	Side Chain Functionality	Side Chain pK_a
glutamic acid	Glu	E		carboxylic acid	4.3
lysine	Lys	K		1° amine	10.5
arginine	Arg	R		guanidine	12.5
proline	Pro	P		none	

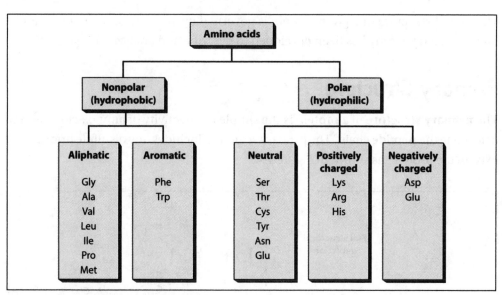

FIGURE 1-1 Classification of amino acids.

FIGURE 1-2 Zwitterionic nature of amino acids.

Nature takes advantage of these diverse amino acids, particularly in the realm of enzyme catalysis, by assembling them together into synergistic arrangements. In contrast to the polysaccharides, which are connected by acetal linkages, amino acids are bound together by a relatively robust amide linkage. Thus the primary structure of proteins can be described as a polyamide backbone embellished with functionalized side chains at regular intervals (Figure 1-3). While there is hindered rotation about the amide C—N bond, there is relatively free rotation about the C—C bonds in the backbone. Thus the polymer can adopt a variety of conformations, the energetics of which are determined by many complex factors, including intermolecular hydrogen bonding, hydrophobic interactions, and solvation effects.

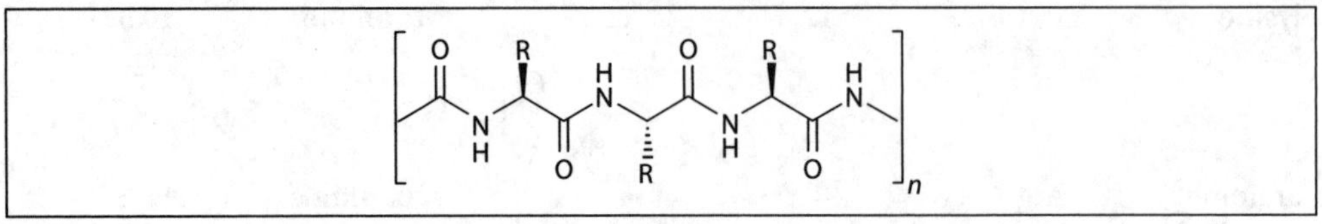

FIGURE 1-3 A polypeptide primary structure.

PROTEIN STRUCTURE

The overall structure of a given protein is governed by an array of parameters, and a hierarchical taxonomy has been developed to describe and analyze these factors.

Primary Structure

The **primary structure** of a protein is the simple connectivity of amino acid to amino acid along the peptide chain. The primary structure includes any disulfide bridges that exist in the protein, as shown in Figure 1-4.

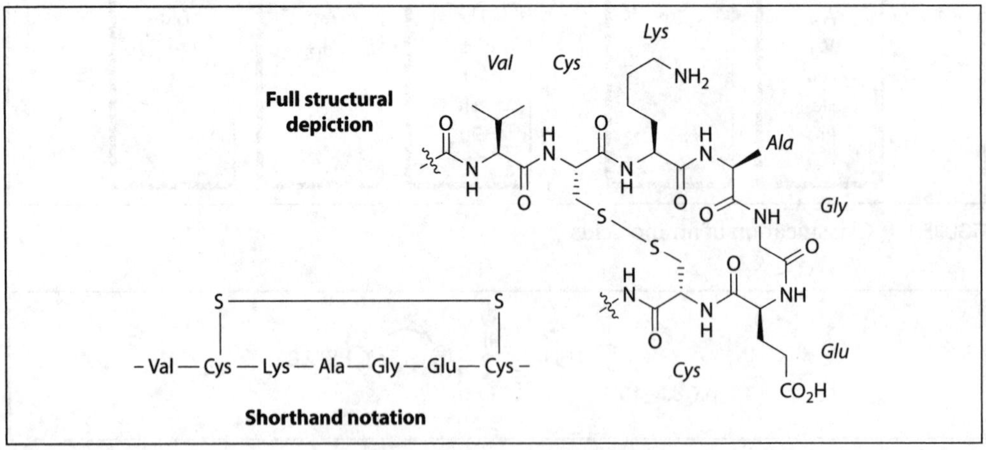

FIGURE 1-4 Primary structure of a peptide fragment, showing a disulfide bridge.

Secondary Structure

The polypeptide strands tend to form well-defined local motifs that constitute the **secondary structure** of proteins. Four of the more common patterns are shown in Figure 1-5. Two types of β-sheets are encountered—an antiparallel sheet, in which the two adjacent strands run in opposite directions, and a parallel sheet constituted of

7

CHAPTER 1:
Structure and
Function of Proteins
and Their
Constituent
Amino Acids

adjacent strands oriented in the same direction; the β-turn motif is seen at the ends of β-sheets. The α-helical motif has a very well-defined pattern, with hydrogen bonding occurring between every fourth amino acid residue, and each turn consisting of 3.6 amino acid residues.

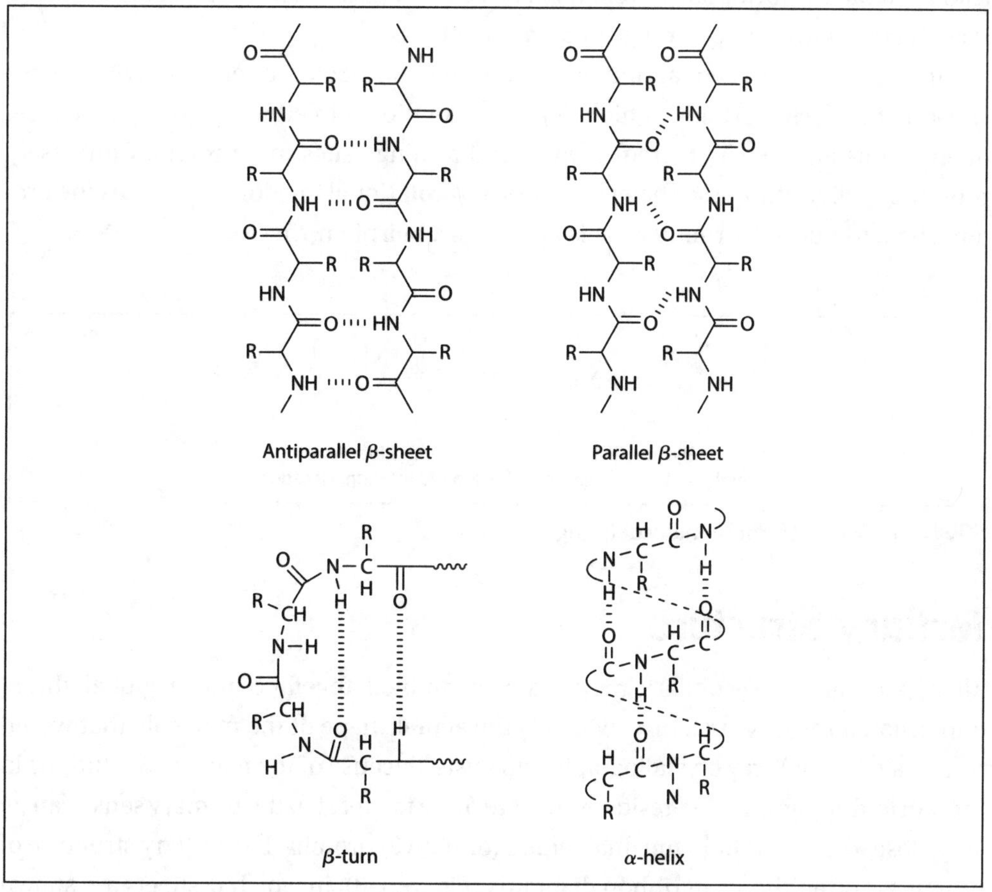

FIGURE 1-5 Four structural motifs in the secondary structure of peptides.

Given the fact that a typical protein is about 300 amino acids long (and can number in the tens of thousands), it is noteworthy that such a small number of secondary motifs constitute such a large proportion of the overall structure of proteins. This is due to the particular conformational constraints along the peptide chain. The peptide bond (i.e., amide bond) itself is planar and not prone to rotation, due to the resonance of the nitrogen lone pair with the carbonyl group (Figure 1-6, left). The other two bonds

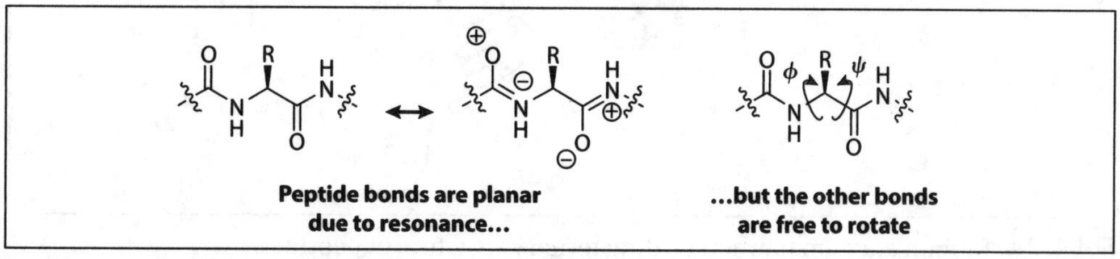

FIGURE 1-6 Conformational constraints in peptides.

(one C—N and one C—C bond) do have some conformational flexibility, and the dihedral (rotational) angles are defined as ϕ for the C—N bond and ψ for the C—C bond (Figure 1-6, right). However, even these bonds do not enjoy unfettered rotational freedom. Due to steric interactions, ϕ and ψ have only certain ranges of values that lead to stable conformations overall. Each secondary motif (e.g., α-helix and β-sheet) is associated with a unique range of ϕ and ψ values.

In this context, two amino acids deserve particular attention. With no α-substituent, glycine exhibits a high degree of rotational freedom (Figure 1-7); consequently, this amino acid is frequently found at hinge sites in a protein. Conversely, proline's cyclic nature essentially shuts down ψ rotational freedom and forces the protein chain to pucker, forming what is known as a hairpin turn.

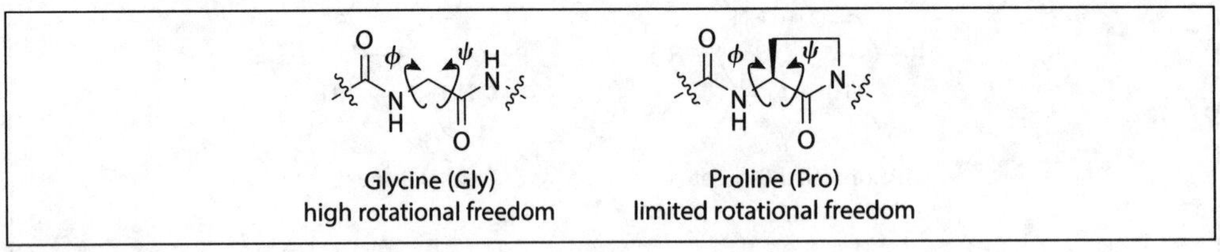

Glycine (Gly)
high rotational freedom

Proline (Pro)
limited rotational freedom

FIGURE 1-7 Two conformationally defining amino acids.

Tertiary Structure

All of the various secondary motifs are assembled together into a global three-dimensional **tertiary structure**, which is the actual shape of the molecule that would be revealed in an X-ray crystallographic analysis. Because of the many convolutions in protein folding, amino acid residues that are quite far apart in the primary sense can be very close to each other in the final folded (or native) protein. The tertiary structure of proteins is often shown in ribbon diagrams (Figure 1-8), in which β-sheets are shown as flat arrows and α-helices are represented as coils, with the less-structured nonrepetitive loops being depicted as ropes connecting the other secondary structures.

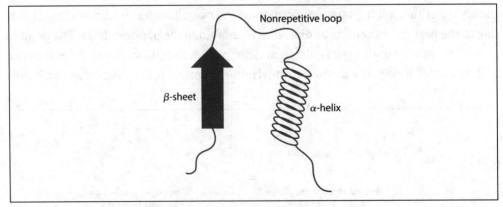

FIGURE 1-8 Ribbon diagram for representing tertiary structure of peptides.

9

CHAPTER 1:
Structure and
Function of Proteins
and Their
Constituent
Amino Acids

Quaternary Structure

Finally, two or more separately folded protein strands may associate with each other to form the active form of a protein, which falls under the category of **quaternary structure**. The conventions and depictional devices for tertiary and quaternary structures are identical—the only difference is that tertiary structure describes the global conformation of a single molecule, whereas quaternary structure describes a supramolecular array of multiple protein molecules.

Protein structures are stabilized by a variety of factors, including covalent bonding (e.g., disulfide bridges) and a host of noncovalent forces, such as hydrogen bonding, pi-pi interactions, and dipole-ion interactions). Regions containing a large number of nonpolar amino acids tend to aggregate together in what is called the **hydrophobic effect**. The origin of this effect lies in the fact that nonpolar side chains cannot form hydrogen bonds with the surrounding water molecules. Consequently, the solvation shell (or cage) around a nonpolar group consists of water molecules with limited mobility, incurring an entropic cost. Having nonpolar groups self-associate therefore minimizes the surface area of the solvent cage.

Any number of environmental factors can disrupt the stabilizing forces and lead to the unfolding (or denaturing) of proteins. These include changes in temperature, ionic strength of the solution, the addition of cosolvents (such as ethanol), and even mechanical agitation.

FUNCTIONS OF PROTEINS

The three-dimensional shape of a protein determines the function of that protein. Proteins have the most diverse functions of any of the biological molecules. Some of those functions include protection, contraction, binding, transport, structural support, acting as hormones, and catalyzing chemical reactions. Many of these functions will be elaborated on in subsequent chapters of this book.

➤ **Protective proteins** have a critical role in the immune system, serving as antibodies. These antibodies come in several different varieties, but they generally work by binding to and inactivating cells displaying molecules that are recognized by the antibody.

➤ **Contractile proteins** are responsible for motor function or movement. In prokaryotic cells these proteins are part of structures such as flagella and cilia. In eukaryotic cells, specialized proteins such as actin and myosin are used for muscle contraction.

➤ **Binding proteins** are highly variable in their function. DNA-binding proteins have critical roles in the regulation of protein synthesis and regulation. Some binding proteins are critical for transportation. Examples include the transport of oxygen by hemoglobin and the transport of electrons by cytochromes.

➤ **Structural proteins** function as their name implies. They provide support within cells and tissues. Structural proteins within cells form microtubules, actin filaments, and intermediate filaments—all critical elements of the cytoskeleton. Proteins critical to support within tissues include collagen and keratin, whose shapes are particularly well suited to providing strength and support.

➤ Many **hormones** have peptide structures. These hormones play a critical role in maintaining homeostasis within the organism. An example of a human peptide hormone is insulin, which regulates blood glucose levels.

➤ Proteins that catalyze chemical reactions are **enzymes**. These will be considered in the following sections.

ENZYME STRUCTURE AND FUNCTION

Enzymes are a special category of proteins that serve as biological catalysts speeding up chemical reactions. The enzymes, often with names ending in the suffix *-ase*, function generally to maintain homeostasis within a cell by determining which metabolic pathways occur in that cell. The maintenance of a stable cellular environment and the functioning of the cell are essential to life.

Enzymes function more specifically by lowering the activation energy (Figure 1-9) required to initiate a chemical reaction, thereby increasing the rate at which the reaction occurs. Most enzymatic reactions are reversible. Enzymes are unchanged during a reaction and are recycled and reused. Enzymes can be involved in catabolic reactions that break down molecules or anabolic reactions that are involved in biosynthesis. The classification of enzymes is based on their reaction type.

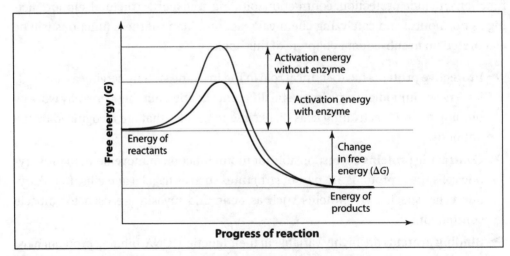

FIGURE 1-9 Increasing rate by lowering the activation energy.

Enzyme Structure

11

CHAPTER 1:
Structure and
Function of Proteins
and Their
Constituent
Amino Acids

As stated earlier, enzymes are proteins and, like all proteins, are made up of amino acids. Interactions between the component amino acids determine the overall shape of an enzyme, and it is this shape that is critical to an enzyme's ability to catalyze a reaction.

The area on an enzyme where it interacts with another substance, called a substrate, is the enzyme's active site. Based on its shape, a single enzyme typically only interacts with a single substrate (or single class of substrates); this is known as the enzyme's specificity. Any changes to the shape of the active site, termed *denaturation*, render the enzyme unable to function. Other sites on the enzyme can be used to bind cofactors and other items needed to regulate the enzyme's activity.

Enzyme Function

The induced fit model is used to explain the mechanism of action for enzyme function seen in Figure 1-10. Once a substrate binds loosely to the active site of an enzyme, a conformational change in shape occurs to cause tight binding between the enzyme and the substrate. This tight binding allows the enzyme to facilitate the reaction. A substrate with the wrong shape cannot initiate the conformational change in the enzyme necessary to catalyze the reaction.

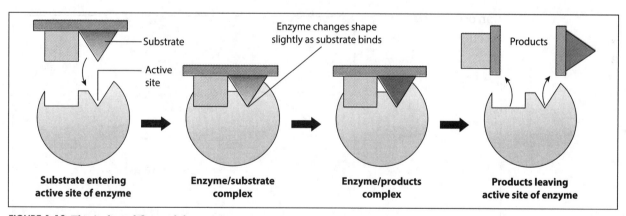

FIGURE 1-10 The induced fit model.

Some enzymes require assistance from other substances to work properly. If assistance is needed, the enzyme has binding sites for cofactors or coenzymes. Cofactors are various types of ions such as iron and zinc (Fe^{2+} and Zn^{2+}). Coenzymes are organic molecules usually derived from water-soluble vitamins obtained in the diet. For this reason, mineral and vitamin deficiencies can have serious consequences on enzymatic functions.

FACTORS THAT AFFECT ENZYME FUNCTION

There are several factors that can influence the activity of a particular enzyme. The first is the concentration of the substrate and the concentration of the enzyme. Reaction rates stay low when the concentration of the substrate is low, whereas the rates increase when the concentration of the substrate increases. Temperature is also a factor that can alter enzyme activity. Each enzyme has an optimal temperature for functioning. In humans this is typically body temperature (37°C). At lower temperatures, the enzyme is less efficient. Increasing the temperature beyond the optimal point can lead to enzyme denaturation, which renders the enzyme useless. Enzymes also have an optimal pH in which they function best, typically around 7 in humans, although there are exceptions. Additionally, extreme changes in pH, ionic strength of the solution, and the addition of cosolvents can also lead to enzyme denaturation. The denaturation of an enzyme is not always reversible.

ENZYME KINETICS

The study of enzyme kinetics involves investigating the effects of various conditions on the reaction rate of enzymes. Most enzymes show an increased reaction rate with increasing substrate concentration until saturation is reached, meaning that increasing substrate concentration no longer increases reaction rate. This relationship can be seen in Figure 1-11.

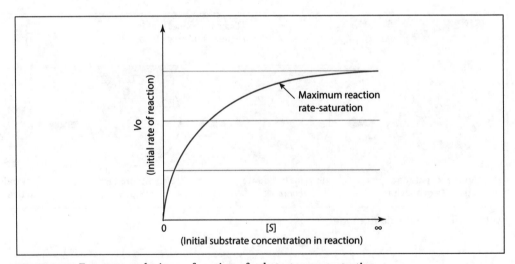

FIGURE 1-11 Enzyme catalysis as a function of substrate concentration.

Michaelis–Menten Kinetics

Enzymes can exhibit a wide variety of kinetic behavior, but one of the most common paradigms is known as the Michaelis–Menten model. In this type of system a substrate

13

CHAPTER 1:
Structure and
Function of Proteins
and Their
Constituent
Amino Acids

(S) and enzyme (E) engage in a pre-equilibrium to form an enzyme-substrate complex (ES)—also called the Michaelis complex—which then undergoes conversion to the product (P).

$$E + S \underset{k_{off}}{\overset{k_{on}}{\rightleftharpoons}} ES \xrightarrow{k_{cat}} E + P \quad \Rightarrow \quad E + S \overset{K_m}{\rightleftharpoons} ES \xrightarrow{k_{cat}} E + P$$

For systems that obey Michaelis–Menten kinetics, when the initial velocity of product formation (v) is plotted against the initial substrate concentration ($\{S\}$), a data set is obtained that can be fit to a rectangular parabolic function, as shown in Figure 1-12. This function asymptotically approaches a maximum velocity (V_{max}) as $\{S\}$ approaches infinity. The concentration corresponding to exactly half the V_{max} is defined as the Michaelis constant, or K_m. On one hand, this constant is a measure of the stability of the Michaelis complex (ES); another interpretation is that K_m represents the concentration of substrate necessary for effective catalysis to be observed. In other words, an enzyme with a very low K_m will catalyze reactions with very low substrate concentrations. Often, K_m is referred to as the binding affinity—that is, enzymes with a low K_m have a high binding affinity. However, the latter description holds true only if $k_{off} \gg k_{cat}$.

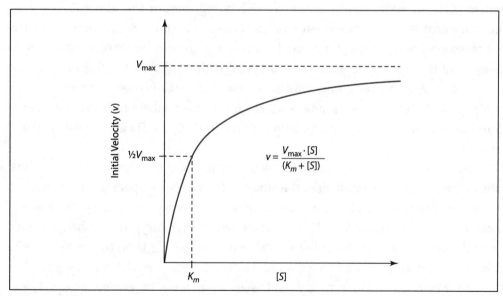

FIGURE 1-12 An enzyme system obeying Michaelis–Menten kinetics.

One classical way to estimate these constants with a linear fit is through the Lineweaver–Burk plot (Figure 1-13), in which the reciprocal of velocity is plotted against the reciprocal of the substrate concentration (for this reason, it is sometimes called a double reciprocal plot). On an L–B plot, the y-intercept is the reciprocal of V_{max}, the x-intercept is the reciprocal of K_m, and the slope is the ratio of K_m to V_{max}.

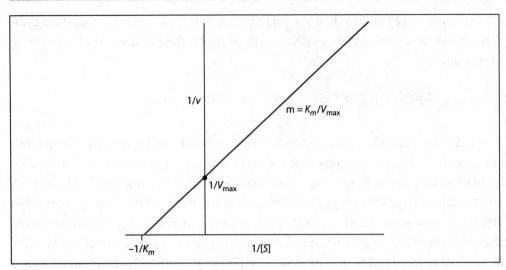

FIGURE 1-13 A Lineweaver-Burk plot.

The catalytic rate constant (k_{cat}) can be estimated from V_{max} through the following relationship:

$$V_{max} = k_{cat} \cdot \{E\}_T$$

where $\{E\}_T$ represents the total number of binding sites, or the sum of bound and unbound enzyme. The catalytic rate constant is also called the turnover number, which is a measure of how many substrate molecules can be converted into product in a given amount of time when the enzyme is saturated with substrate. The units of k_{cat} are sec^{-1}, and the reciprocal of this value is a measure of the time it takes for one enzyme molecule to turn over (i.e., become available for the next substrate molecule). Therefore, enzymes with high k_{cat} values turn over very quickly (i.e., in a very short amount of time).

The ratio of k_{cat}/K_m is often used as a measure of the enzyme's efficiency: the higher the ratio, the more efficient the enzyme. If an enzyme operates on a variety of substrates, this ratio can also reflect the selectivity of an enzyme for one substrate over another. For example, the k_{cat}/K_m ratio exhibited by chymotrypsin for phenylalanine is on the order of 10^5, whereas the k_{cat}/K_m ratio for glycine is on the order of 10^{-1}, meaning chymotrypsin shows a millionfold selectivity for phenylalanine vs. glycine.

The Michaelis–Menten model is based on a few simplifying assumptions, including

1. **The steady-state approximation**, which assumes that the concentration of ES remains constant even though the concentration of substrate and product are changing
2. **The free ligand approximation**, which assumes that the concentration of the free substrate approximates the total substrate concentration, a premise that holds as long as the enzyme concentration is well below K_m

15

CHAPTER 1:
Structure and
Function of Proteins
and Their
Constituent
Amino Acids

3. **The rapid equilibrium approximation**, which assumes the turnover rate (k_{cat}) is much smaller than the reverse equilibrium rate constant (k_{off})

Cooperativity

The reaction rate of an enzyme can be influenced by multiple substrate binding sites. When enzymes have multiple substrate binding sites, the affinity of those binding sites can be altered upon binding to a single site. For example, hemoglobin has four binding sites. The binding of oxygen to the first binding site increases the affinity of the other binding sites on hemoglobin. This is termed **cooperative binding**. In some cases, binding of one substrate decreases the affinity of other bonding sites. This is called negative cooperativity.

Control of Enzyme Activity

It is critical to be able to regulate the activity of enzymes in cells to maintain efficiency. This regulation can be carried out in a variety of ways.

FEEDBACK REGULATION

In addition to an active site, allosteric enzymes have another site for the attachment of regulatory molecules. Many enzymes contain allosteric binding sites and require signal molecules such as repressors and activators to function. Feedback regulation, illustrated in Figure 1-14, acts somewhat like a thermostat to regulate enzyme activity. As the product of a reaction builds up, repressor molecules can bind to the allosteric site of the enzyme, causing a change in the shape of the active site. The consequence of this binding is that the substrate can no longer interact with the active site of the enzyme, and the activity of the enzyme is temporarily slowed or halted. When the product of the reaction declines, the repressor molecule dissociates from the allosteric site. This allows the active site of the enzyme to resume its normal shape and normal activity.

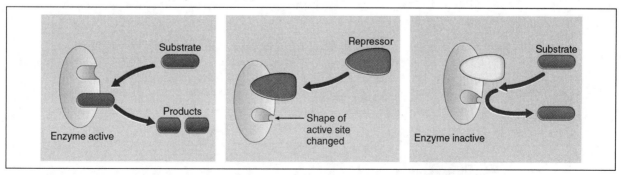

FIGURE 1-14 Allosteric inhibition of an enzyme. Repressors can be used to regulate the activity of an enzyme. *Source:* From George B. Johnson. *The Living World*, 3rd ed., McGraw-Hill, 2003; reproduced with permission of The McGraw-Hill Companies.

Some allosteric enzymes stay inactive unless activator molecules are present to allow the active site to function.

ENZYME INHIBITION

Inhibitor molecules also regulate enzyme action. A competitive inhibitor is a molecule that resembles the substrate in shape so much that it binds to the active site of the enzyme, thus preventing the substrate from binding. This halts the activity of the enzyme until the competitive inhibitor is removed or is outcompeted by an increasing amount of substrate. Noncompetitive inhibitors bind to allosteric sites and change the shape of the active site, thereby decreasing the functioning of the enzyme. Increasing levels of substrate have no effect on noncompetitive inhibitors, but the activity of the enzyme can be restored when the noncompetitive inhibitor is removed.

In contrast to competitive inhibition, which allows an inhibitor to bind to the active site in order to block substrate binding, during uncompetitive inhibition an inhibitor binds to the enzyme if the substrate is already bound. During mixed inhibition, the inhibitor may bind whether the enzyme is bound to the substrate or not.

COVALENT MODIFICATIONS

One means of covalent modification of enzymes involves the transfer of an atom or molecule to the enzyme from a donor or proteolytic cleavage of the amino acid sequence of the enzyme. The phosphorylation (transfer of inorganic phosphate) of enzymes by kinases and the dephosphorylation of enzymes by phosphatases are examples of covalent modification.

Zymogens are enzyme precursors found in an inactive form. In order for the zymogen to be activated, a biochemical change must occur to expose the active site of the enzyme. This activation often involves proteolytic cleavage of the enzyme and occurs in the lysosomes of eukaryotic cells. The digestive enzyme pepsin is secreted in zymogen form (called pepsinogen) to prevent the enzyme from digesting proteins in the cells of the pancreas where the enzyme is produced.

CHAPTER 2

Transmission of Genetic Information from the Gene to the Protein

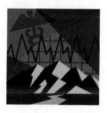

Read This Chapter to Learn About

➤ Nucleic Acid Structure and Function

➤ DNA Replication

➤ Mutations and DNA Repair

➤ The Central Dogma

➤ Ribonucleic Acid

➤ Transcription

➤ Translation

➤ Chromosome Organization

➤ Control of Gene Expression

➤ Recombinant DNA and Biotechnology

Deoxyribonucleic acid (DNA) is the genetic, or hereditary, material of the cell. The information encoded in DNA ultimately directs the synthesis of proteins within cells. When expressed, these proteins determine nearly all critical biological characteristics. When a cell divides, DNA self-replicates to ensure that progeny cells receive the same DNA instructions as the parent cell.

NUCLEIC ACID STRUCTURE AND FUNCTION

DNA is a nucleic acid polymer consisting of the nucleotide monomers seen in Figure 2-1. Nucleosides contain the sugar deoxyribose and a nitrogenous base. When a nucleoside is phosphorylated by adding a phosphate group (PO_4), it is referred to as a nucleotide. There are four nitrogenous bases used to make DNA nucleosides and nucleotides: adenine (A), thymine (T), cytosine (C), and guanine (G). Each nucleoside or nucleotide differs only by the nitrogenous base used. In total, there are four possible nucleotides used to produce DNA.

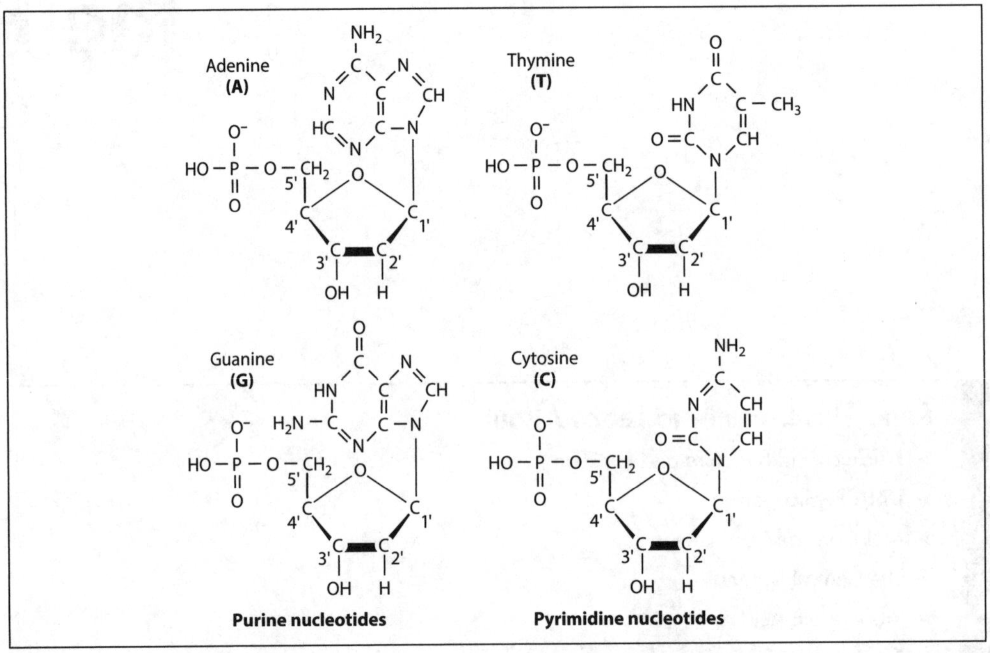

FIGURE 2-1 Nucleotide structure. All nucleotides contain a sugar, a PO_4, and a nitrogenous base. *Source:* From Sylvia S. Mader, *Biology*, 8th ed., McGraw-Hill, 2004; reproduced with permission of The McGraw-Hill Companies.

The nitrogenous bases of each nucleoside or nucleotide are classified as a purine or pyrimidine based on their chemical structure. A purine is a double-ringed structure, whereas pyrimidines are single-ringed structures. The nitrogenous bases adenine and guanine are purines; cytosine and thymine are pyrimidines.

Because of the complementary structure of base pairing, the genetic information can be transmitted via DNA replication.

The Double Helix

James Watson and Francis Crick proposed a model for the structure of DNA in 1953. By analyzing information from the studies of others, they knew that DNA existed in a double-stranded configuration and that the amount of A and T in a DNA molecule was

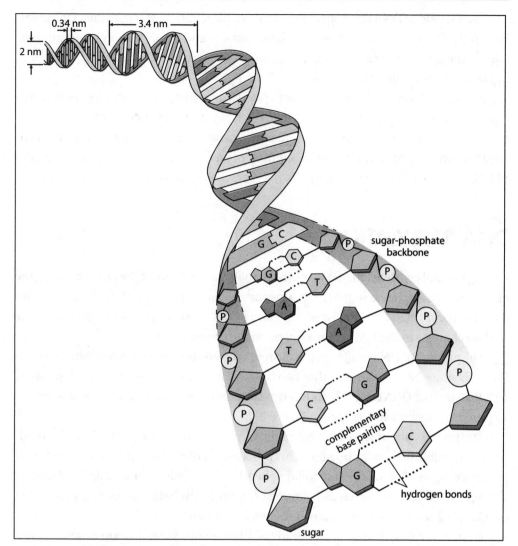

FIGURE 2-2 DNA double helix. The Watson and Crick model of DNA structure shows two strands of DNA that run antiparallel to each other. *Source:* From Sylvia S. Mader, *Biology*, 8th ed., McGraw-Hill, 2004; reproduced with permission of The McGraw-Hill Companies.

always the same, as was the amount of C and G. They then developed a model of DNA structure seen in Figure 2-2.

A single strand of DNA has a sugar-phosphate backbone (where the nucleotides bond together using phosphodiester bonds). Two strands of DNA are hydrogen bonded together via their nitrogenous bases, and this process is called hybridization. The idea of complementary base pairing is essential to this model. Complementary base pairing means that a purine must pair with a pyrimidine. An A on one strand of DNA always bonds to a T on another strand of DNA using two hydrogen bonds. A C on one strand always bonds to a G on another strand using three hydrogen bonds. This base pairing holds together the two strands of DNA, which then twist to take on a double-helix conformation. Knowing the sequence of bases in one DNA strand makes it possible to determine the sequence of bases in the complementary strand.

Each strand of DNA has a specific polarity or direction in which is runs. This polarity is referred to as 5' and 3'. The complementary strand of DNA always runs antiparallel, in the opposite direction of the original strand. So if one DNA strand runs 5' to 3', the other strand of the double helix runs 3' to 5'.

Strands of DNA can be forcefully separated during denaturation. Heat is the most common variable to cause denaturation of the DNA strands, which involves the breaking of the hydrogen bonds holding the base pairs together. The use of denaturing techniques is one way to estimate the GC content of an organism. Following denaturation of DNA, the complementary base pairs may reestablish, or reanneal, to each other.

DNA REPLICATION

During normal cell division, it is essential that all components of the cell, including the chromosomes, replicate so that each progeny cell receives a copy of the chromosomes from the parent cell. The process of replicating DNA must happen accurately to ensure that no changes to the DNA are passed on to the progeny cells.

The process of DNA replication is termed **semiconservative replication**. One double helix must be replicated so that two double helices result—one for each progeny cell. Because the DNA double helix has two strands, each strand can serve as a template to produce a new strand as seen in Figure 2-3.

The process of semiconservative replication has three basic steps. First, the original DNA double helix must unwind. This process is achieved using the enzymes topoisomerase (gyrase) to relax supercoiling ahead of the replication fork and helicase at the replication fork. Single-strand binding proteins follow helicase, binding to the DNA and keeping the strands separated at the replication fork.

Next, the hydrogen bonds that hold the nitrogenous bases together must be broken. This "unzips" the double helix in a localized area of the chromosomes called the origin of replication.

Finally, each template strand produces a complementary strand of DNA using the typical rules of complementary base pairing. The primase enzyme initiates the process; however, DNA polymerase is the key enzyme in this process. This enzyme bonds to the DNA template and chemically reads the nucleotide sequence while assembling the complementary free nucleotides to produce the new strand. The synthesis of DNA occurs in both directions moving outward from the origin of replication in replication forks. In eukaryotic cells, there are multiples origins of replication.

As DNA is synthesized during replication, the DNA polymerase reads the template DNA strand from the 3' to 5' direction, which means that the new DNA being synthesized runs in the 5' to 3' direction. Because one DNA template runs in the 3' to 5' direction, DNA polymerase is able to read it and produce a continuous complementary strand called the leading strand. However, the other DNA template runs in the 5' to 3' direction, so the complementary strand (the lagging strand) is synthesized in a

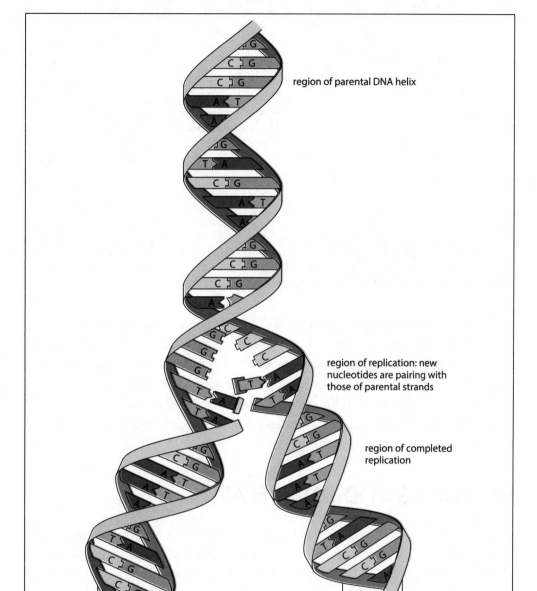

region of parental DNA helix

region of replication: new
nucleotides are pairing with
those of parental strands

region of completed
replication

old
strand

new
strand

daughter molecule

new
strand

old
strand

daughter molecule

FIGURE 2-3 Semiconservative replication of DNA. During DNA replication, the DNA double helix unwinds and each strand serves as a template for the formation of a new strand. *Source:* From Sylvia S. Mader, *Biology*, 8th ed., McGraw-Hill, 2004; reproduced with permission of The McGraw-Hill Companies.

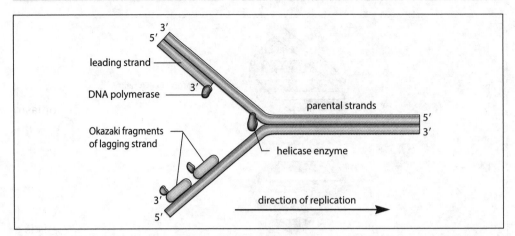

FIGURE 2-4 Okazaki fragments. DNA replication is continuous on the leading strand of DNA and discontinuous on the lagging strand, resulting in the formation of Okazaki fragments on the lagging strand. *Source:* From Sylvia S. Mader, *Biology*, 8th ed., McGraw-Hill, 2004; reproduced with permission of The McGraw-Hill Companies.

discontinuous manner because the replication form is moving against the direction of DNA synthesis, as seen in Figure 2-4. In order to synthesize the discontinuous strand of DNA, a primer (a short sequence of nucleotides) must bind to the DNA. Then DNA polymerase begins to synthesize the new DNA strand until it runs into the next primer. This results in small pieces of DNA, termed **Okazaki fragments**, which must eventually be linked together. The primers are eventually degraded and the Okazaki fragments are linked using the enzyme DNA ligase.

MUTATIONS AND DNA REPAIR

During the process of DNA replication, it is possible for DNA polymerase to produce errors by adding a nucleotide that is not complementary to the DNA template or by adding or deleting nucleotides on the new DNA strand. Certain segments of DNA are more susceptible to mutations than others, and these susceptible areas where mutations tend to occur more frequently are referred to as hot spots. Luckily, DNA polymerase has a proofreading ability that usually detects these errors and repairs them using exonuclease activity. However, if these errors are not corrected, there are permanent changes to the DNA known as mutations.

In some cases, a mutation that cannot be repaired successfully triggers cellular apoptosis to destroy the damaged cell. When this mechanism does not engage, the mutations remain and can be passed on to progeny cells. Mutations occur spontaneously at a rate of one per billion nucleotides, but there is significant variation among organisms in this rate. Although these odds sound quite good, keep in mind that the DNA in a single human cell has about 3 billion nucleotides. This means mutations inevitably occur each time the DNA is replicated. Mutations are often harmless, but in some cases they can code for faulty proteins that can drastically alter the functioning of cells. This can lead to serious consequences such as genetic disease or cancer.

THE CENTRAL DOGMA

DNA is the hereditary information of the cell, which is located within chromosomes in the nucleus of eukaryotic cells. A gene is a segment of DNA located on a chromosome that has information to encode for a single protein. Proteins are made in the cytoplasm of the cell with assistance from ribosomes, but unfortunately the genes carrying the instructions cannot leave the nucleus, nor can the ribosomes, which assist in protein synthesis, enter the nucleus.

To get around this problem, the DNA message in the nucleus is converted to an intermediate ribonucleic acid (RNA) message that can travel out of the nucleus to the cytoplasm and be read by the ribosomes to produce a protein. Protein synthesis is a two-step process: the conversion of DNA to RNA is transcription, and the conversion of RNA to a protein is translation. The process describes the flow of genetic information in the cell and is the central dogma of molecular biology.

DNA → RNA → protein

RIBONUCLEIC ACID

RNA is another form of nucleic acid and is a critical player in the process of protein synthesis. RNA molecules are very similar to DNA with a few exceptions, as shown in the following table.

Differences Between DNA and RNA		
	DNA	**RNA**
Number of strands	2, double helix	single
Sugar used in the nucleotide	deoxyribose	ribose
Nitrogenous bases used	adenine, thymine, guanine, cytosine	adenine, uracil, guanine, cytosine

Within the cell, there are three types of RNA: ribosomal RNA (rRNA), transfer RNA (tRNA), and messenger RNA (mRNA). Each type has a specific role in the process of protein synthesis. Both rRNA and tRNA are considered noncoding. The functions of each type of RNA are show in the following table:

Types of RNA	
Type of RNA	**Function**
Ribosomal (rRNA)	rRNA is made in the nucleolus of the nucleus. It is a structural component of ribosomes.
Transfer (tRNA)	tRNA is located in the cytoplasm of the cells. It is used to shuttle amino acids to the ribosome during the process of translation.
Messenger (mRNA)	mRNA is copied from DNA and serves as the messenger molecule to carry the DNA message to the ribosomes in the cytoplasm.

TRANSCRIPTION

The first step of protein synthesis is the production of mRNA from the DNA. This process of transcription initially resembles the process of semiconservative DNA replication. At the point where transcription is to begin, the DNA double helix unwinds. In this local area, the hydrogen bonds holding together the base pairs must break. Because only one strand of mRNA needs to be produced, only one strand of the DNA serves as a template.

The enzyme RNA polymerase recognizes sequences of DNA called promoters and binds to them. The RNA polymerase chemically reads the sequence of DNA and assembles the complementary RNA nucleotides in the 5′ to 3′ direction. The rules of complementary base pairing during transcription are similar to that of DNA replication, with one major change: RNA uses the base uracil (U) instead of thymine (T). If the DNA contains the base A, then the complementary RNA will contain the base U (not T), whereas C and G will pair together. RNA polymerase continues to synthesize the complementary RNA strand until it reaches a termination sequence on the DNA. At this point, the RNA molecule is released and the DNA double helix reforms. The process of transcription can be seen in Figure 2-5.

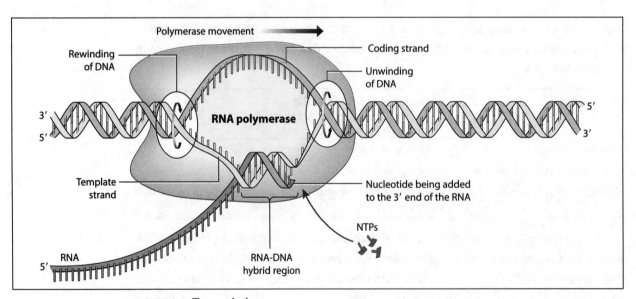

FIGURE 2-5 Transcription.

RNA Modification

Once RNA has been produced from the DNA template, it must be modified before it can be translated into a protein. First, a 5′ cap is added to the 5′ end of the RNA. This cap is a chemically modified nucleotide that helps regulate translation. Next, a poly-A tail is added to the 3′ end of the RNA. This tail consists of many A nucleotides placed on the end of the RNA. The purpose of the tail is to prevent exonuclease degradation of the RNA molecule.

Although some of eukaryotic chromosomal DNA has information that is needed to code for proteins, the majority of the DNA does not have information to code for proteins. The coding DNA is termed **exons**, and the noncoding DNA is termed **introns**. Unfortunately, the introns are located within the exons, disrupting their sequence.

For many years, introns were regarded as "junk DNA" as their functions were not well understood. Currently, it is known that introns have functions such as regulating translation, acting as mobile genetic elements, and allowing for alternate splicing patterns. The acquisition of introns also seems to be an important part of eukaryotic evolution.

During transcription, the RNA that is copied from the DNA contains the sequences of both the introns and the exons. Prior to translation, the introns must be removed, and the exons must be spliced together to form functional mRNA. This is achieved using spliceosomes. Each **spliceosome** is composed of proteins termed small nuclear ribonucleoproteins (snRNPs) and small nuclear RNAs (snRNAs), which perform the actual splicing of exons. The snRNAs are examples of ribozymes, which are catalytic RNA molecules.

Several unique RNAs can be produced by splicing the same exons in different sequences. Figure 2-6 demonstrates the RNA splicing process. Once the splicing is complete, the mRNA molecule moves through the nuclear pores to the cytoplasm where translation will occur.

The Genetic Code

Once the mRNA has been produced, it must be translated into a protein. In this case, there is a "language" barrier. The mRNA is written using a 4-letter code (A, U, C, and G), while proteins are made using a 20-letter code (there are 20 different amino acids used to make proteins). So how does a 4-letter language get converted to a 20-letter language? The mRNA is read as codons, three nucleotides at a time. Each codon has the information to specify for one amino acid. Mathematically, there are four nucleotides in the mRNA, and if every combination of 3 letters is used, there will be 64 possible codons, all of which are listed in the genetic code seen in Figure 2-7. Because there are only 20 amino acids used to make proteins, there is an overlap, or redundancy, in the code where more than one codon can code for the same amino acid. The significance of the redundancy of the genetic code will become apparent when mutations are discussed.

Knowing the sequence of codons on the mRNA makes it possible to use the genetic code to decipher the sequence of amino acids that will be used to build the protein in translation. Any change to the DNA, which, in turn, changes the mRNA codons, can potentially change the order of amino acids and thus the shape and function of the intended protein.

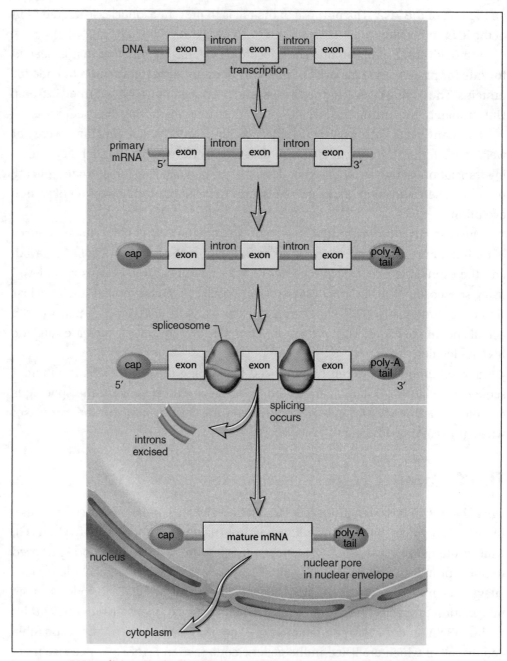

FIGURE 2-6 RNA splicing. During mRNA processing, introns are removed from the mRNA and the exons are spliced together. Capping and the addition of a poly-A tail are also part of mRNA processing. *Source:* From Sylvia S. Mader, *Biology*, 8th ed., McGraw-Hill, 2004; reproduced with permission of The McGraw-Hill Companies.

TRANSLATION

The process of translation occurs in the cytoplasm. The codons on the mRNA are read, and the appropriate amino acids needed to produce the protein are assembled. This process requires assistance from various enzymes, ribosomes, and tRNA.

First letter	Second letter: U	Second letter: C	Second letter: A	Second letter: G	Third letter
U	UUU } Phe UUC } UUA } Leu UUG }	UCU } UCC } Ser UCA } UCG }	UAU } Tyr UAC } UAA Stop UAG Stop	UGU } Cys UGC } UGA Stop UGG Try	U C A G
C	CUU } CUC } Leu CUA } CUG }	CCU } CCC } Pro CCA } CCG }	CAU } His CAC } CAA } Gln CAG }	CGU } CGC } Arg CGA } CGG }	U C A G
A	AUU } AUC } Ile AUA } AUG Met or start	ACU } ACC } Thr ACA } ACG }	AAU } Asn AAC } AAA } Lys AAG }	AGU } Ser AGC } AGA } Arg AGG }	U C A G
G	GUU } GUC } Val GUA } GUG }	GCU } GCC } Ala GCA } GCG }	GAU } Asp GAC } GAA } Glu GAG }	GGU } GGC } Gly GGA } GGG }	U C A G

FIGURE 2-7 The genetic code. The codons on mRNA can be read on the genetic code to predict the sequence of amino acids produced by a particular mRNA. *Source:* From Eldon D. Enger, Frederick C. Ross, and David B. Bailey, *Concepts in Biology*, 11th ed., McGraw-Hill, 2005; reproduced with permission of The McGraw-Hill Companies.

Ribosomes

Eukaryotic ribosomes are composed of two subunits, one large and one small, of rRNA and various proteins. Once the ribosome assembles on the mRNA, there are two RNA binding sites inside the ribosome: the peptidyl (P) site and the aminoacyl (A) site.

Transfer RNA

The tRNA molecules shuttle the appropriate amino acids to the ribosomes as dictated by the codons on the mRNA. The tRNA itself is a piece of RNA folded into a specific configuration. On one end, the tRNA contains an anticodon with a sequence complementary to the codon on the mRNA. For example, if the codon on the mRNA reads CAU, the anticodon on the tRNA will read GUA. On the other end of the tRNA, a specific amino acid is attached. The aminoacyl-tRNA synthetases are responsible for attaching amino acids to their corresponding tRNA.

Based on the genetic code there are 64 codons with three serving as stop codons, leaving 61 remaining functional codons. This would suggest that there would need to be 61 varieties of tRNAs with anticodons to match these mRNA codons. However, this is not the case. The tRNAs display wobble pairing where the third base of the anticodon

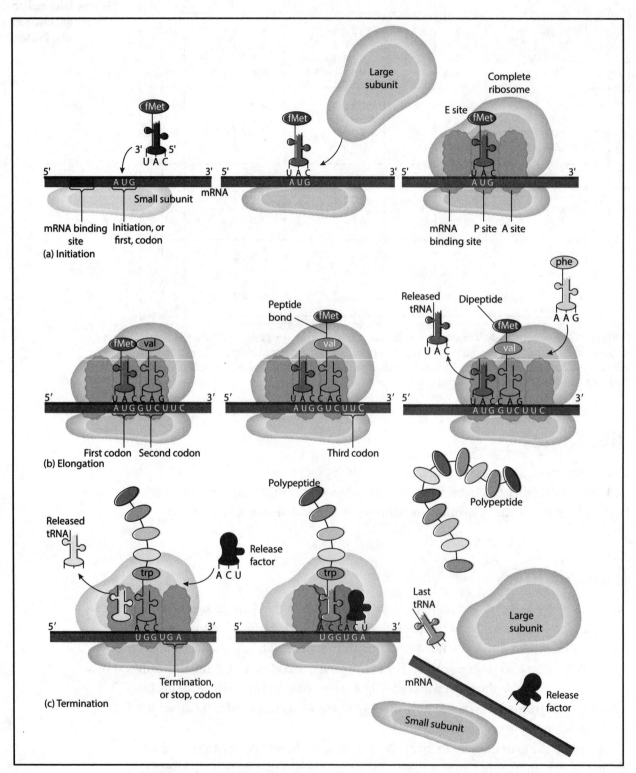

FIGURE 2-8 Translation.

can bind to the third base of the codon in a noncomplementary way. For example, a tRNA displaying the anticodon UAG would be expected to bind to a codon with the full complementary sequence AUC. However, that same UAG anticodon on the tRNA could also bind to a codon with the sequence AUU where the third base is not a standard match of complementarity.

The Steps of Translation

Translation occurs as a three-step process. First, the ribosome must assemble on the mRNA. Next, the amino acids dictated by the codons must be brought to the ribosome and bonded together in the direction of the N terminus to C terminus. Finally, the resulting protein must be released from the ribosome. The entire process of translation can be seen in Figure 2-8.

INITIATION

The process of translation begins when the ribosome assembles on the mRNA and requires a variety of initiation factors. The location for ribosomal assembly is signaled by the start codon (AUG) found on the mRNA. The small ribosomal subunit then binds to the mRNA. The first tRNA enters the P site of the ribosome. This tRNA must have the appropriate anticodon (UAC) to hydrogen bond with the start codon (AUG). As seen in the genetic code, the amino acid specified by the start codon is methionine. Thus the first amino acid of every protein will be methionine. Now the large subunit of the ribosome can assemble on the mRNA.

ELONGATION

At this point, the P site of the ribosome is occupied, but the A site is not. A tRNA bearing the appropriate anticodon to bind with the next codon of the mRNA will enter the ribosome and hydrogen bond to the codon. A key enzyme will be used at this point to form a peptide bond between the two amino acids in the P and A sites. This enzyme is peptidyl transferase. The two amino acids are now attached to the tRNA in the A site. The tRNA in the P site moves to the E site and breaks off (leaving behind its amino acid) and leaves the ribosome. The ribosome then moves over one codon to the right, putting the remaining tRNA in the P site and leaving an empty A site. This process of a new tRNA entering, a peptide bond forming between amino acids, the tRNA in the P site leaving, and the ribosome shifting over by one codon will occur over and over again, producing a growing peptide.

TERMINATION

There are three mRNA codons (UAA, UAG, and UGA) that serve as stop codons and do not code for amino acids. When one of these codons reaches the A site of the ribosome, release factors block the A site and the protein is released from the ribosome. The ribosomal subunits will dissociate. This signals the end of translation. In some cases, it is necessary for the released protein to be modified before it can be functional. These modifications most often include phosphorylation, but other forms of modification are possible. This process often occurs in the endoplasmic reticulum or the Golgi complex of eukaryotic cells.

CHROMOSOME ORGANIZATION

In eukaryotic cells, DNA is organized in linear chromosomes. Humans have 23 pairs, or a total of 46 chromosomes, per somatic (nonreproductive) cell. A single chromosome consists of one DNA double helix wrapped around specialized histone proteins that form chromatin. There are additional proteins that serve regulatory and enzymatic functions within the chromosomes. Each chromosome contains an enormous amount of DNA, all of which must fit into the nucleus of the cell. Organizing the DNA around histones and other specialized proteins helps compact, or supercoil, the DNA, as shown in Figure 2-9. During cell division, the chromatin coils even more to form a compact chromosome. When chromosomes replicate in preparation for cell division, the new copy stays attached to the original at a location called the centromere.

At the end of each chromosome, there are repetitive sequences of DNA called telomeres that act as a sort of protective cap for the ends of the chromosomes. During each round of cell division, the telomeres become shorter. If all are working properly, the cell initiates apoptosis when the telomeres shorten or erode too much, leaving the critical nucleotides at the end of the chromosomes open to damage. This mechanism is necessary so that older cells are destroyed before they incur too much damage. In cancerous cells, this mechanism fails, allowing the cells to achieve immortality.

Chromatin can be further categorized according to how tightly it is coiled. Lightly coiled chromatin is often found in areas being actively transcribed and is more specifically referred to as euchromatin. Heterochromatin is more tightly coiled and serves a variety of regulatory functions. Centromeres and telomeres are examples of heterochromatin.

Repetitive DNA Sequences

Repetitive sequences of DNA are found within the genome in more than a single copy. These repetitive sequences can be categorized as tandem repeats and interspersed repeats. Tandem repeats are copies of repetitive DNA that occur adjacent to each other on the chromosome. An example of a tandem repeat is satellite DNA that is often found in centromeres and heterochromatin.

Transposable elements (transposons) are an example of interspersed repeats. These pieces of DNA have the ability to become mobile and insert themselves into

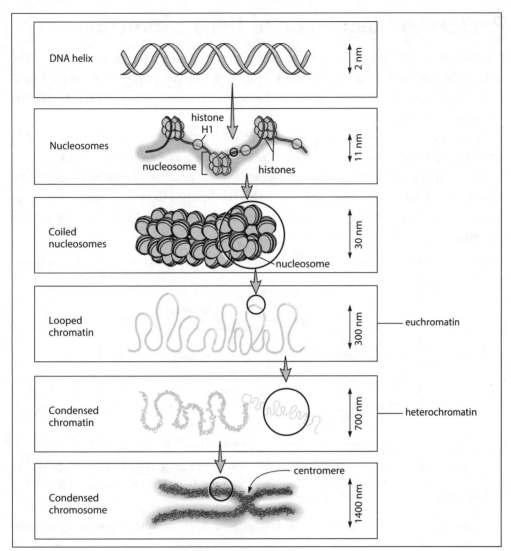

FIGURE 2-9 Chromosome structure. Chromosomes exhibit multiple levels of organization. *Source:* From Sylvia S. Mader, *Biology*, 8th ed., McGraw-Hill, 2004; reproduced with permission of The McGraw-Hill Companies.

specific genes, which is why they are sometimes called jumping genes. The insertion of a transposon into a specific gene causes a mutation that will disrupt the coding sequence in a similar way to a large frameshift (insertion) mutation.

CONTROL OF GENE EXPRESSION

Gene expression refers to the control over which genes are transcribed and translated. Each cell has many genes, and it is not necessary for every cell to express every gene it has. To be efficient, cells are selective about which genes they express, synthesizing only the proteins that are necessary at a given time.

Prokaryotic Regulation of Gene Expression

In eukaryotic cells transcription and translation are restricted to separate parts of the cell so that translation cannot occur until transcription is complete. Prokaryotic cells do not have separate locations for these processes, so they are able to couple their transcription and translation.

The regulation of bacterial gene expression is primarily by operons, as seen in Figure 2-10, which control the access of RNA polymerase to the genes to be transcribed. They do this primarily via repressor proteins. The *lac* operon model proposed by François Jacob and Jacques Monod was the first to describe the role of repressors in the expression of the enzyme beta-galactosidase that is needed for lactose metabolism in bacteria.

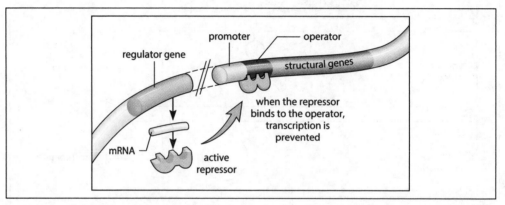

FIGURE 2-10 Bacterial operon system. The operon system is used to regulate gene expression in prokaryotic cells. *Source:* From Sylvia S. Mader, *Biology*, 8th ed., McGraw-Hill, 2004; reproduced with permission of The McGraw-Hill Companies.

There are many different operons that have been characterized, but they all have some basic features:

➤ A promoter sequence on the DNA where RNA polymerase must bind. If the promoter is inaccessible, the gene is not transcribed.

➤ An operator sequence on the DNA where a repressor protein can bind, if present. When a repressor is bound to the operator, the promoter sequence is blocked such that RNA polymerase cannot access the site.

➤ A regulator gene that produces a repressor protein when expressed.

➤ Structural genes that are the actual genes being regulated by the operon.

Operons come in two basic categories: inducible and repressible. Inducible operons are normally "off," while repressible operons are normally "on." In a negative inducible operon, the repressor binds to the operator so that transcription is always prevented unless an inducer molecule is present. When the inducer is present, it binds to the repressor, preventing the repressor from binding to the operator. This allows transcription to occur. In negative repressible operon systems, the repressor is always inactive such that transcription always occurs. Only when a corepressor is present to interact with the repressor can transcription be inhibited. When the repressor and corepressor are bound, they can then interact with the operator site and prevent access by RNA polymerase, thus turning off transcription.

Some operon systems operate using positive control. In those systems, activator proteins bind to DNA, causing transcription. Positive inducible operons require the binding of an inducer to an activator. When this occurs, transcription can be activated. In positive repressible operons, the activator proteins normally bind to the DNA. When an inhibitor is bound to the activator, it cannot bind to DNA and transcription is not activated.

Eukaryotic Control of Gene Expression

Gene expression can be regulated on a permanent level due to a process called differentiation. Because nearly all of the cells within the body are specialized, it makes sense that these cells really only need to express the genes related to that cell's particular function. Even though all cells have the same genes, each specialized cell is only capable of expressing a small subset of those genes. So although brain cells possess the gene to produce the protein insulin, they are unable to express this gene because it is not needed for the functioning of a brain cell and it would be inefficient to make an unnecessary protein. The process of differentiation happens early in development and is thought to generally be an irreversible process. Cells that have yet to differentiate are referred to as stem cells.

Once a cell has differentiated and selected a set of genes to express, genes within this set can be regulated on a minute-to-minute basis. The set of proteins being expressed in a given cell at a given time is referred to as the proteome. There are a number of ways to regulate the process of transcription and translation. These methods can completely prevent gene expression, or if gene expression does occur, there are methods to control the rate of the process, in turn influencing the amount of protein that is produced. The table "Mechanisms for Regulating Gene Expression" summarizes the major mechanisms for the control of gene expression.

TRANSCRIPTIONAL REGULATION

One way to control the expression of a particular gene is by physically regulating access to the gene. For transcription to occur, DNA binding proteins (also called transcription factors) must be able to bind to the promoter sites on DNA. Recall that each chromosome is coiled. If the coiling is particularly tight in a specific region, the transcription factors are unable to access the gene, thus preventing transcription and the expression of the gene. If the chromosome was to loosen its coiling, transcription factors would be able to access the promoter region. These transcription factors must bind to enhancer or silencer DNA sequences, which ultimately determine if the gene will be expressed and the rate of expression.

An extreme example of how the coiling of chromosomes affects gene expression is a process called X chromosome inactivation that occurs in females. Gender is determined by the sex chromosomes, X and Y. Females have a pair of X chromosomes inherited from each parent, while males have one X inherited from their mother and a Y inherited from their father. In females, one of the two X chromosomes in each cell is randomly selected for inactivation. The X chromosome to be inactivated is coiled so tightly that RNA polymerase will never be able to access the genes, and thus no information on the inactive X chromosome is ever expressed.

Methylation. Gene expression can also be influenced by patterns of DNA methylation. This process involves the addition of methyl groups to C or A nucleotides in the DNA. This pattern of methylation is responsible for regulating gene expression in cells and for preventing differentiated cells from reverting to an undifferentiated stem cell form. While many of the methylation patterns are deleted during zygote formation, some of these patterns of DNA methylation that regulate gene expression are heritable. DNA methylation is also an important part of the development of cancer.

POST-TRANSCRIPTIONAL REGULATION

When transcription does occur, a variety of other regulatory methods can be used to determine if translation will ultimately occur. The RNA that is produced during transcription must be spliced and modified before it is translated. If this does not occur, no protein is made and the gene is not expressed. Furthermore, even if the mRNA is properly modified, the rate at which it leaves the nucleus (via nuclear pores) influences if and how quickly it is translated. The faster the mRNA enters the cytoplasm, the more it is translated, leading to an increased amount of protein produced.

TRANSLATIONAL CONTROL

Once in the cytoplasm, the mRNA begins to degrade quickly, usually within minutes. One reason for this quick degradation is that enzymes begin destroying the poly-A tail that was added during RNA modification in the nucleus. Without the poly-A tail, translation cannot occur. The longer the tail is, the longer the mRNA exists for translation and the more protein is made. The shorter the tail, the less protein made.

POST-TRANSLATIONAL REGULATION

Once transcription and translation are complete, a protein exists. However, there is one last way to regulate gene expression at this point. In some cases, the protein is inactivated immediately following synthesis. In other cases, the protein may not go through its normal modification procedure, thus rendering it useless. The mechanisms for regulating gene expression can be seen in the following table.

Mechanisms for Regulating Gene Expression	
Stage at Which Regulation Occurs	**Mechanisms Used**
Transcriptional regulation	Coiling of chromosomes to physically prevent or allow the access of transcription factors and RNA polymerase to the promoter regions of DNA
Post-transcriptional regulation	Whether or not mRNA is properly spliced Control over the rate at which mRNA leaves the nucleus via nuclear pores
Translational regulation	Life span of mRNA, which is influenced by the length of the poly-A tail added during RNA modification in the nucleus
Post-translational regulation	Degradation of protein immediately following synthesis Failure to properly modify the protein, rendering it useless

Cancer as a Failure of Cellular Controls

A typical cell divides about 50 times before its telomeres shorten to the point where the chromosome is risking damage upon subsequent cell divisions. Once the telomeres shorten to a threshold point, apoptosis (programmed cell death) occurs in the cell. Some cells have the ability to bypass cell death and thus become immortal. This is a critical characteristic of cancer cells.

Cancer often develops by a failure of normal cellular controls. The gene products of proto-oncogenes are one of several mechanisms to regulate the cell cycle. Mutation to a proto-oncogene causes activation to an oncogene. The gene product of the oncogene does not properly regulate the cell cycle, which can lead to cancer. Certain viruses are known to be oncogenic viruses, meaning that the viral DNA inserts into human chromosomes, disrupting proto-oncogenes.

Tumor suppressor genes are protective mechanisms that produce proteins that can suppress tumor formation. When these genes are mutated, their protective function is lost, which can cause development of cancer.

RECOMBINANT DNA AND BIOTECHNOLOGY

A DNA molecule that contains DNA from two or more sources is termed **recombinant DNA** (*rDNA*). An organism that contains recombinant DNA is termed **transgenic**. Recombinant DNA technology is a field that is advancing exponentially. It has wide-ranging applications, including pharmaceutical development, gene therapy, medical applications, forensic analysis, agricultural applications, bioremediation, and more.

Recombinant DNA can be created in a variety of ways in nature. However, when it is created in the lab, some concerns related to safety and ethics surface. These concerns include the consequences of the potential release of rDNA into nature, interaction of created recombinant organisms with wild type organisms, safety of recombinant organisms in the food chain, and the ethics of altering the DNA of organisms. While studies generally show that there are minimal safety concerns with recombinant organisms, this is a relatively new field of research and more years of data will need to be collected before a final conclusion can be made.

The techniques and applications of recombinant DNA technology are extensive, but a brief review of the key technologies and tools will be presented here.

Restriction Enzymes

Restriction enzymes, or endonucleases, act as DNA scissors. They are found naturally in bacteria, where they function as a defense mechanism to disable foreign DNA. These restriction enzymes have been isolated from bacteria and are used for research purposes. There are many different restriction enzymes (at least 1,000), and each has a specific recognition sequence. This means that they recognize a specific DNA sequence and then make a cut in the DNA at that point. These cuts can go directly through both strands of DNA producing blunt ends, or they can make single-stranded cuts on the DNA resulting in sticky ends as seen in Figure 2-11. Researchers can use particular restriction enzymes to cut specific sequences of DNA in a predictable manner. DNA from more than one source can be cut with the same restriction enzyme. The resulting fragments can then be pasted together using the enzyme DNA ligase. The result is recombinant DNA.

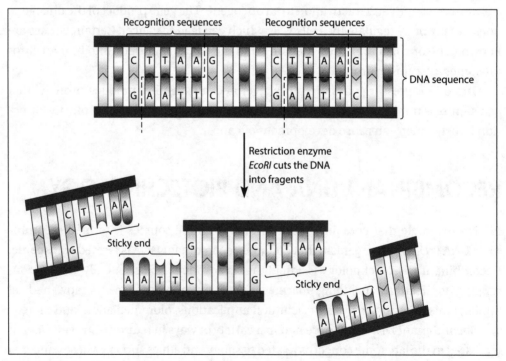

FIGURE 2-11 Restriction enzyme activity.

Production of rDNA

Plasmids are small, self-replicating loops of DNA found naturally in bacterial cells. These plasmids can be isolated and manipulated in the lab to produce recombinant DNA. The recombinant plasmid can then be reintroduced into bacteria in a natural process called transformation that allows bacteria to take in plasmids from their environment. Any foreign DNA that has been inserted into the plasmid is expressed (meaning the proteins that it encodes for will be made) by the bacterial cell.

If a researcher wanted to take a gene from a specific species and insert it into a plasmid, the first step would be to use the same restriction enzyme to cut the circular plasmid and to excise the gene of interest. The DNA ligase enzyme could be used to "glue" the gene into the plasmid that will serve as a vector to carry the gene to another cell. Now the plasmid could be introduced into a bacterial cell by transformation. Then the bacterial cell will begin to express the human gene and produce the human protein.

Gene cloning refers to producing multiple copies of a particular gene. Introducing a recombinant plasmid into a bacterial cell and allowing for bacterial replication would qualify as gene cloning. Viruses can also be engineered to serve as a vector to carry foreign genes. These viruses can be introduced into host cells that replicate the recombinant viral DNA, thus cloning the gene.

While transformation is more easily achieved in bacterial cells, it is possible to use a variety of methods to transform eukaryotic cells.

DNA Libraries

When genes have been cloned into vectors, a library can be produced. In this context, a DNA library refers to a population of organisms in which each carries a unique DNA sequence carried by a vector. There are multiple types of DNA libraries that can be produced. Genomic libraries refer to a population of clones that collectively contain the entire genome or a particular organism.

In complementary DNA (cDNA) libraries, the DNA carried by the vectors has been created using mRNA as a starting point. The mRNA is collected, and the enzyme reverse transcriptase is used to convert the mRNA to DNA form. The DNA created is called complementary DNA (cDNA). The cDNA is then cloned into a vector. The significance of cDNA is that it allows one to work with the genes that were being actively expressed (in the form of mRNA) under specific conditions.

Mutant libraries are helpful in determining the function of genes. This type of library is formed by forcing mutations in the population of the library. The library can then be screened and differences in function can be compared. Additionally, knockout mutants can be helpful in analyzing gene function. These mutants are altered to provide a loss of function to a gene. The knockout can be compared to wild type to see differences in phenotype and functioning.

Detection of rDNA

Gel electrophoresis is a method of separating DNA or RNA based on molecular weight. There are many variations on this technique, but the basic principle is consistent. An electrical current is applied to the gel containing samples, and the smaller fragments move more quickly through the gel, while larger fragments migrate more slowly through the gel. Once the separation has occurred, the fragments can be visualized using assorted staining methodologies. Gel electrophoresis can also be used for the separation of proteins based on weight and charge.

During gene cloning and library production, it is critical to be able to confirm that the DNA of interest has in fact been cloned. While there are a variety of ways to do this, Southern blotting is frequently used. In Southern blotting, the first step requires treatment of the sample with restriction enzymes followed by the separation of DNA via gel electrophoresis. Following this step, the DNA in the gel is denatured and is transferred to a membrane. Finally, the membrane containing the DNA is exposed to a probe. The probe hybridizes to the DNA sample when it finds a complementary match. A variety of techniques can be used to visualize the hybridization. In addition to Southern blotting, there are other blotting techniques that can be used to detect RNA and proteins when needed.

DNA Amplification

Polymerase chain reaction (PCR) is a technique used to make multiple copies of a DNA target sequence. This technology revolutionized DNA technology and has countless applications. Essentially, PCR is a manipulation of the natural processes of DNA replication. In the PCR procedure seen in Figure 2-12, the target DNA sample to be copied is mixed with the appropriate ingredients for DNA replication: primers (short sequences of engineered DNA that bind to a target sequence to initiate the reaction), nucleotides, and a thermostable DNA polymerase. The mixture of ingredients is cycled through a heating and cooling process. The heating separates the DNA double helix, and the cooling allows the primers to hybridize so that DNA polymerase can begin synthesis of the complementary strands. In this way, one copy of DNA has become two. In the next cycle of heating and cooling, the two copies will become four. Within a fairly brief number of cycles (and only a couple of hours) millions of copies of the target DNA can be created.

There are many variations on the PCR procedure, including methods for amplification of cDNA. One of particular interest is real-time PCR (rtPCR), also called quantitative PCR (qPCR). One limitation of traditional PCR techniques is that while they provide detection of a sample, they do not provide quantitation of samples. In rtPCR, the sample is simultaneously amplified and quantified.

DNA Sequencing

DNA sequencing reactions can be performed to determine the sequence of an unknown DNA sample. Early forms of sequencing relied on chain termination methods. During these reactions, the unknown DNA is mixed with a primer, nucleotides, and DNA polymerase. The DNA sample is heated to denature the two strands of the double helix. Primers then hybridize to their target sequence, and this allows DNA polymerase to begin replication. This reaction is done four times, once for each of the four nucleotides (A, T, C, and G). Each time the reaction is performed, a modified version of a single nucleotide is added. This modified nucleotide is missing a 3′ hydroxyl group, and once it is incorporated into a DNA strand, no other nucleotides

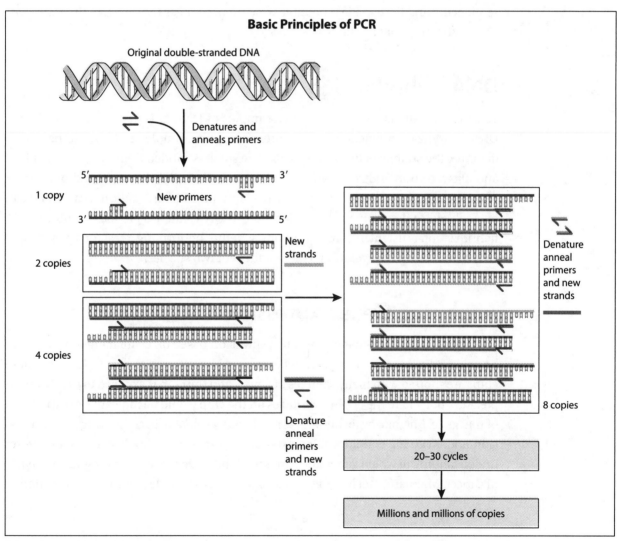

FIGURE 2-12 Polymerase chain reaction.

can be added to it, effectively terminating replication. When the reaction is run the first time, using T for example, all four normal nucleotides are added, as well as some of the modified T. Each time a modified T is added to a DNA strand by DNA polymerase, the reaction stops. The end result is fragments of multiple sizes that were synthesized by DNA polymerase. This same procedure is repeated using modified A, C, and G. In the end, the fragments produced by each of the four reactions can be separated based on their size by gel electrophoresis. These fragments on the gel can then be analyzed by a computer to indicate the original sequence of the DNA sample.

Because of the cost and time involved with chain termination sequencing, newer methods have been developed. Methods such as shotgun sequencing and high throughput sequencing typically use restriction enzymes to fragment DNA prior to sequencing, and multiple reactions can be run simultaneously. These changes to sequencing methodology have drastically decreased the time and cost associated with sequencing and have made it possible to sequence longer runs of DNA than was possible with traditional methods.

DNA Hybridization

To assess the similarities between two samples of DNA, it is necessary to perform a DNA hybridization reaction. In this procedure, two samples of DNA are heated to denature the strands of the double helix. The single-stranded DNA samples are mixed and allowed to hybridize, or anneal, with each other. Hybridization will only occur between complementary nucleotides. The amount of hybridization that occurs can be analyzed to determine how similar the two DNA samples are to each other. DNA hybridization is useful in many situations, whether performing a test for a genetic disease or analyzing the evolutionary relatedness of two species.

Analyzing Gene Expression

The ability to monitor changes in gene expression based on cellular environment can be achieved using microarrays. A microarray is also referred to as a DNA chip. These chips are spotted with many samples of genes, and the chip is exposed to a cDNA sample. Any spot where the cDNA hybridizes on the chip would be indicative of expression of that gene. Microarray technology is particularly valuable in comparing gene expression under varying conditions. For example, microarray technology has led to better understanding of which genes are expressed (and not expressed) during various types of cancer. Microarray technology can also be used to help determine gene function.

Transmission of Heritable Information from Generation to Generation and Processes That Increase Genetic Diversity

DNA IS THE GENETIC MATERIAL

A series of historic experiments collectively provided evidence that DNA is the genetic material of living things. A brief summary of those experiments follows.

Frederick Griffith worked with *Streptococcus pneumoniae* that exist in two forms: a virulent form (termed **smooth**) and a nonvirulent form (termed **rough**). He injected various combinations of smooth and rough *S. pneumoniae* into mice and observed the consequences, seen in Figure 3-1. Of note was that the injection of rough *S. pneumoniae* (which should not be virulent) and dead, smooth *S. pneumoniae* (which also should not be virulent) caused death in mice. The conclusion was that the dead, smooth bacteria were passing to the rough bacteria something that caused virulence, which the rough bacteria took up and expressed. Griffith called this the transforming principle.

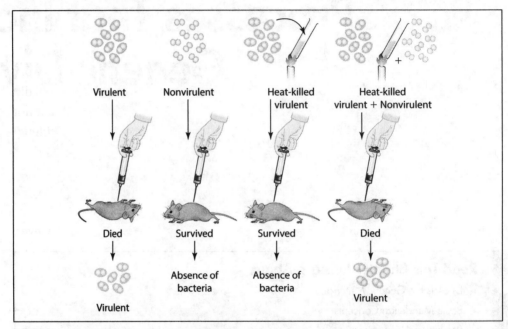

FIGURE 3-1 Griffith's experiments on the transforming principle.

Oswald Avery, Colin MacLeod, and Maclyn McCarthy followed up on Griffith's work by determining what the transforming principle was. Their work relied on the elimination of specific components in *S. pneumoniae* in order to determine which was responsible for transformation. Their results made it clear that DNA was the transforming factor.

Alfred Hersey and Martha Chase provided conclusive evidence that DNA is the genetic material of cells. They utilized the T2 bacteriophage and were able to radioactively label the DNA (using ^{32}P) and proteins (using ^{35}S) of T2 so that they could be tracked as T2-infected *Escherichia coli*, as seen in Figure 3-2. Following infection, they were able to track which material (DNA or proteins) entered the *E. coli*. In this way it was determined that DNA was the genetic material.

43

CHAPTER 3:
Transmission of
Heritable
Information from
Generation to
Generation and
Processes That
Increase Genetic
Diversity

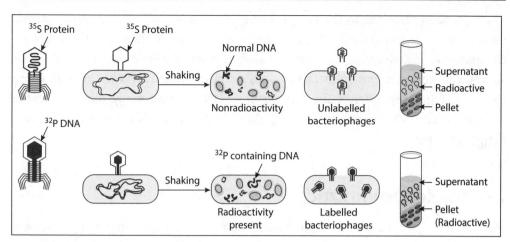

FIGURE 3-2 Hershey and Chase experiments.

BASIC MENDELIAN CONCEPTS

The basic principles of genetics were proposed by Gregor Mendel in the 1860s. His work with traits in pea plants led him to propose several theories of inheritance. Mendel did all his work and postulated his theories at a time when the genetic material had not even been discovered, so the fact that his theories hold true today could be considered quite a stroke of luck.

An understanding of some basic terminology is essential to discuss genetics. The exact genetic makeup of an individual for a specific trait is referred to as the genotype, while the physical manifestation of the genetic makeup is referred to as a phenotype for a specific trait. A gene has information to produce a single protein or enzyme. However, genes can exist in different forms termed **alleles**. In some cases, mutations can cause the production of alleles that produce faulty enzymes needed for metabolism. This leads to a class of genetic disorders known as inborn errors of metabolism.

Through his studies of pea plants, Mendel formulated several laws to explain how particular traits were inherited. These laws addressed issues concerning how specific traits were sorted and passed on to progeny and how some traits exerted dominance over others.

Mendel's Law of Segregation

One of Mendel's most important contributions was the **law of segregation**. There are several important ideas in this law. These ideas can be summarized as follows:

➤ For every given trait, an individual inherits two alleles for the trait (one from each parent).

➤ As an individual produces gametes, the two alleles segregate so that each gamete contains only a single allele per trait. During fertilization, each gamete contributes one allele per trait, providing the offspring with two alleles per trait.

There are exceptions to the law of segregation. These include the alleles carried on sex chromosomes in males. Because males contain one X chromosome and one Y chromosome, the male does not have two alleles per trait for genes on the sex chromosomes. Another exception is that mitochondria contain their own DNA (in single copy) that is inherited separately from chromosomal DNA. Occasionally, alleles from the mitochondrial DNA may incorporate into the chromosomal DNA in a process termed **genetic leakage**.

Complete Dominance

Mendel also proposed the concept of **dominance** to explain how some traits are expressed, whereas others are hidden. Individuals can inherit two of the same allele (homozygous) or two different alleles (heterozygous) for any given trait. In the heterozygous individual, only one allele is normally expressed, while the other allele is hidden. The dominant allele is the one expressed, whereas the recessive allele is hidden in the presence of a dominant allele. When individuals are heterozygous for a particular trait, their phenotype appears dominant, yet they still carry and can pass on the recessive allele via their gametes. A recessive phenotype is only observed when the individual is homozygous for the recessive allele. Keep in mind that dominant traits are not necessarily more common or more advantageous than recessive traits. Those labels only refer to the pattern of inheritance that the allele follows and say nothing about the frequency of advantageousness of the allele. The most common allele in the population is usually referred to as wild type.

By convention, a single letter is selected to represent a particular trait. The dominant allele is always notated with a capital letter, and the recessive allele is notated with a lowercase letter. An example of possible allelic combinations can be seen in the following table.

Possible Allelic Combinations		
Alleles Inherited	**Genotype**	**Phenotype**
AA	Homozygous dominant	Dominant
Aa	Heterozygous	Dominant
aa	Homozygous recessive	Recessive

PREDICTING GENOTYPES

When the genotypes of both parents are known for a specific trait, the genotypes of the potential offspring can be determined. The tool used for this is known as the **Punnett square**.

45

CHAPTER 3:
Transmission of
Heritable
Information from
Generation to
Generation and
Processes That
Increase Genetic
Diversity

Punnett Squares

A monohybrid cross is a breeding between two parents (the P generation) in which a single trait is studied. The offspring of this cross are called the F_1 (first filial) generation. A breeding between two F_1 offspring produces the next generation, F_2, and so on. The potential gametes of each parent are determined and every possible combination of gametes is matched up on a matrix (the Punnett square) to determine every possible genotype of the potential offspring. A ratio of the offspring is expressed as dominant:recessive.

Mendel worked with many traits in the pea plant. He found that when he crossed a true breeding (homozygous) plant of a dominant phenotype to a true breeding plant of a recessive phenotype, 100% of the F_1 offspring had the dominant phenotype. However, when he bred two of the F_1 offspring, he found that 75% of the F_2 offspring had the dominant phenotype, yet 25% had the recessive phenotype. Although the recessive phenotype disappeared in the F_1 generation, it reappeared in the F_2 generation. The F_1 offspring were all heterozygous. When two heterozygotes are bred, the offspring will always show Mendel's observed 3:1 phenotypic ratio. A cross between two heterozygotes that results in a 3:1 phenotypic ratio can be seen in Figure 3-3.

TEST CROSSING

The genotype of a parent with a dominant phenotype can be determined using a method known as a **testcross** (also called a backcross). An organism with the dominant phenotype may be either homozygous or heterozygous. In the testcross, the parent with the dominant phenotype is always crossed to a homozygous recessive mate. The outcome of the phenotypic ratio of the offspring reveals the genotype of the unknown parent. If 100% of the offspring have the dominant phenotype, then the unknown parent is homozygous dominant. If the offspring display a 1:1 ratio, the genotype of the unknown parent is heterozygous. The possible outcomes of a testcross can be seen in Figure 3-4.

Mendel's Law of Independent Assortment

A dihybrid cross considers the inheritance of two different traits at the same time. The same rules of the monohybrid cross apply as long as the traits involved meet certain criteria. Those criteria are developed from **Mendel's law of independent assortment**, which states the following:

➤ The alleles must assort independently during gamete formation, meaning that the distribution of alleles for one trait has no influence on the distribution of alleles for the other trait.

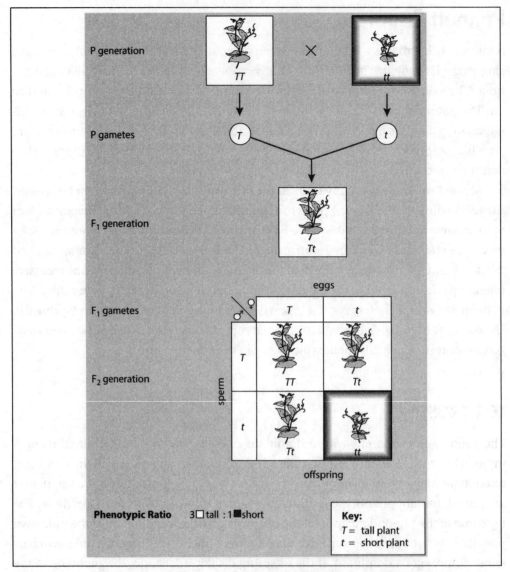

FIGURE 3-3 Monohybrid cross. The crossing of two heterozygous individuals leads to the typical 3:1 phenotypic ratio observed by Mendel. *Source:* From Sylvia S. Mader, *Biology*, 8th ed., McGraw-Hill, 2004; reproduced with permission of The McGraw-Hill Companies.

➤ If two genes are linked, meaning they occur on the same chromosome, they do not assort independently and thus are inherited together, changing the expected outcomes in the offspring.

Two unlinked traits can be considered together in a Punnett square. When two traits are involved in a dihybrid cross, each trait is assigned a different letter. To predict the possible offspring, all possible gamete combinations of each trait for the parents must be considered. Suppose two parents have the genotypes *AABB* and *aabb*. All F_1 offspring will be *AaBb*. If two F_1 offspring are bred, a 9:3:3:1 ratio will be seen in the F_2 generation. See Figure 3-5 for an example of a dihybrid cross.

47

CHAPTER 3:
Transmission of
Heritable
Information from
Generation to
Generation and
Processes That
Increase Genetic
Diversity

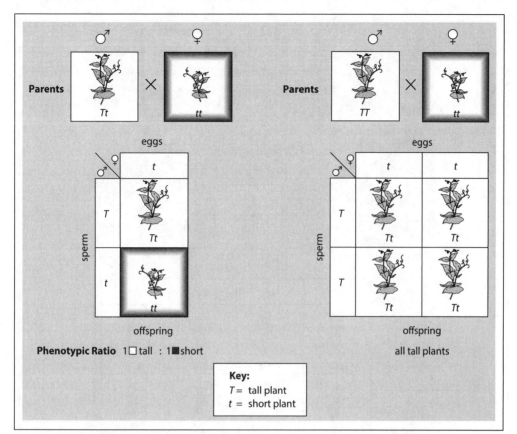

FIGURE 3-4 Testcross outcomes. (a) If the dominant phenotype parent is heterozygous, the ratio observed in the testcross is 1:1. (b) If the dominant phenotype parent is homozygous, all of the offspring exhibit the dominant phenotype. *Source:* From Sylvia S. Mader, *Biology*, 8th ed., McGraw-Hill, 2004; reproduced with permission of The McGraw-Hill Companies.

EXCEPTIONS TO MENDEL'S LAWS

Although Mendel's laws tend to be good predictors of inheritance for some genetic situations, sometimes these laws do not apply. Not every trait operates according to a simple dominant/recessive pattern or in a completely predictable manner. A summary of the genetic situations that are not predicted by Mendel's models can be found in the table that follows.

Linked Genes

The location of a gene on a chromosome is referred to as the **locus** of the gene. Genes that are linked occur on the same chromosome, which means that if one allele is found in a gamete, the other is too since they are on the same chromosome. In the case of linkage, the combination of gametes produced is not as diverse as would be the case with nonlinked alleles. In some cases, the loci of the alleles are so close together that

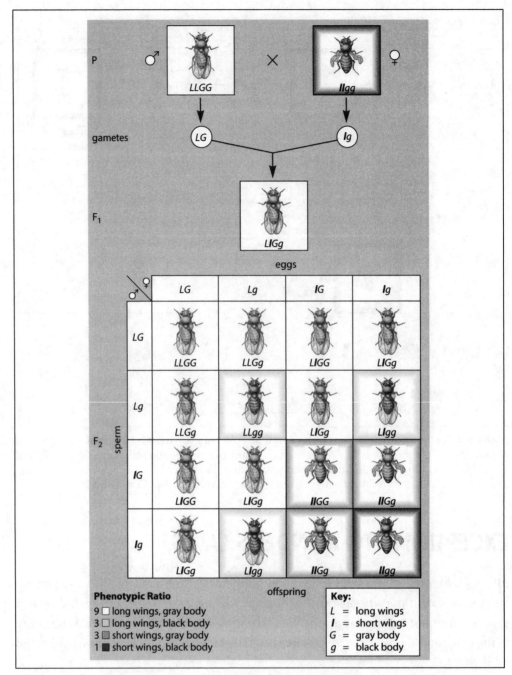

FIGURE 3-5 In a dihybrid cross, the inheritance of two unlinked traits are considered simultaneously. In this cross, Mendel's 9:3:3:1 phenotypic ratio is observed. *Source:* From Sylvia S. Mader, *Biology*, 8th ed., McGraw-Hill, 2004; reproduced with permission of The McGraw-Hill Companies.

they are always inherited together. However, if the loci of the alleles are far away from each other on the chromosome, then there is a possibility for crossing over and genetic recombination to occur. This process will be discussed in more detail with meiosis in a later section.

49

CHAPTER 3:
Transmission of
Heritable
Information from
Generation to
Generation and
Processes That
Increase Genetic
Diversity

A Summary of Possible Genetic Situations		
Genetic Situation	**Key Characteristics**	**Examples**
Simple dominant/recessive inheritance	One allele is dominant over the recessive allele. The only way to express the recessive phenotype is to be homozygous recessive. Individuals who are homozygous dominant or heterozygous express the dominant phenotype.	Mendel's traits observed in pea plants
Linked genes	These are separate genes located on the same chromosome. They do not assort independently and are generally inherited together. In the case that the linked genes are located far from each other on the same chromosome, there is a possibility for the genes to recombine during crossing over in meiosis.	Two genes located on the same chromosome
Multiple alleles	Some traits have more than two alleles to select from in the gene pool. Although an individual can receive only two alleles per trait (one from each parent), multiple alleles increase the diversity in the population.	Human blood type
Incomplete dominance	An individual who is heterozygous is expected to have a dominant phenotype. In incomplete dominance, both alleles are expressed somewhat so that the individual expresses a phenotype that is intermediate of the dominant and recessive phenotypes.	Snapdragon flower color
Codominance	An individual inherits two different alleles that are both dominant. Both alleles will be fully expressed, leading to an individual that expresses both dominant phenotypes.	Type AB blood in humans
Polygenic traits	More than one gene influences a single trait. This leads to multiple potential phenotypes.	Hair and skin color in humans
Epistasis	One gene can mask the presence of an expected phenotype of another gene.	Fur color in Labrador retriever dogs
Sex linkage	Recessive traits located on the single X chromosome in males are expressed, while they must be inherited on both X chromosomes to be expressed in women.	Color blindness

Multiple Alleles

For the traits Mendel observed with pea plants, there were always two alleles. One was dominant and one was recessive. Although an individual can inherit only two alleles (one from each parent) for any given trait, there is the possibility that there may be more than two alleles to select from in the gene pool, which consists of all genotypes in the population. These new alleles arise due to mutation and increase diversity in the population.

Human blood type is an example of multiple alleles. The ABO system has three alleles: I^A, I^B, and i. The alleles I^A and I^B are dominant, whereas the allele i is recessive. Each allele codes for either the presence or absence of particular antigens on the surface of red blood cells. With simple dominant/recessive traits, two phenotypes are expected—a dominant phenotype and a recessive phenotype. Any time multiple alleles are involved with a trait, more than two potential phenotypes will be expected. This is the case in blood type where four phenotypes can be observed: type A, type B, type AB, and type O.

Incomplete Dominance

According to Mendelian rules, a heterozygous individual always expresses the dominant phenotype. If alleles behave by incomplete dominance, this is not the case. Flower color in snapdragons is a classic example. If the allele R codes for red flowers and the allele r codes for white flowers, Mendelian rules would predict that the heterozygote (Rr) would have red flowers. However, because this trait behaves according to incomplete dominance, both alleles will be expressed to some degree, leading to a pink (intermediate) phenotype in the heterozygous offspring. In the case of incomplete dominance, only two alleles are involved, yet there are three potential phenotypes that can arise.

Codominance

Codominance is similar to incomplete dominance. For this to occur, the trait involved must first have multiple alleles and more than one of them must be dominant. If a heterozygous individual inherits two different dominant alleles, both alleles are expressed, leading to an individual who has both phenotypes (as opposed to a blended phenotype seen with incomplete dominance).

Human blood type is an example of codominance as well as multiple alleles. Should an individual inherit the genotype of $I^A I^B$, they will display the A phenotype as well as the B phenotype. In this case, the result is type AB blood. The following table contains more details on human blood type.

	The Genetic Basis of Human Blood Types	
Blood Type	**Potential Genotypes**	**Antigens Found on the Red Blood Cell Surface**
Type A	$I^A I^A$ or I^Ai	A
Type B	$I^B I^B$ or I^Bi	B
Type AB	$I^A I^B$	A and B
Type O	Ii	none

51

CHAPTER 3:
Transmission of
Heritable
Information from
Generation to
Generation and
Processes That
Increase Genetic
Diversity

Polygenic Traits

Generally, a single gene influences one trait. **Polygenic traits** involve gene interaction. This means that more than one gene acts to influence a single trait. Skin color and hair color are both examples of polygenic traits in humans. Because more than one gene is involved, the number of potential phenotypes is increased, resulting in continuous variation.

Epistasis

Epistasis is a unique genetic situation where one gene interferes with the expression of another gene. In many cases, epistasis can lead to the masking of an expected trait. An example is coat color in Labrador retrievers. These dogs have black, chocolate, or yellow fur. In addition to the gene that controls fur color, the *B* gene, there is another allele that controls how pigment is distributed in the fur, the *E* gene. The *B* gene produces an enzyme that processes brown pigment to black pigment. Dogs that have the genotype *BB* or *Bb* produce black pigment, while those with the genotype *bb* produce brown pigment. The *E* gene allows the pigment to be deposited into the hair follicle. If the Labrador is *EE* or *Ee*, it is able to deposit the pigment. However, dogs with the genotype *ee* will not. Therefore, the gene *B* determines if a dog produces black or brown pigment, but these phenotypes can be expressed only if the dog is homozygous dominant or heterozygous for the *E* gene. Any dog that is homozygous recessive for the *E* gene, *ee*, will be yellow.

Pleiotropy

Pleiotropy occurs when a single gene influences two or more other traits. Most frequently, the effects of pleiotropy are seen in genetic diseases. In sickle cell disease, the mutation in the hemoglobin gene results in the production of hemoglobin protein with a reduced oxygen-carrying ability. This, in turn, affects multiple organ systems in the body, explaining the multiple symptoms of the disease.

Sex Linkage

When alleles are found on the X and Y sex chromosomes, the normal rules of genetics may not apply. Although the sex chromosomes do contain genes to influence gender, there are other traits found on these chromosomes that have nothing to do with gender. Women inherit an XX genotype, whereas men inherit an XY genotype. In men, traits that occur on the sex chromosomes are the exception to the normal rule of always having two alleles per trait. Because the sex chromosomes in men are not a true pair, they do not have two alleles per trait on their sex chromosomes. The Y chromosome contains relatively few genes as compared to the X chromosome.

When a recessive trait is located on the X chromosome, women must receive two copies of the recessive allele (one from each parent) to express the recessive trait.

However, men who inherit a recessive allele on their only X chromosome will express the recessive phenotype. Color blindness and hemophilia are examples of traits that are sex linked. While women can express these traits, to do so they must receive the recessive alleles on both X chromosomes (meaning they must receive it from both of their parents). Therefore, these traits are more commonly observed in men, as they only need to receive the recessive trait on their single X chromosome.

Women who are heterozygous for a trait on the X chromosome do not express the trait; yet they are carriers for this and can pass the traits to their sons. Since women are genotypically XX, every egg cell they make contains the X chromosome. Men are XY and thus half their sperm contain the X chromosome and half contain the Y. In males, the Y chromosome must come from the father and the X comes from the mother.

PEDIGREE ANALYSIS

A **pedigree** is a diagram used to help determine a pattern of inheritance over multiple generations. In pedigrees, males are indicated by a square and females by a circle. Individuals in the pedigree who are affected by a certain trait are indicated by shading in the square or circle. Those that are not affected are indicated by no shading in the square or circle. In some cases, a square or circle may be half shaded, and this is to indicate a carrier or a heterozygote. Horizontal lines indicate matings, and vertical lines show offspring. An example of a pedigree indicating recessive inheritance is seen in Figure 3-6.

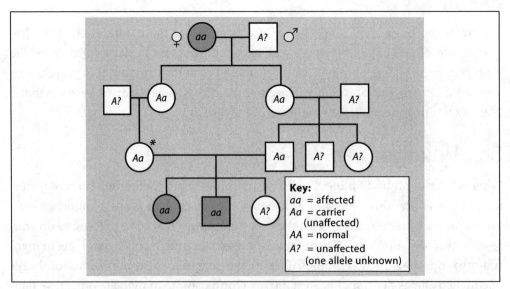

FIGURE 3-6 This pedigree shows a recessive pattern of inheritance. *Source:* From Sylvia S. Mader, *Biology*, 8th ed., McGraw-Hill, 2004; reproduced with permission of The McGraw-Hill Companies.

53

CHAPTER 3:
Transmission of
Heritable
Information from
Generation to
Generation and
Processes That
Increase Genetic
Diversity

If a pedigree shows many more males than females being affected, sex-linked inheritance should be suspected. If males and females both seem equally affected, look for skipping of generations. Dominant traits usually appear in each generation, whereas recessive traits often skip generations.

ENVIRONMENTAL INFLUENCES ON GENES AND EPIGENETICS

Although some genes behave according to very predictable rules, there are many cases where some external or internal environmental factor can interfere with the expression of a particular genotype. Penetrance of a genotype is a measure of the frequency at which a trait is actually expressed in the population. If a trait were described at 80% penetrance, it would mean that 80% of the people with the genotype for the particular trait would have the phenotype associated with the genotype. While some traits always show 100% penetrance, others do not. Within an individual, expressivity is a measure of the extent of expression of a phenotype. This means that, in some cases, expression of a phenotype is more extreme than others.

There are many examples of how the environment affects the expression of a particular phenotype. Hydrangea plants may have the genotype to produce blue flowers, but depending on the acidity of the soil that they are grown in (an environmental factor), they may express a different phenotype than expected (such as pink flowers). Women who have the BRCA 1 and 2 alleles are at a high but not guaranteed risk for developing breast cancer, meaning that something other than the allele determines the expression of the allele.

Many traits cannot be predicted by genotype alone (like intelligence, emotional behavior, and susceptibility to cancer). In many cases, the interaction of genes and the environment is a complicated relationship that is impossible to predict. Factors in humans such as age, gender, diet, and so forth are all factors known to influence the expression of certain genotypes. This is the concern of the field of epigenetics.

Epigenetics involves the study of heritable changes in gene expression that are not caused by DNA sequence changes. These changes can have many sources but frequently involve patterns of DNA methylation and histone modification that influence gene expression. These changes may involve down-regulation or up-regulation of gene expression. These patterns that influence gene expression are referred to as the epigenome, and they may be heritable for many generations. However, the epigenome is known to show change over time, particularly during the process of cellular differentiation during embryonic development.

GENETIC VARIABILITY DURING CELL DIVISION

The cell is the basic unit of structure and function in an organism. For life to continue, cells must divide and reproduce. Cell division in eukaryotes happens through two processes: mitosis and meiosis. Mitosis is normal cell division used for growth and the replacement of cells. In mitosis, a parent cell is copied to produce two identical daughter cells.

There are times that producing genetically identical offspring cells is not appropriate, such as during sexual reproduction. During the process of sexual reproduction, genetically diverse gametes must be created. These gametes are produced by the process of meiosis. Both mitosis and meiosis have many features in common. The processes of mitosis and meiosis will be considered in detail in Chapter 7.

Cytoplasmic Inheritance

Recall that certain organelles such as mitochondria contain their own DNA. This DNA is circular and in single copy; therefore, there are no pairs of alleles—just a single copy of each allele. Any genes present on mitochondrial DNA will be inherited by the daughter cells during cytokinesis of mitosis or meiosis. Unlike chromosomal inheritance, any genes passed through mitochondrial DNA will not follow the normal Mendelian laws of genetics.

Mistakes in Meiosis

While the technicalities of meiosis will be discussed in Chapter 7, this section will discuss the consequences of meiotic mistakes in the context of factors that influence genetic variability. Mistakes that happen during meiosis can have drastic consequences. Because the gametes are used for reproduction, any chromosomal damage to the gametes is passed on to the next generation. There are several ways in which mistakes can occur, changing the number of chromosomes or damaging them.

If chromosomes fail to separate properly during meiosis, a nondisjunction has occurred. This leads to gametes that have the wrong number of chromosomes. If those gametes are fertilized, the resulting embryo will have the wrong diploid number. An example of this is Down syndrome, which often is the result of a nondisjunction in the female gamete. If a female egg contains 24 chromosomes instead of the expected 23 and is fertilized by a normal sperm, the resulting embryo has 47 chromosomes, which is one more than expected. This condition is referred to as a **trisomy**. In the case where a gamete is missing a chromosome as the result of a nondisjunction and is fertilized by a normal gamete, the result is an embryo with 45 chromosomes. This is termed a **monosomy**. With the exception of Down syndrome, which is a trisomy of human chromosome 21 (which is very small) and certain trisomies and monosomies of the

55

CHAPTER 3:
Transmission of
Heritable
Information from
Generation to
Generation and
Processes That
Increase Genetic
Diversity

sex chromosomes (X and Y), most embryos with trisomies and monosomies do not survive development.

Other forms of chromosomal damage can occur in meiosis. They typically have serious if not fatal consequences. They are as follows:

➤ **Deletion.** This occurs when a portion of a chromosome is broken off and lost during meiosis. Although the total chromosome number is normal, some alleles are lost.

➤ **Duplication.** This is when a chromosome contains all of the expected alleles and then receives a duplication of some alleles.

➤ **Inversion.** When a portion of a chromosome breaks off and reattaches to the same chromosome in the opposite direction, this is termed *inversion*.

➤ **Translocation.** This occurs when a piece of a chromosome breaks off and reattaches to another chromosome.

MUTATIONS

Mutations occur naturally through the process of DNA replication, but certain factors can greatly increase the spontaneous mutation rate. These factors are referred to as mutagens. The mutagens that are linked to development of cancer are called carcinogens. Should any of these mutations occur in gametes (germ cells), they would be considered heritable and are passed on to the next generation.

Mutations change the coding sequence of DNA. When the DNA changes, the mRNA codons change, and the amino acid sequence of the protein made may change. In some cases, this may produce a protein that functions better than the one intended by the DNA (thus providing an advantage), one that functions equivalently to the intended protein, or in the worst case, a protein that functions worse than the intended protein or does not function at all. Recall that mutations happen spontaneously and that the rate of mutation is increased by exposure to mutagens.

Mutations can occur in several ways—by the change in a single nucleotide, the mispairing of nucleotides, the addition or deletion of a nucleotide, or the movement of nucleotides. While these changes typically happen at the DNA level, there can also be transcription and translation errors that occur.

Point Mutations

When a single nucleotide is swapped for another, the resulting mutation is termed a **point (substitution) mutation**. This ultimately changes a single codon on the mRNA. In some cases, this mutation is silent, meaning that if the codon is changed and still codes for the intended amino acids, there will be no detectable consequence. However, sometimes even a single point mutation can have major consequences. If the new codon (a missense codon) codes for a different amino acid than what was intended, the new protein may not function properly. This can lead to a genetic disease such as sickle cell. It is also possible for a change in a single nucleotide (nonsense codon) to produce a stop codon in a new location, causing a nonsense mutation. In this case, the protein produced would be too short and most likely nonfunctional.

Frameshift Mutations

A **frameshift mutation** is the result of the addition or deletion of nucleotides. Unlike the point mutation where the overall number of nucleotides does not change, adding or deleting changes the number of nucleotides. Because mRNA is read in codons, an addition or deletion alters all of the codons from the point of the mutation onward. This disrupts the reading frame of the mRNA. Since many codons are changed, the frameshift mutation generally produces a damaged or nonfunctional protein.

EVOLUTION

Evolution simply means change. The changes referred to are genetic ones, thus putting the concept of mutation at the center of the process of evolution. Evolution is something that occurs over time, so a single individual does not evolve, but populations of individuals do evolve. **Microevolution** deals with genetic changes within a population, whereas **macroevolution** is concerned with changes that occur to a species on a larger scale over a longer period of time.

Mechanisms for Evolution

A variety of factors are responsible for the microevolution of a particular population. Natural selection, based on mutation, tends to be the major driving force for evolution, while genetic drift and gene flow can also influence the process.

MUTATION

New alleles are created **by mutation**. These new alleles code for proteins that may be beneficial, neutral, or detrimental as compared to the original protein intended by the allele. New alleles that code for beneficial proteins can provide advantages that are ultimately selected for by natural selection and are passed to the next generation, whereas detrimental alleles are selected against.

NATURAL SELECTION

A central concept to the process of how evolution occurs is that of Darwin's **natural selection**. Natural selection explains the increase in frequency of favorable alleles from

57

CHAPTER 3:
Transmission of
Heritable
Information from
Generation to
Generation and
Processes That
Increase Genetic
Diversity

one generation to the next. This results from differential reproductive success in which some individuals reproduce more often than others and thus are selected for. This increases the frequency of their alleles in the next generation. Those that reproduce less decrease the frequency of their alleles in the next generation.

Fitness Concept. The concept of **evolutionary fitness** is key to natural selection. In this context, fit refers to the reproductive success of an individual and their allelic contribution to the next generation. Those individuals who are more fit are more evolutionarily successful because their genetic traits are passed to the next generation, thus increasing the frequency of specific alleles in the gene pool.

Over generations, selective pressures that are exerted on a population can lead to adaptation. When selective pressures change, some organisms that may have been considered marginally fit before may now have increased fitness under the new conditions. Further, those individuals that may have been very fit previously may drastically decrease their fitness. Their genetic adaptations will be selected against. While individuals cannot change their genetics, over time, the population changes genetically, which is termed **adaptation**.

Differential Reproductive Success and Competition. Competitive interactions within a population are another critical factor for natural selection. The ability to outcompete other individuals for resources, including mates, is a key feature of fitness. In any given population, some individuals are better able to compete for resources and are considered more fit than others. This leads to **differential reproductive success**. This concept assumes that mating in the population is random. In some cases, such as with humans, mating is nonrandom, which leads to another form of selection to be discussed shortly.

Competition between species can also influence the evolutionary progression of all species involved. In some cases, symbiotic relationships exist where two species exist together for extended periods of time. In mutualistic relationships, both species benefit from the association. In parasitic relationships, one species benefits at the expense of the other species. In commensalism, one species benefits while the other species is relatively unharmed.

When two species are competing for the same ecological requirements or niche, the reproductive success and fitness, as well as the growth of one or both populations, may be inhibited based on the ability to compete for resources. This will change the microevolutionary course of the population.

GENE FLOW

When individuals leave a population, they take their alleles with them, resulting in **gene flow**. This can decrease genetic variation within the gene pool of the population, ultimately affecting the evolution of the population. Outbreeding occurs with the individuals that leave the population. They can add diversity to the gene pool of their new populations by adding alleles to it.

GENETIC DRIFT

Genetic drift involves changes to the allelic frequencies within a population due to chance. Although this is generally negligible in large populations, it can have major consequences in smaller populations. The bottleneck effect is a form of genetic drift where catastrophic events may wipe out a large percentage of a population. When the population is small, the few remaining alleles in the gene pool may not be characteristic of the larger population. The founder effect is a form of genetic drift that occurs when a small number of individuals leave a larger population and form their own small population where inbreeding is necessary. The new population only has the diversity brought to it by the founding members.

GENETIC BASIS FOR EVOLUTION AND THE HARDY–WEINBERG EQUATION

The **Hardy–Weinberg equation** can be used to calculate allelic frequencies within a population given the population is large and microevolution is not occurring—not necessarily a realistic situation. The Hardy–Weinberg equation is expressed as

$$p^2 + 2pq + q^2 = 1$$

where p represents the frequency of a dominant allele and q represents the frequency of a recessive allele such that $p + q = 1$.

The equation can be used to show the frequency of homozygous dominant individuals (p^2), the frequency of heterozygotes ($2pq$), and the frequency of homozygous recessive individuals (q^2). Given information on the frequency of a single allele, all other pieces within the equation can be determined. Although these frequencies are temporarily accurate, any evolution occurring within the population would shift these predicted values.

For Hardy–Weinberg allelic frequencies to hold true, it is necessary that certain criteria be met. If any of these criteria are violated, the allelic frequencies will change over time. Any of the following will negate Hardy–Weinberg equilibrium:

➤ Nonrandom mating
➤ Gene flow
➤ Populations with a small number of individuals
➤ Mutations
➤ Bottleneck effect
➤ Founder effect

59

CHAPTER 3:
Transmission of
Heritable
Information from
Generation to
Generation and
Processes That
Increase Genetic
Diversity

TYPES OF NATURAL SELECTION

For any given trait, there can be several different phenotypes. If two phenotypes are present for a particular trait, dimorphism is the case. If three or more phenotypes are seen for a particular trait, polymorphism is at work. For example, flower color in snapdragons exhibits polymorphism with red, white, and pink phenotypes. Some phenotypes can be considered intermediates (like pink flowers) or can be extremes from either end of the intermediate phenotype (like red and white flowers). When natural selection occurs, it may select for intermediate phenotypes, either extreme phenotype, or both extreme phenotypes as seen in Figure 3-7.

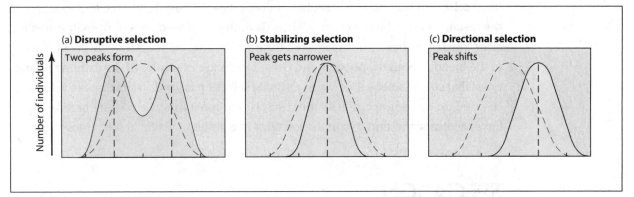

FIGURE 3-7 Types of natural selection. (a) In disruptive selection, the extreme phenotypes are selected for, whereas the intermediate phenotype is selected against. (b) In stabilizing selection, the intermediate phenotype is favored. (c) In directional selection, one extreme phenotype is favored. *Source:* From George B. Johnson, *The Living World*, 3rd ed., McGraw-Hill, 2003; reproduced with permission of The McGraw-Hill Companies.

Directional Selection

In **directional selection**, an allele that is considered advantageous is selected for. The allelic frequency continues to shift in the same direction generation after generation. In this case, one allele that produces an extreme phenotype is selected for. The selection of antibiotic resistance alleles in bacteria is an example of directional selection. Over time, selective pressures can result in an entire population possessing the same allele for a particular trait.

Stabilizing Selection

Stabilizing selection leads to favoring the alleles that produce an intermediate phenotype. Human birth weight would be an example of stabilizing selection. Babies of an intermediate weight are favored over those who are too small to survive or too large to be easily delivered.

Disruptive Selection

In some cases, the environment favors two extreme phenotypes simultaneously. In this case, **disruptive selection** occurs, where individuals with either extreme phenotype are favored, while those with the intermediate forms of the alleles are selected against. Over time, the continued selection of both extremes may eventually lead to the evolution of two distinct species.

Artificial Selection

When particular alleles are purposely selected for based on nonrandom mating, **artificial selection** occurs. The breeding of domesticated dogs is an excellent example of the results of artificial selection. All breeds of dogs are members of the same species, all of which have been selectively bred from wolves for specific traits that are appealing to the breeder. Both toy poodles and Great Danes are examples of the extreme phenotypes that can be selected for when artificial selection is used. Traits that are artificially selected for are not necessarily the result of the most fit alleles. Many breeds of dog have medical conditions or predispositions as a result of artificial selection.

SPECIATION

Natural selection can ultimately result in the formation of new species. By definition, a species is a group of individuals who can breed with each other and not with members of other species. When a population becomes geographically isolated from each other, members of the same species may evolve differently in different locations. This type of speciation is referred to as allopatric. Even when geographic barriers do not exist to divide a population, there are factors that can ultimately prevent some members of the population from breeding with others. This is sympatric speciation. Over time, they may evolve into two different species that can no longer breed with each other.

There are a variety of mechanisms that occur to prevent interbreeding between species. When these mechanisms do not work, hybrid species may occur.

Prezygotic Isolation

Prezygotic isolation mechanisms occur to prevent fertilization between the gametes of members of two different species. They are as follows:

➤ **Temporal isolation.** Two different species may live in the same environment but have different breeding seasons or may have overlapping breeding seasons but breed during different times of the day.

61

CHAPTER 3:
Transmission of
Heritable
Information from
Generation to
Generation and
Processes That
Increase Genetic
Diversity

➤ **Ecological isolation.** The two species live in different habitats and thus rarely encounter each other to breed.

➤ **Behavioral isolation.** The mating behaviors of the two species are not compatible with each other.

➤ **Reproductive isolation.** Even if members of different species attempt to mate, their reproductive structures may not be compatible.

➤ **Gamete isolation.** The gametes of one species cannot fertilize the gametes of the other species, so reproduction is unsuccessful even if successful copulation occurs.

Postzygotic Isolation

If prezygotic isolation mechanisms fail, there are a variety of mechanisms that occur after fertilization to prevent successful reproduction between members of different species. The postzygotic isolation mechanisms are as follows:

➤ **Hybrid inviability.** If fertilization occurs between the gametes of two different species, the zygote will not be able to continue in development.

➤ **Hybrid sterility.** If fertilization and subsequent development successfully occurs, the hybrid offspring is sterile and unable to reproduce.

➤ **Hybrid breakdown.** Some hybrid offspring are fertile and can reproduce. However, the second-generation offspring are infertile.

TYPES OF EVOLUTION

The evolutionary process can proceed in a variety of directions or patterns such as convergent, divergent, and parallel evolution. These gradual and random changes in the genome are how evolutionary time is measured.

Convergent Evolution

When two populations exist in the same type of environment that provides the same selective pressures, the two populations will evolve in a similar manner via **convergent evolution**. While the populations may not be closely related, they may develop similar analogous structures to allow them to function in similar environments. Fish in Antartica have evolved the ability to produce specialized glycoproteins that serve as a sort of antifreeze to prevent their tissues from freezing in the low-temperature water. Fish on the opposite side of the world, in the Arctic, have evolved the same kind of antifreeze protection mechanism. Genetic studies show that the two species of fish produce antifreeze proteins that are very different from each other, which strongly suggests that two independent events led to the evolution of these mechanisms.

Divergent Evolution

In an individual population, it is possible that individuals within the population evolve differently. Over time, this may lead to the development of new species via divergent evolution. In many cases, changes to the population or geographic isolation may cause different adaptations within the population. This sort of evolution can lead to homologous structures. Vertebrate limbs are an excellent example of divergent evolution. The forearms of different vertebrate species have different structures and functions; however, they all diverged from a common origin.

Parallel Evolution

When two species share the same environment, the evolution of one species can affect the evolution of the other species. This is called **parallel evolution** or coevolution. Any changes to one species will require adaptations to the other species for them to continue to exist in the same environment. An example might be how the predation patterns of birds might influence the evolution of butterfly species sharing the same space. Some butterflies have evolved the ability to store poisonous chemicals that deter birds from eating them, while other butterflies simply mimic the poisonous ones to avoid being preyed upon.

CHAPTER 4

Principles of Bioenergetics and Fuel Molecule Metabolism

Read This Chapter to Learn About

➤ Bioenergetics

➤ Carbohydrates

➤ Cellular Metabolism

➤ Fatty Acid and Protein Metabolism

BIOENERGETICS

Bioenergetics refers to the initial and final energy states of biomolecules. Understanding the key principles of bioenergetics is important because it allows people to determine the direction and extent to which specific biochemical reactions will or will not occur. The three primary factors that determine chemical reactions are total heat content (enthalpy), disorder (entropy), and the energy available to do work (free energy).

Adenosine Triphosphate

All living things harvest energy from various biomolecules (primarily carbohydrates and fatty acids) in controlled ways to sustain life. The energy extracted from food is

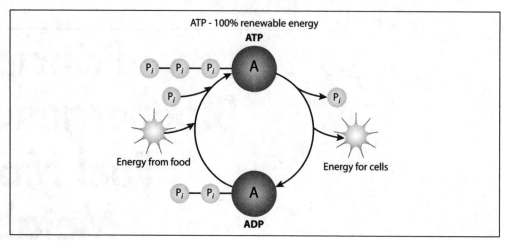

FIGURE 4-1 The structure of ATP and ADP.

used to build complex molecules and for energy storage. The preferred source of potential energy for cells is **adenosine triphosphate** (ATP). The hydrolysis of ATP provides energy that can be coupled to other reactions in the cell to increase their thermodynamic favorability.

The structure of ATP can be seen in Figure 4-1. ATP is a hybrid molecule consisting of the nitrogenous base adenine (found in nucleotides), the sugar ribose, and three phosphate groups (P_i). The breaking of the bond that attaches the last P_i to the molecule results in the release of energy that is used in a variety of cellular processes. The resulting molecule is adenosine diphosphate (ADP). A P_i must be reattached to ADP to regenerate ATP. Unfortunately, the process of adding a P_i to ADP is not a simple one. The chemical reactions of cellular respiration are used to achieve this goal.

CARBOHYDRATES

As the name suggests, **carbohydrates** are formally hydrates of carbon. For example, the well-known chemical formula for glucose ($C_6H_{12}O_6$) can be expressed as a whole-number ratio of carbon and water: $C_6(H_2O)_6$. In living systems, carbohydrates feature in a wide variety of roles, including reservoirs of chemical energy, structural polymers, and tags for cell recognition.

Monosaccharides

Carbohydrates tend to be sorted into four categories: monosaccharides, disaccharides, oligosaccharides, and polysaccharides. Among these, the basic building blocks are the **monosaccharides**, or simple sugars. From a functional group standpoint, these compounds can be thought of as polyhydroxyketones and aldehydes—in other words, each sugar contains one carbonyl group and several hydroxyl groups. If the carbonyl group

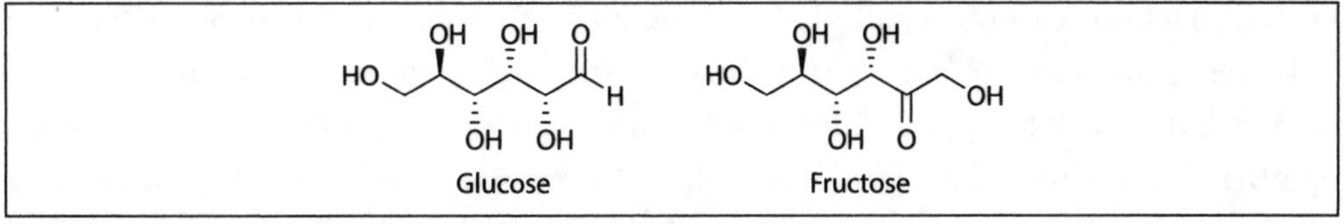

FIGURE 4-2 The simple sugars glucose and fructose.

is at the end of the chain (i.e., an aldehyde), then the sugar is termed an **aldose**; if the carbonyl is internal, then the sugar is a **ketose**. Furthermore, sugars are characterized by the number of carbons in the backbone. Thus three-carbon sugars are generically classified as **trioses**, with the next higher homologs being **tetroses** (four carbons), **pentoses** (five carbons), and **hexoses** (six carbons). By this definition, glucose is an aldohexose, whereas fructose is a ketohexose (Figure 4-2).

In terms of stereochemistry, the simple sugars fall into two broad categories: D-sugars and L-sugars, whereby the former represent the lion's share of naturally occurring sugars. The D-aldoses derive from D-glyceraldehyde (Figure 4-3). Note that

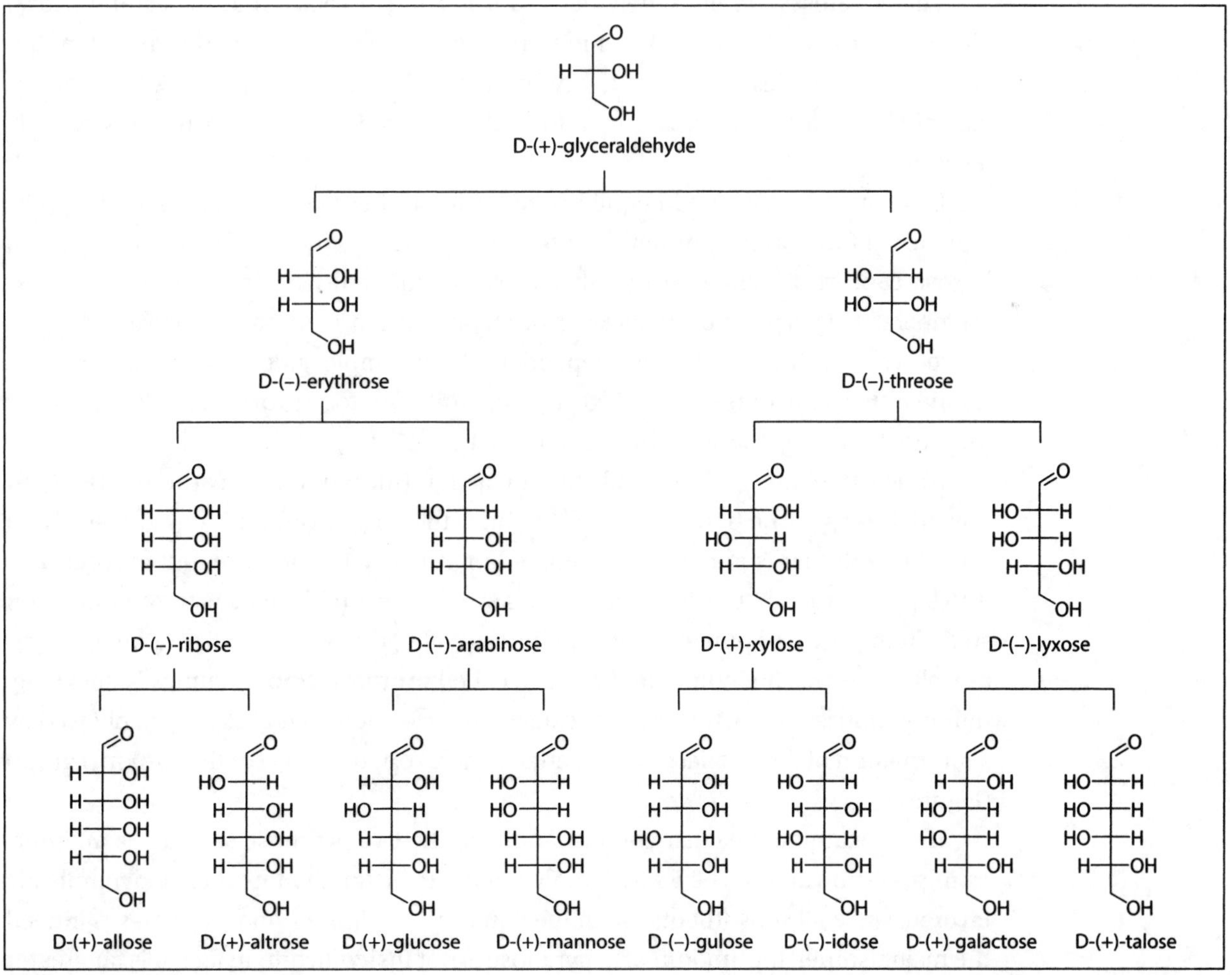

FIGURE 4-3 The family of D-aldoses.

the lowest chiral carbon in all of these sugars has the same stereochemistry. The L-aldoses (not shown) are mirror images (or enantiomers) of their D-aldose counterparts—for example, L-glucose is the enantiomer of D-glucose. In a similar vein, members within the same family are diastereomers—for example, D-glucose is a diastereomer of D-mannose, and D-ribose is a diastereomer of D-xylose.

The designation of D-glyceraldehyde stemmed from the fact that it rotated polarized light in a right-handed fashion (i.e., it was dextrorotatory). However, not all of the D-sugars are dextrorotatory. Therefore, an additional nomenclature tag is frequently used with a simple sugar to indicate how it rotates light. Thus D-(−)-erythrose is a derivative of D-glyceraldehyde, but the minus sign indicates it rotates polarized light to the left (i.e., levorotatory). On the other hand, D-(+)-galactose is a derivative of D-glyceraldehyde that happens to be dextrorotatory. In other words, D- and L- indicate whether the sugar is derived from D- or L-glyceraldehyde, while (+)- and (−)- indicate whether the sugars are dextrorotatory or levorotatory, respectively. Please note that both of these designations are completely independent of the R/S convention for naming chiral centers.

The D-ketoses are ultimately derived from dihydroxyacetone (an achiral triose) via D-erythrulose (Figure 4-4). Among the ketoses, D-fructose is the most familiar congener. The D-designation of D-erythrulose is derived from comparison of its single chiral center to that of D-glyceraldehyde. Interestingly, D-erythrulose is actually levorotatory.

In solution, sugars are in equilibrium between the open-chain form and a cyclic hemiacetal form, a transformation catalyzed by either acid or base. Any pentose and hexose can, in principle, form either a five-membered ring (a furanose) or a six-membered ring (a pyranose); however, often one form predominates for a given sugar. The outcome is highly substrate-dependent. For example, glucose forms almost predominantly the pyranose ring (Figure 4-5), while fructose provides a 1:2 mixture of furanose and pyranose structures, respectively.

Notice that the hydroxyl substituent at C1 (the anomeric carbon) can point toward the top or the bottom face of the ring—the former isomer is designated β and the latter α. Either isomer can be prepared in pure crystalline form, but in solution a 9:16 equilibrium mixture of $\alpha : \beta$ isomers is eventually established. As the composition shifts from pure α or pure β to the equilibrium ratio, the bulk optical rotation changes as well—thus this phenomenon has been called **mutarotation**. Chemically speaking, mutarotation is nothing more than an acid-catalyzed hemiacetal cleavage, followed by a reformation of the hemiacetal with attack on the opposite face of the carbonyl group (Figure 4-6).

If you examine the chair conformations of the two pyranose structures, an interesting question arises. The β form would appear to be much more thermodynamically favored, since all substituents are in the equatorial attitude—and while this is indeed the major isomer, the amount of α-pyranose is not insignificant. In fact, it is far greater

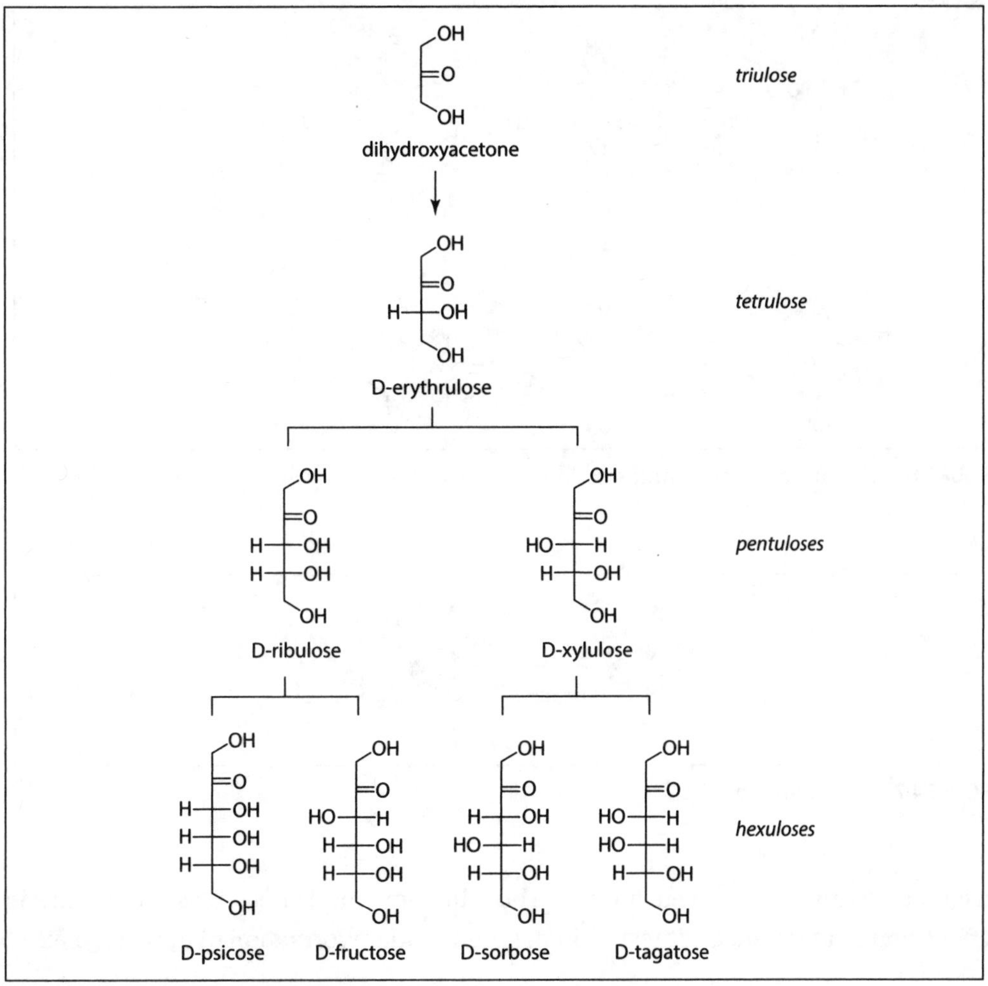

FIGURE 4-4 The D-family of ketoses.

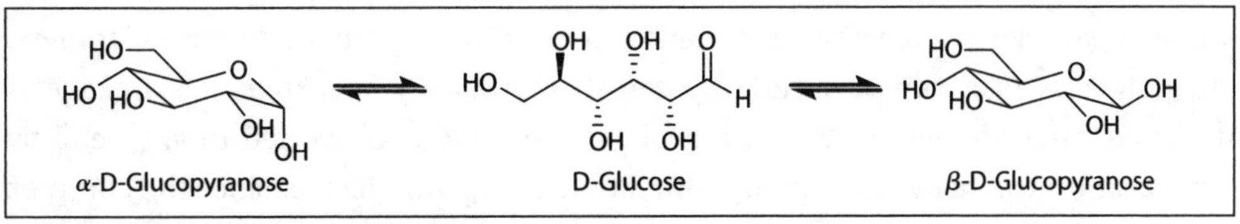

FIGURE 4-5 Equilibrium mixture of open-chain and pyranose forms of D-glucose.

than would be predicted by steric factors alone. Therefore, some other factor must be playing a role in privileging this axial hydroxyl substituent.

The answer lies in dipole-dipole interactions. If you examine Newman projections of both isomers, sighting down the bond between C1 and the ring oxygen (Figure 4-7), you find that the β-isomer places the C1 hydroxyl group in a position that bisects the lone pairs on the ring oxygen. This, in turn, brings the dipole of the hydroxyl group and ring oxygen into coalignment—a situation that is electrostatically disfavored. On the other hand, the α-isomer allows for the two dipoles to adopt a more favorable

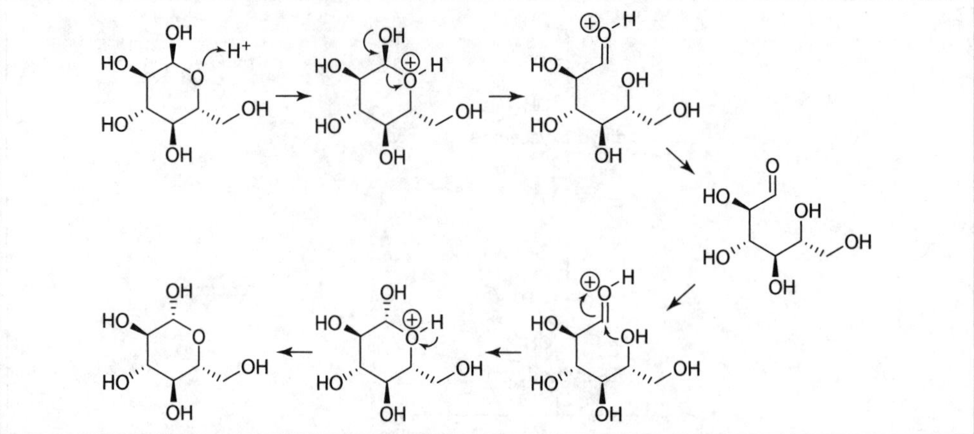

FIGURE 4-6 The mechanism of mutarotation.

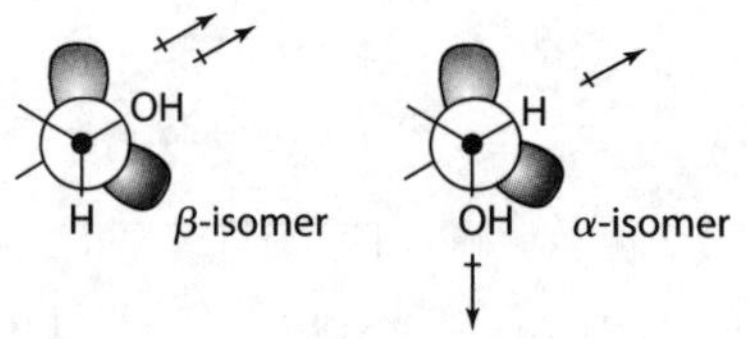

FIGURE 4-7 The anomeric effect.

alignment with respect to each other. This phenomenon is known as the **anomeric effect**, and in many sugars it results in the predominant formation of the α-isomer.

Disaccharides and Oligosaccharides

Simple sugars can link together via the anomeric carbon to produce dimers, oligomers, and polymers (aka complex carbohydrates). Chemically speaking, this linkage is produced when the hemiacetal of one sugar molecule is converted to an acetal by condensation with a hydroxyl group from another sugar molecule. Since the complex carbohydrates can involve many different monomers, the simple sugars have been given three-letter abbreviations (see table) to simplify the nomenclature of di-, oligo-, and polysaccharides (not unlike the three-letter abbreviations for amino acids).

In addition to the identity of the sugars involved, these higher-order carbohydrates are characterized by the configuration at the anomeric carbon (i.e., α vs. β), as well as the hydroxyl group used to form the acetal linkage (specified by the carbon bearing the hydroxyl group). For example, the disaccharide sucrose (Figure 4-8) is a dimer of α-D-glucose and β-D-fructose, and the two are linked via the 1-hydroxy group of glucose and the 2-hydroxy group of fructose. Therefore, the systematic name for sucrose is α-D-Glc-(1→2)-β-D-Fru.

When multiple simple sugars are connected, oligosaccharides are formed, such as lacto-N-tetraose (LNT, Figure 4-9), a type of human milk oligosaccharide (HMO)

The Common Simple Sugars and Their Abbreviations			
Aldoses		**Ketoses**	
pentoses		*pentuloses*	
D-ribose	Rib	D-ribulose	Rul
D-arabinose	Ara	D-xylulose	Xul
D-xylose	Xyl		
D-lyxose	Lyx		
hexoses		*hexuloses*	
D-allose	All	D-psicose	Psi
D-altrose	Alt	D-fructose	Fru
D-glucose	Glc	D-sorbose	Sor
D-mannose	Man	D-tagatose	Tag
D-gulose	Gul		
D-idose	Ido		
D-galactose	Gal		
D-talose	Tal		

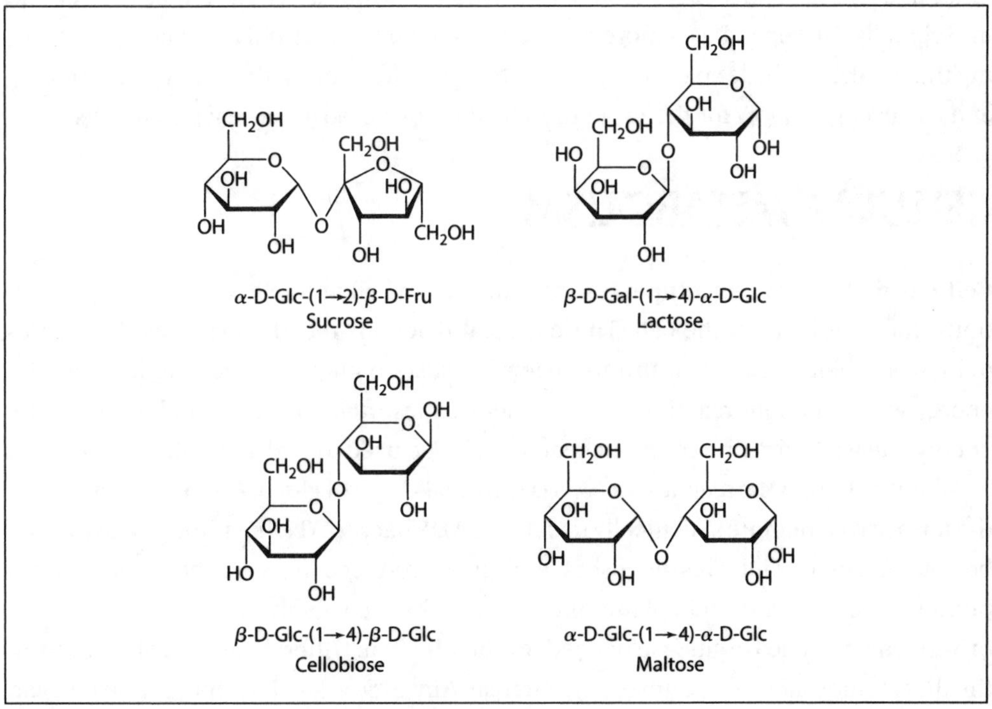

FIGURE 4-8 Four naturally abundant disaccharides.

implicated in the development of the early immune system and the modulation of gastrointestinal microbiota.

Polysaccharides

Finally, **polysaccharides** consist of much longer arrays of covalently connected simple sugars, which can be a diverse array of components or a repeating identical monomer. For example, cellulose is constructed from β-D-glucose connected by a $1 \rightarrow 4$ linkage

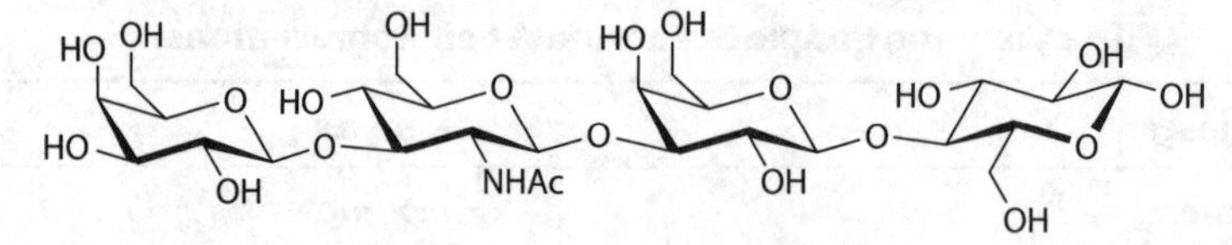

FIGURE 4-9 Lacto-N-tetraose (LNT), an oligosaccharide.

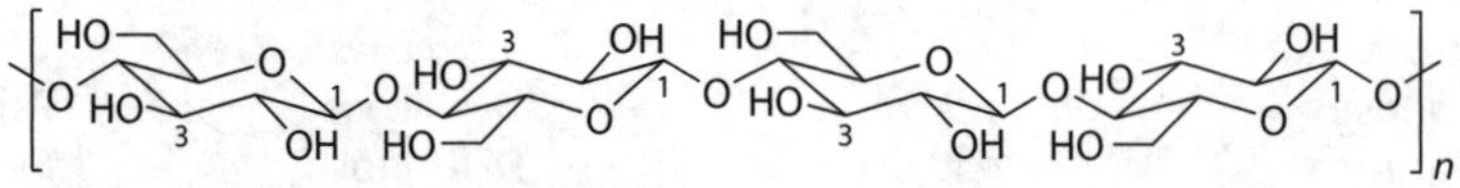

FIGURE 4-10 Cellulose, a polysaccharide.

(Figure 4-10). The very flat geometry afforded by this arrangement lends cellulose its structural characteristics (strong, fibrous polymer with high tensile strength) crucial to the integrity of plant cell walls. Glycogen is another polysaccharide of critical importance as a storage molecule in vertebrates, where it is found in abundance in liver and muscle cells. Glycogen has a more compact shape than other polysaccharides, meaning that it takes up little space in terms of storage. Additionally, the many nonreducing ends in glycogen allow for the rapid mobilization of stored glucose when needed.

CELLULAR METABOLISM

Cellular metabolism encompasses the sum total of all anabolic and catabolic reactions that occur within the cell. These critical reactions rely on a variety of enzymes to increase their rate to an appropriate level to sustain life. Anabolic reactions require energy, while catabolic reactions release energy. These reactions are coupled so that the energy released from one catabolic reaction can be used to fuel an anabolic reaction.

A critical catabolic reaction in cells is the breakdown of glucose to release energy in the form of ATP, or more specifically to convert ADP back to ATP. In animals, glucose can be obtained in the diet. This glucose is ultimately produced in the anabolic reactions of photosynthesis that occur in plants and is stored as starch. As animals ingest starch, it is broken down to release glucose needed for metabolism. Other sources of glucose from the diet include lactose, maltose, and sucrose. Any excess glucose that is ingested can be stored as glycogen for later use as a source of glucose. Glycogen is stored primarily in cells of the liver and muscles.

The breakdown of glucose occurs in the process of cellular respiration that must be done by all living organisms. Cellular respiration can be done aerobically (using oxygen) or anaerobically (without oxygen). The aerobic pathway has a much higher ATP yield than the anaerobic pathway. The production of ATP in either pathway relies on the addition of a P_i to ADP. This can be achieved through substrate level phosphorylation when ATP synthesis is directly coupled to the breakdown of glucose or via oxidative phosphorylation where ATP synthesis involves an intermediate molecule.

Glucose and Glycogen

From a biological perspective, the relationship between **glucose** and **glycogen** is a critical one. **Glycogenesis**, glycogen synthesis, occurs when blood glucose levels are high, typically after a meal, and relies on the enzyme glycogen synthase. **Glycogenolysis**, glycogen breakdown, occurs when blood sugar levels are low and relies on the enzyme glycogen phosphorylase. The reactions of glycogenesis and glycogenolysis can be seen in Figure 4-11.

The regulation of glycogenesis and glycogenolysis is a complex mechanism that involves the hormones insulin and glucagon, both secreted by the pancreas. Insulin exerts its effects by binding to cell receptors, which initiates a phosphorylation cascade that ultimately increases the rate of glucose uptake into cells, activates the enzymes required for glycogenesis, and inhibits the enzymes of glycogenolysis. Glucagon is antagonistic to insulin. As glucagon binds to its receptors, adenylate cyclase converts ATP to the second messenger cAMP, which in turn amplifies the original signal and leads to the release of glucose molecules from glycogen.

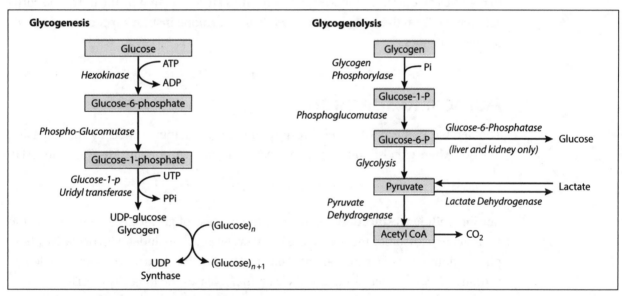

FIGURE 4-11 Glycogenesis and glycogenolysis.

In addition to the regulatory roles of glucagon and insulin, the hormone epinephrine also has an influence. In the presence of epinephrine secreted from the adrenal medulla, glycogenolysis is stimulated, while glycogenesis is inhibited. This occurs because epinephrine activates adenylate cyclase in liver and muscle cells.

Gluconeogenesis

To keep glucose levels relatively stable and fuel metabolism, organisms must be able to generate glucose in addition to the glucose they can extract from stored glycogen.

While glucose can be obtained in the diet of animals from other molecules such as starch, lactose, maltose, and sucrose, it can also be generated from other noncarbohydrate molecules in the process of gluconeogenesis. The primary variables that encourage gluconeogenesis are low carbohydrate dieting, extreme activity levels, and fasting/starvation. In mammals, the process occurs primarily in the liver.

The steps of **gluconeogenesis** have some resemblance to glycolysis in reverse. These reactions and the enzymes that catalyze them can be seen in Figure 4-12. The potential starting materials for gluconeogenesis include pyruvate, lactate, glycerol, some amino acids, and some fatty acids.

Regulation of gluconeogenesis is influenced by allosteric effectors and hormones. ATP, adenosine monophosphate (AMP), and acetyl-CoA all serve as allosteric modulators. High levels of lactate, glycerol, acetyl-CoA, and amino acids stimulate the process levels of acetyl-CoA (high levels increase gluconeogenesis) and levels of ADP (high levels discourage gluconeogenesis). Depending on the starting substrate, the process may begin in either the mitochondria or cytoplasm and conclude in the endoplasmic reticulum of the cell. Glucose transporters ultimately move the newly synthesized glucose to the cell's cytoplasm. Gluconeogenic enzymes are stimulated by the hormone cortisol secreted from the adrenal cortex, while the hormone insulin suppresses synthesis of these enzymes.

Aerobic Respiration

The aerobic pathway of cellular respiration can be demonstrated by the following reaction where glucose and oxygen interact to produce carbon dioxide, water, and ATP:

$$C_6H_{12}O_6 + 6O_2 \; \rightarrow \; 6CO_2 + 6H_2O + ATP$$

Aerobic cellular respiration begins with the process of glycolysis, is followed by the citric acid cycle (sometimes called the Krebs cycle), and concludes with oxidative phosphorylation in the electron transport chain. The electron transport chain is fueled by protons (H^+) and electrons and is the step that releases the majority of ATP.

During glycolysis and the citric acid cycle, glucose is systematically broken down and small amounts of ATP are generated by substrate level phosphorylation. Carbon dioxide is released as a waste product. However, the most important part of these steps is that the breakdown of glucose allows for electron carrier molecules to collect protons and electrons needed to run the electron transport chain, where ATP is produced in mass quantities.

Electron carrier molecules are a critical part of cellular respiration. These electron carrier molecules include nicotinamide adenine dinucleotide (NAD^+) and the flavoprotein flavin adenine dinucleotide (FAD). When these molecules pick up electrons and protons, they are reduced to NADH and $FADH_2$. The reduced forms of the carrier molecules deliver protons and electrons to power the electron transport chain. Once

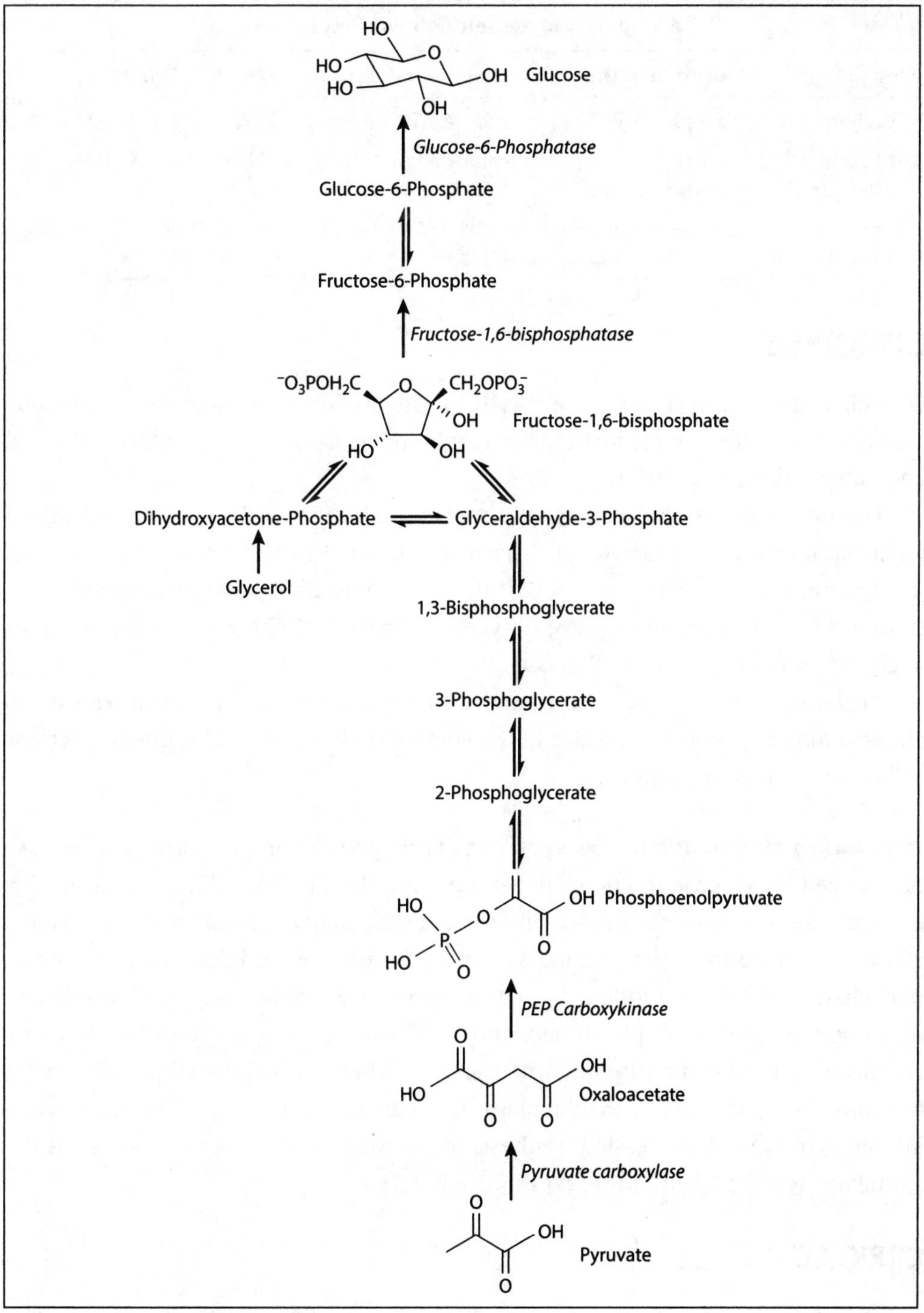

FIGURE 4-12 Gluconeogenesis.

these items are delivered to the electron transport chain, the molecules return to their oxidized forms, NAD^+ and FAD.

An overview of all the reactions of aerobic cellular respiration, including key starting and ending products, is shown in the following table.

A Summary of Aerobic Cellular Respiration			
Step	Location in the Cell	Starting Products	Ending Products
Glycolysis	Cytoplasm	Glucose, ATP, ADP, NAD$^+$	Pyruvate, ATP, NADH
Citric acid cycle	Matrix of mitochondria	Acetyl-CoA, ADP, NAD$^+$, FAD	CO_2, ATP, NADH, FADH$_2$
Electron transport chain	Cristae membrane of mitochondria	NADH, FADH$_2$, O_2, ADP	NAD$^+$, FAD, H$_2$O, ATP

GLYCOLYSIS

Overall, the process of **glycolysis** breaks down glucose into two molecules of pyruvate. This happens in the cytoplasm of the cell and is the starting step for both aerobic and anaerobic cellular respiration.

During the process, 2 ATP molecules are invested while 4 ATP molecules are gained via substrate level phosphorylation. This results in a net gain of 2 ATP for the process. In addition, NAD$^+$ is reduced to NADH that will be used in a later step (the electron transport chain) for oxidative phosphorylation. Figure 4-13 shows the major reactions of glycolysis and the enzymes that catalyze them.

At the end of glycolysis, the pyruvate molecules can be further broken down either aerobically or anaerobically. In the aerobic pathway, the subsequent reactions will occur in the mitochondria.

Regulation of Glycolysis. The regulation of glycolysis is complex, primarily because of the need for glucose in energy generation and the need for glucose as a starting molecule for synthesis to other biomolecules. The major regulatory mechanism is allosteric regulation of the glycolysis enzymes hexokinase (inhibited by glucose-6-phosphate), PFK-1 (inhibited by citrate and ATP; activated by fructose-2,6-bisphosphate, fructose-6-phosphate, and AMP), and pyruvate kinase (inhibited by acetyl-CoA and ATP; activated by fructose-1,6-biphosphate and AMP). Additionally, the hormones glucagon and insulin play roles in the regulation of glycolysis. Glucagon inhibits glycolysis by repressing synthesis of fructose-2,6-biphosphate, while insulin stimulates synthesis of fructose-2,6-biphosphate.

CITRIC ACID CYCLE

The two pyruvate molecules remaining at the end of glycolysis are actively transported to the mitochondria, specifically to the matrix of the mitochondria. The structure of a mitochondrion, illustrated in Figure 4-14, is important to its function in cellular respiration. A key feature of this organelle is its double membrane. The space between the inner and outer membrane is termed the **intermembrane space**. The space bounded by the inner membrane is a liquid called the matrix, and it is here where the citric acid cycle occurs. The folded inner membrane is called the cristae membrane and is the site of the next step in the process, the electron transport chain.

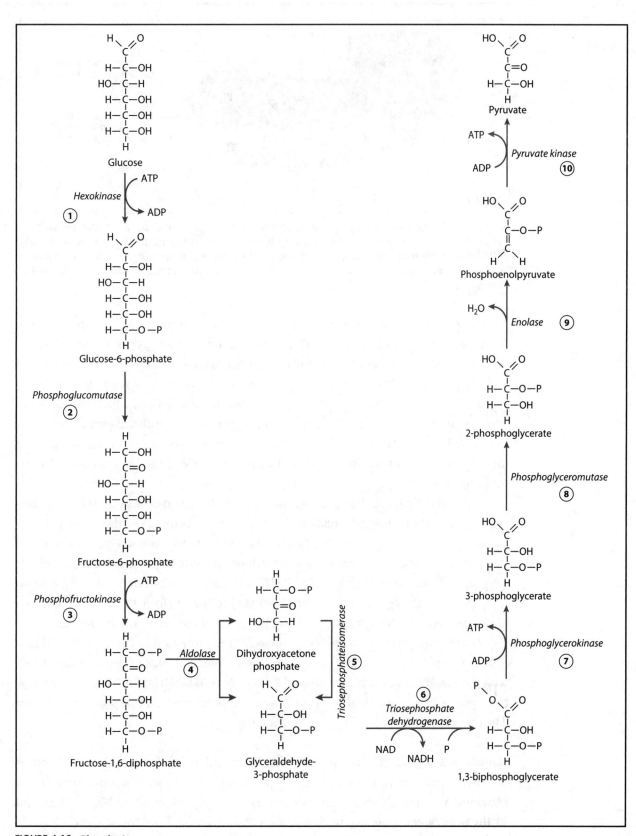

FIGURE 4-13 Glycolysis.

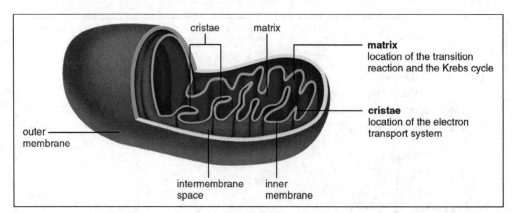

FIGURE 4-14 Mitochondrion structure. A mitochondrion is bound by a double membrane. Pyruvate decarboxylation and the Krebs cycle occur within the matrix of the mitochondria, and the electron transport chain occurs within the cristae membrane. *Source:* From Sylvia S. Mader, *Biology*, 8th ed., McGraw-Hill, 2004; reproduced with permission of The McGraw-Hill Companies.

Once in the mitochondria, pyruvate molecules are modified to enter into the reactions of the citric acid cycle. This modification, termed **pyruvate decarboxylation**, involves the oxidation of pyruvate and the release of CO_2 as illustrated at the top of Figure 4-15. The remnants of pyruvate are a two-carbon acetyl group. Coenzyme A (CoA) is added to the acetyl group, creating acetyl-CoA, which is capable of entering the citric acid cycle. These modifications to pyruvate also allow for the reduction of NAD^+ to NADH that will be used later in the electron transport chain. Because there are two pyruvate molecules, this step produces $2\ CO_2$, 2 acetyl-CoA, and 2 NADH molecules.

The acetyl-CoA that has been formed enters the **citric acid cycle** by combining with a four-carbon molecule (oxaloacetate), which forms the six-carbon molecule citric acid. The remaining reactions of the citric acid cycle are seen in Figure 4-15. These reactions include the removal of the two carbons that entered as acetyl-CoA, which are released as CO_2; the production of one ATP molecule via substrate level phosphorylation; and the rearrangement of the intermediate products to form the starting molecule of oxaloacetate. In this way, the cycle is able to continue. In addition, the rearrangement of intermediates in the process allows for the reduction of NAD^+ to NADH and FAD to $FADH_2$. Because there are 2 acetyl-CoA molecules, this cycle must turn twice with the result being the production of $4\ CO_2$, 2 ATP, 6 NADH, and 2 $FADH_2$. The glucose has been fully broken down into CO_2, which is released. At this point, the process continues with the electron transport chain.

Regulation of the Citric Acid Cycle. The regulation of the citric acid cycle is achieved primarily through substrate availability and allosteric modulation of key enzymes. Additionally, the cycle is dependent on the availability of NAD^+, FAD, and ADP. The enzymes subjected to allosteric regulation within the citric acid cycle include citrate synthase, isocitrate dehydrogenase, and α-ketoglutarate dehydrogenase.

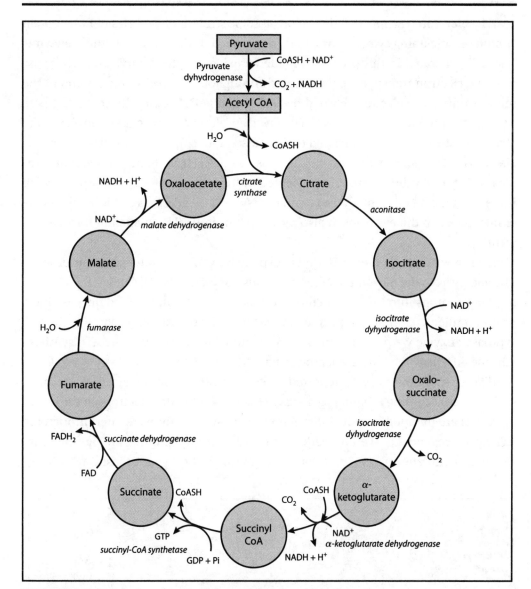

FIGURE 4-15 Pyruvate decarboxylation and the citric acid cycle.

Further, the activities of pyruvate dehydrogenase and pyruvate carboxylase operate outside of the citric acid cycle but have major influence on the regulation of the cycle.

THE ELECTRON TRANSPORT CHAIN AND OXIDATIVE PHOSPHORYLATION

During glycolysis and the citric acid cycle, NAD^+ and FAD have been reduced to NADH and $FADH_2$. Once they are reduced, they move toward the electron transport chains located in the cristae membrane of the mitochondria. They are oxidized by releasing the electrons and protons they carry to the electron transport chain. At this point, the oxidized forms of NAD^+ and FAD return to glycolysis and the citric acid cycle to be used again and again.

The **electron transport chain** (Figure 4-16) is structurally a series of four protein complexes, including cytochromes, that are associated with an ATP synthase enzyme. The ATP generated in this process is made by oxidative phosphorylation. There are multiple electron transport chains located throughout the cristae membrane of the mitochondria. The electrons carried by NADH and $FADH_2$ enter the chain and pass through the protein complexes. NADH delivers its electrons to the first complex in the chain; the electrons are then passed to the subsequent complexes. $FADH_2$ delivers its electrons to the second complex and then passes the electrons to the subsequent complexes. Eventually the electrons are accepted by the terminal electron acceptor, which is the oxygen inhaled through the respiratory system (hence the aerobic label). As the oxygen picks up the electrons, it also picks up 2 protons (H^+), which in turn creates water.

The **chemiosmotic theory** is used to explain how ATP is produced in this process. The energy from the movement of the electrons donated by NADH and $FADH_2$ is used to pump protons into the intermembrane space. These protons build up, creating a proton gradient, referred to as proton motive force. The protons move through the ATP synthase enzyme via passive transport. As protons moves through the ATP synthase enzyme, ADP is phosphorylated, producing ATP.

The exact amount of ATP reported as being produced in the electron transport chain varies according to source. For every NADH that donates electrons to the chain, 3 protons are pumped into the intermembrane space, 3 protons reenter through the ATP synthase, and 2.5 ATP are made. For every $FADH_2$, 2 protons are pumped into the intermembrane space, 2 protons reenter through the ATP synthase, and 1.5 ATP

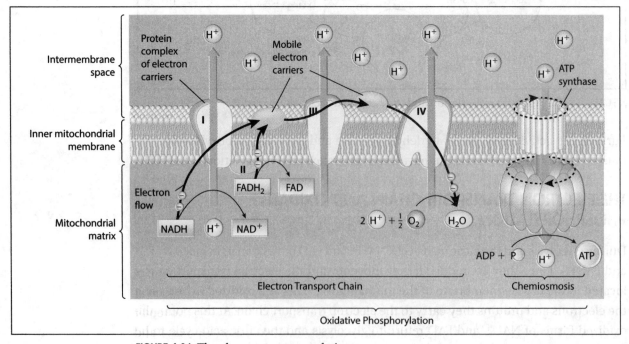

FIGURE 4-16 The electron transport chain.

are made. Theoretically, a grand total of 28 ATP are produced in the electron transport chain. Combining this range of ATP with the 4 ATP produced by substrate level phosphorylation in glycolysis and the citric acid cycle leads to an approximate grand total of 30 to 36 ATP made in aerobic cellular respiration per glucose molecule. A summary of ATP made throughout the process of aerobic respiration can be seen in the following table.

ATP Production in Aerobic Cellular Respiration		
Step of Aerobic Cellular Respiration	Products of Previous Steps	ATP Made During Chemiosmotic Phosphorylation in the Electron Transport Chain
Glycolysis	2 NADH 2 ATP	2 NADH = 5 ATP (however, the net gain will be approximately 3 ATP due to the use of ATP to actively transport pyruvate to the mitochondria)
Citric acid cycle (including pyruvate decarboxylation)	8 NADH 2 FADH2 2ATP	8 NADH = 20 ATP 2 FADH2 = 3 ATP
Total	4 ATP (substrate level phosphorylation from glycolysis and the citric acid cycle)	28 ATP (oxidative phosphorylation from the electron transport chain)

If oxygen is not available to accept electrons, the electrons in the electron transport chain will build up, essentially shutting down the electron transport chain. Not only does ATP production drastically decline, but now that NADH cannot be oxidized to NAD$^+$ by the electron transport chain, there is not enough NAD$^+$ to continue glycolysis. In this case, the use of **fermentation** (a part of the anaerobic pathway) will be necessary to complete the oxidation of NADH to NAD$^+$ in order to continue glycolysis.

Regulation of Oxidative Phosphorylation. The magnitude of the proton motive force is the primary regulator of the flow of electrons through the electron transport chain. Increases to the proton motive force cause a decrease in the rate of electron flow, and decreases in the proton motive force cause an increase in the rate of electron flow. Additionally, the ADP concentration within a cell influences the rate of electron transport. During times of increased energy needs, such as during physical exertion, the rate of proton flow through ATP synthase and the rate of electron flow will increase.

Oxidative Stress. The process of oxidative phosphorylation can lead to the release of activated oxygen from the mitochondria. The reactive oxygen species that result must either be broken down enzymatically via antioxidants or the cells must be able to repair the damage caused by the reactive oxygen species. Superoxide dismutase, catalase, and gluthathione peroxidase are all known cellular antioxidants.

Oxidative stress occurs when the cell cannot keep up with the breakdown of, or management of damage from, reactive oxygen species. While minor oxidative stress can be tolerable to cells, increasing levels of oxidative stress can be particularly problematic. Even moderate oxidative stress can trigger apoptosis in cells. Oxidative stress also appears to be implicated in a variety of diseased conditions, including neurodegenerative diseases such as Alzheimer's, Parkinson's, and Huntington's diseases.

Anaerobic Pathways

There are times when oxygen is either not available or not utilized by cells to perform aerobic respiration. For animals, this may occur for brief episodes when the oxygen demands of the cells cannot be met for brief periods of time. Unfortunately, the use of anaerobic respiration produces very little ATP as compared to aerobic cellular respiration and thus cannot meet the ATP demands of larger organisms for extended periods of time. However, in some smaller organisms such as certain bacteria and yeasts, anaerobic respiration is used permanently or for lengthy periods of time.

The first step in the anaerobic pathway is glycolysis. Once glycolysis occurs and pyruvate is generated, the **anaerobic pathway** continues with a second step, fermentation. Depending on the organism, fermentation can occur in one of two ways—lactic acid fermentation or alcoholic fermentation. The primary benefit of either type of fermentation is that it allows for the oxidation of NADH to NAD$^+$ that is necessary for glycolysis to continue in the absence of functional electron transport chains. It is important to note that fermentation itself produces no ATP. The only ATP created during anaerobic respiration (glycolysis and fermentation) is from the glycolysis step. Therefore, it is absolutely critical to regenerate the NAD$^+$ needed to continue with glycolysis. The total net gain of ATP from anaerobic respiration is 2 ATP as compared to 32 from complete aerobic respiration.

LACTIC ACID FERMENTATION

Lactic acid fermentation occurs in some types of bacteria and fungi as well as in the muscle cells of animals when oxygen levels are not sufficient to meet the demands of aerobic respiration. In this step, pyruvate is reduced to lactic acid, thus regenerating the NAD$^+$ needed to continue glycolysis.

ALCOHOLIC FERMENTATION

Some organisms such as certain bacteria and yeast use **alcoholic fermentation**. In this step, pyruvate is decarboxylated, which produces CO_2, and then reduced to form ethanol. As with lactic acid fermentation, NAD$^+$ is recycled so that glycolysis may continue.

Pentose Phosphate Pathway

In contrast to the catabolic nature of glycolysis, the **pentose phosphate pathway** provides an anabolic alternative to glycolysis. The detailed steps of the pathway can be seen in Figure 4-17. The results of the pentose phosphate pathway are (1) the generation of NADPH, which can be used in anabolic reactions such as fatty acid synthesis in cells, (2) the production of ribose-5-phosphate, which is used for the synthesis of nucleotides, and (3) the production of erythrose-4-phosphate, which is used for synthesis of aromatic amino acids. The pentose phosphate pathway is most active in cells

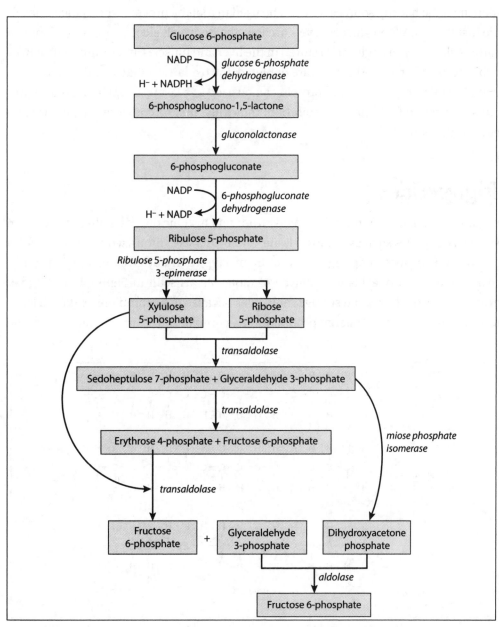

FIGURE 4-17 Pentose phosphate pathway.

that perform high levels of lipid synthesis and in cells that are at high risk for oxidative damage.

FATTY ACID AND PROTEIN METABOLISM

To this point, glucose has been discussed as the only starting material for cellular respiration. However, there are times when glucose may not be available to cells in sufficient quantities. If cellular respiration were to stop completely due to a lack of glucose, death would occur quickly due to a lack of sufficient energy supplies. For this reason, there must be backup sources that can be used to fuel the process when glucose levels are insufficient. When glucose levels are low, the body will elect to use other forms of carbohydrates such as glycogen stored in the liver and muscles and to stimulate gluconeogenesis. When those reserves are depleted, the oxidation of fatty acids can be used to fuel cellular respiration, and protein can be used as a last resort. When fats and proteins are used to fuel cellular respiration, they must first be converted to glucose or a glucose derivative.

Triglycerides

Organisms can acquire their fatty acids from fats in their diet, fats already stored in specialized tissues such as adipose tissue, and from fats synthesized in the body from carbohydrates. In considering the structure of a typical triacylglycerol, or triglyceride, there are three fatty acids and a glycerol molecule, as seen in Figure 4-18. **Triglycerides** are particularly good storage molecules because their complete oxidation leads to more than twice the energy production as compared to carbohydrate or protein

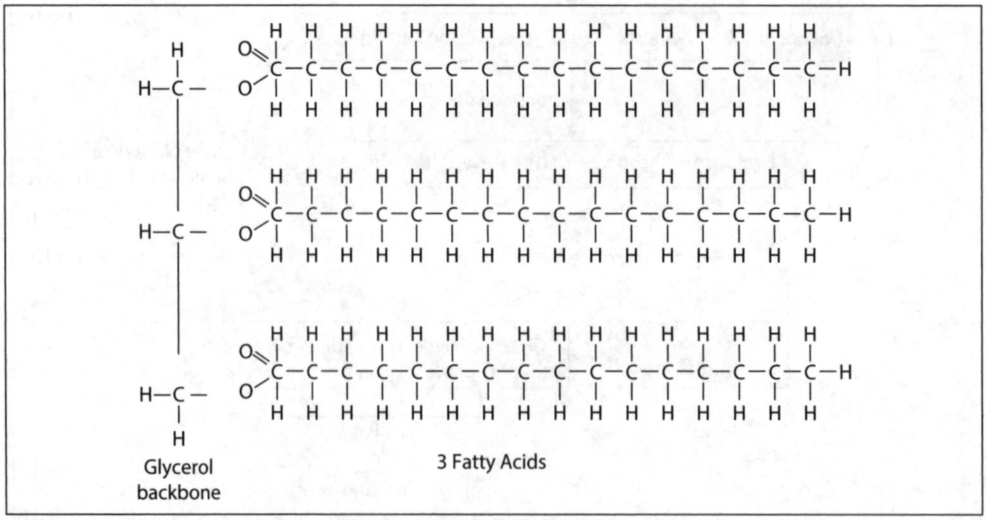

FIGURE 4-18 Structure of a triglyceride.

oxidation. Additionally, their relative chemical inertness allows them to be stored in large amounts in the cell without risk of undesirable chemical reactions with other molecules of the cell.

BIOSYNTHESIS OF FATS

Excess carbohydrates in animals are converted to triglycerides in the smooth endoplasmic reticulum of cells. The process of **lipogenesis** involves the conversion of acetyl-CoA to fatty acids using fatty acid synthases to polymerize the fatty acid chains. To synthesize unsaturated fatty acids, a desaturation reaction is required to introduce a double bond into the fatty acid chain. Once synthesized, the fatty acids can then be converted to triglycerides. These are secreted from the liver once they are packaged in lipoproteins.

DIGESTION AND TRANSPORT OF FATS

Because triglycerides are insoluble in water, they do present some challenges in terms of chemical digestion. They require emulsification via bile salts prior to enzymatic breakdown in the intestine. Following chemical digestion, transport is also a challenge and is achieved by using carrier proteins to counter their insolubility. The result is a chylomicron. Within the blood, lipoproteins are used to transport a variety of lipid types between tissue and organs.

β-OXIDATION OF FATTY ACIDS

Once in cells, fatty acids can be converted by β-**oxidation**, a four-step process that occurs in the mitochondria, into acetyl-CoA, which can enter the citric acid cycle. β-oxidation of fatty acids also produces NADH and $FADH_2$. This process varies slightly depending on the structure of the fatty acid. Recall that saturated fatty acids contain a maximum number of hydrogens in their hydrocarbon chains, whereas unsaturated fatty acids have double covalent bonds in their chains leading to less than the maximum number of hydrogens present. The structure of saturated and unsaturated fatty acids can be seen in Figure 4-19. Saturated fatty acids with an even number of carbons are the most straightforward conversion to acetyl-CoA via ß-oxidation, but unsaturated fatty acids or fatty acids with an uneven number of carbons can also be converted with some modification. In vertebrates, acetyl-CoA can be converted to ketone bodies when glucose is not available.

Protein Metabolism

Just as fatty acid can be converted into molecules appropriate for use during cellular respiration, proteins also can be converted. As proteins are broken down into amino acids by peptidases during the digestive process, they can be chemically modified

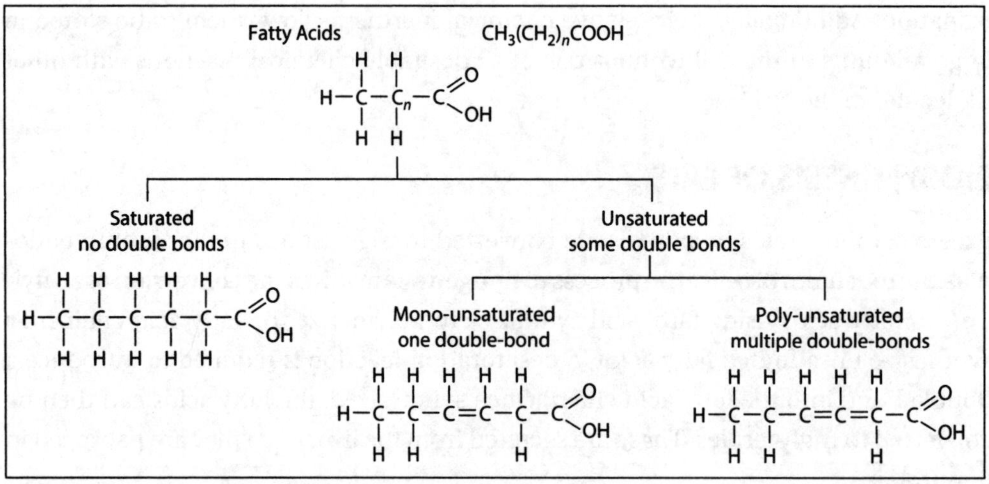

FIGURE 4-19 Saturated and unsaturated fatty acids.

within cells into α-keto acids and then converted into acetyl-CoA, pyruvate, or various intermediates of the citric acid cycle.

Unit I Minitest

20 Questions   **30 Minutes**

This minitest is designed to assess your mastery of the content in Chapters 1 through 4 of this volume. The questions have been designed to simulate actual MCAT questions in terms of format and degree of difficulty. They are based on the content categories associated with Foundational Concept 1, which is the theme of this unit. They are also designed to test the scientific inquiry and reasoning skills that the test makers have identified as essential for success in medical school.

In this test, most of the questions are based on short passages that typically describe a laboratory experiment, a research study, or some similar process. There are also some questions that are not based on passages.

Use this test to measure your readiness for the actual MCAT. Try to answer all of the questions within the specified time limit. If you run out of time, you will know that you need to work on improving your pacing.

Complete answer explanations are provided at the end of the minitest. Pay particular attention to the answers for questions you got wrong or skipped. If necessary, go back and review the corresponding chapters or text sections in this unit.

Now turn the page and begin the Unit I Minitest.

Directions: *Choose the best answer to each of the following questions. Questions 1–4 are not based on a passage.*

1. Which of the following statements BEST explains why your body prefers to perform aerobic respiration as opposed to anaerobic respiration?

   A. Anaerobic respiration does not allow for NADH to be recycled to NAD^+.

   B. Aerobic respiration requires less of an ATP investment than anaerobic respiration does.

   C. Aerobic respiration produces far more ATP than anaerobic respiration.

   D. Aerobic respiration is easier for cells to perform than anaerobic respiration.

2. If you replaced the thymine in a double helix with radioactive thymine and you allowed DNA replication to occur once, which of the following results would you expect?

   A. The DNA would not be radioactive in either of the double helices.

   B. The mRNA made from the double helices would be radioactive.

   C. The DNA in each of the double helices would be radioactive.

   D. The DNA in one of the double helices would be radioactive but not in the other one.

3. The glucose made by a plant is used by the plant to produce all the other molecules that the plant needs, such as proteins, lipids, and nucleic acids. Which statement would be correct about how plants make these other molecules?

   A. Glucose has all the elements needed to make all of the other molecules.

   B. Glucose has all of the elements needed to produce lipids, but must obtain other elements to produce proteins and nucleic acids.

   C. Glucose has all of the elements needed to produce lipids and proteins, but must obtain other elements to produce nucleic acids.

   D. None of these statements are correct.

4. In Mendel's experiments with the pea plant, the gene for height exists in two allelic forms designated T for tall stature and t for short stature. In the second generation of a cross between a homozygous tall parent (TT) and a homozygous short parent (tt), the phenotypic ratio of dominant to recessive pea plants is

   A. $1:1$

   B. $2:1$

   C. $3:1$

   D. $4:1$

Questions 5–8 are based on the following passage.

Passage I

Approximately 0.04% of Caucasians are born with cystic fibrosis. This disease is one of the most common recessive genetic diseases and is often fatal. Cystic fibrosis is characterized by the accumulation of abnormally thick mucus throughout the body and the loss of excess amounts of salt via sweat. The thick mucus builds up and causes major problems in the lungs, which often become infected, and can cause digestive abnormalities such as malnutrition and blockages through the intestinal tract. The severity of the disease is variable and many other potential complications can arise.

The gene involved in cystic fibrosis is a mutated allele of the cystic fibrosis transmembrane regulator (CFTR). There are at least 900 known mutations of this gene that can lead to cystic fibrosis. The normal CFTR gene produces the CFTR protein that is a transmembrane chloride channel in cells of the lungs, digestive tract, skin, and reproductive tract. One mutation termed delta F508 has a single amino acid change in the protein that marks it for destruction before it ever reaches the membrane to complete its function. Without the proper CFTR in the membrane of cells, the chloride and sodium ion balance is altered such that not enough water leaves the cells to produce mucus of the proper consistency. The thick mucus that results accumulates and causes multiple problems, including the trapping of bacteria that can cause infections. While there is no cure for cystic fibrosis, better management strategies have increased the life span of people with this genetic disease.

5. Many potential treatments are being evaluated for cystic fibrosis. Of the items listed, which would appear to have the BEST chance of preventing the symptoms of the disease in an affected person?
   A. the use of a drug that increases the production of CFTR
   B. the use of a drug that prevents CFTR from being degraded when it reaches the lysosomes
   C. the use of a drug that increases nutrient absorption in the small intestine
   D. the use of a drug that activates a chloride cell channel other than CFTR

6. The CFTR protein is 1,480 amino acids in length. How many codons must have been present in the mRNA used to make the protein?
   A. 493
   B. 1480
   C. 1481
   D. 4440

7. If two parents do not have cystic fibrosis but are carriers for the disease, what are their odds of having a child with cystic fibrosis?
   A. 0%
   B. 25%
   C. 50%
   D. 75%

8. Pancreatic insufficiency occurs in some cystic fibrosis patients. This means that there is a lack of digestive enzymes being secreted from the pancreas to the small intestine. Trypsin levels in particular are quite reduced. What items would the individual have a hard time digesting due to a lack of trypsin?
   A. proteins
   B. carbohydrates
   C. sugar
   D. fats

Questions 9–12 are based on the following passage.

Passage II

Within the cells of the body, mitochondria are present in variable numbers. Some cell types have a few of these organelles, and other cell types have hundreds of mitochondria. An interesting feature of mitochondria that distinguishes them from other organelles is that they have their own DNA, termed *mitochondrial DNA (mtDNA)*. The mtDNA is completely distinct from the nuclear chromosomes and is presumed to have evolved separately from the nuclear DNA. Mitochondrial DNA is circular and consists of 37 genes coding for proteins, transfer RNA (tRNA), and ribosomal RNA (rRNA). Each mitochondrion has about five copies of the mtDNA. All of the mitochondria within the body's cells are descendents of the mitochondria present in an egg cell before it was fertilized. Because all mitochondria are derived from those present in an egg cell, they contain the mtDNA from the mother. Sperm contribute no mitochondria or mtDNA to the egg cell during fertilization. This mode of inheritance is often called maternal inheritance.

While mtDNA composes a small portion of the cell's total DNA, it is subject to mutation and several diseases are known to be caused by mutations to mtDNA. One of those diseases is Leber's optic atrophy, which causes deterioration of the optic nerve and a progressive loss of central vision. Most people with this condition have inherited both normal mtDNA as well as mtDNA that carries the mutation. When the number of mutated mitochondria outnumber the normal mitochondria, symptoms of the disease occur.

9. The number of mitochondria in a particular cell type probably relate to
    A. the size of the cell and the amount of space available
    B. the number of proteins the cell needs to produce
    C. the amount of materials in the cell that need to be degraded and removed
    D. the amount of ATP the cell needs to produce

10. Men with mtDNA mutations that cause a disease
    A. will pass them on only to their sons
    B. will pass them on only to their daughters
    C. will pass them on to both sons and daughters about 50% of the time
    D. will never pass them on to their children

11. Endosymbiotic theory explains why mitochondria have their own DNA. This theory essentially states that at one point, free-living prokaryotic cells were engulfed by another cell, eventually becoming mitochondria. The BEST support for this theory is that
    A. mitochondria are membrane-bound organelles
    B. mitochondrial DNA resembles that of prokaryotic DNA
    C. mitochondria have more than one copy of their DNA
    D. mitochondria are found in multiple copies in each cell

12. Mitochondrial DNA within the cells of a given organism is derived from a single source. Which of the following processes should NOT occur within mtDNA?
    A. transcription
    B. translation
    C. crossing over and recombination
    D. spontaneous mutation

Questions 13–16 are based on the following passage.

Passage III

Nitric oxide (NO) is a remarkable gas that acts as a signaling molecule throughout the body. It is produced by vascular endothelium, smooth muscle, and cardiac muscle cells. Because the half-life of NO is only a few seconds, its effects are short lived, but it is nevertheless essential to many of the body's regulation processes. A few of the known roles of NO include control over blood vessel dilation and pressure, involvement in inflammation, neurotransmission, and the regulation of apoptosis (programmed cell death). It is suspected that NO has many other roles in the body that are yet to be completely understood.

Nitric oxide is produced in cells when a group of enzymes know as nitric oxide synthases (NOS) convert the amino acid L-arginine to L-citrulline. NO is produced as a by-product of the reaction. The activity of NO is modulated by cyclic guanine monophosphate (cGMP). When present, cGMP increases the vasodilating abilities of

NO. The expression of phosphodiesterase (PDE) enzymes causes the degradation of cGMP that suppresses the function of NO.

Because NO acts as a smooth muscle vasodilator, a variety of pharmaceuticals that act on NO have been developed. Nitroglycerin, which decreases the amount of oxygen flowing to the myocardium of the heart, is often used to manage the chest pain of angina that is associated with coronary artery disease. Drugs for erectile dysfunction (ED) such as Viagra, Cialis, and Levitra all work by enhancing NO function and increasing vasodilation and blood flow in the penis during sexual stimulation. Even the nutritional supplement industry has tried to manipulate the effects of nitric oxide. Bodybuilders and athletes have been using what are termed NO hemodilators, alleging that these supplements increase blood flow to muscles, making them look larger and recover faster after injury.

13. You would expect that drugs such as Viagra work by
    A. inhibiting PDE enzyme activity.
    B. decreasing cGMP activity.
    C. decreasing NOS activity.
    D. acting as an antagonist to L-arginine.

14. Cyclic GMP is a modified form of a
    A. protein
    B. sugar
    C. nucleotide
    D. lipid

15. Some of the advertisements for NO hemodilator supplements imply that the product contains NO. What would be the MOST likely ingredient of these supplements?
    A. The products would have to contain NO to have any of the alleged effects in the body.
    B. Since the half-life of NO is so brief, the product most likely contains L-arginine, which can be converted to L-citrulline and NO in the cells.
    C. The products would most likely contain the PDE enzyme.
    D. The products would contain L-citrulline and NO.

16. One of the contraindications for men taking ED drugs is that they should not be combined with nitroglycerin. What might be an immediate problem observed with men taking nitroglycerin and ED drugs?
    A. Both drugs cause vasodilation by increasing NO levels. This could cause blood pressure to drop to dangerous levels.
    B. The ED drugs might increase the heart rate to dangerous levels.
    C. The drugs might inhibit immune function and inflammatory responses.
    D. The two drugs might interact, having toxic results for the liver and kidneys.

Question 17 is not based on a passage.

17. If a DNA codon, reading from the 5′ end, is C-A-T, then the base sequence of the corresponding anticodon, reading from the 5′ end, will be
    A. C-A-U
    B. G-T-A
    C. A-U-G
    D. A-T-G

Questions 18–20 are based on the following data.

The generalized events in DNA replication can be depicted by the following flowchart:

Double helix → Nicking of a strand → Unwinding → Destabilization and relief of pressure → Initiation → Elongation → Closing of nicks

18. Between which two steps would the enzyme *DNA polymerase* be used?
    A. Double helix → Nicking of a strand
    B. Nicking of a strand → Unwinding
    C. Initiation → Elongation
    D. Elongation → Closing of nicks

19. Between which two steps would the enzyme *topoisomerase* be used?
    A. Double helix → Nicking of a strand
    B. Nicking of a strand → Unwinding
    C. Initiation → Elongation
    D. Elongation → Closing of nicks

20. Between which two steps would the enzyme *DNA ligase* be used?
    A. Double helix → Nicking of a strand
    B. Nicking of a strand → Unwinding
    C. Initiation → Elongation
    D. Elongation → Closing of nicks

This is the end of the Unit I Minitest.

Unit I Minitest Answers and Explanations

1. **The correct answer is C.** The primary difference between aerobic and anaerobic cellular respiration is the amount of ATP generated. Anaerobic respiration generates far less ATP per glucose molecule than aerobic respiration.

2. **The correct answer is C.** During semiconservative replication, the DNA helix unwinds so that both strands of DNA can serve as a template. Both strands are copied, producing two double helices. Each one consists of a template strand and a newly synthesized strand.

3. **The correct answer is B.** This question requires a general knowledge of the chemical makeup of the major macromolecules of the cell. Glucose contains only carbon, hydrogen, and oxygen. Generally, lipids contain the same three elements. Proteins always contain C, O, H, and N and perhaps some other elements depending on the amino acids used. Nucleic acids contain C, O, H, N, and phosphorus.

4. **The correct answer is C.** This problem requires a Punnett square to be performed for each generation. For the first generation, the Punnett square for the genetic cross of $TT \times tt$ or:

	T	*T*
t	*Tt*	*Tt*
t	*Tt*	*Tt*

In the first generation, the *T* and *t* gametes unite to produce individuals with a *Tt* (heterozygous) genotype. In the second generation, the Punnett square is conducted for the genetic cross of $Tt \times Tt$ or:

	T	*t*
T	*TT*	*Tt*
t	*Tt*	*tt*

The phenotypic results from this cross are that three of the four pea plants will be tall (*TT*, *Tt*, and *Tt*) and one of the four is short (*tt*). Thus the phenotypic ratio of dominant to recessive pea plants is 3 : 1, given by choice C.

5. **The correct answer is D.** If a person has cystic fibrosis, his or her CFTR gene is mutated and produces a faulty version of the CFTR protein. Increasing the production of the mutated CFTR would not improve the condition. The passage indicates that some mutations of CFTR produce proteins that are misdirected and destroyed instead of being sent to the cell membrane. A drug that stops the destruction of CFTR might sound helpful; but if it doesn't additionally get the CFTR to the membrane where it is needed, it won't be beneficial. Increasing nutrient absorption in the small intestine would be helpful in countering some of the malnutrition problems that cystic fibrosis patients often have. However, it would lead to an improvement only in that one symptom. Activating an additional chloride channel other than CFTR might help restore ion and water balance to produce mucus of the appropriate consistency.

6. **The correct answer is C.** A codon is a sequence of three nucleotides found on the mRNA that specifies particular amino acids to be added to a protein. The genetic code lists all possible codons. One codon always specifies one amino acid. If the protein is 1480 amino acids long, you might suspect that the mRNA had 1480 codons. However, there would be an additional codon present that served as the stop codon. The stop codon does not code for an amino acid, but instead signals the end of translation and the release of the protein. Therefore, 1481 codons would be present on the mRNA.

7. **The correct answer is B.** Carriers are heterozygotes. In the case of a recessive inheritance, a carrier will not necessarily know that they are carrying a single allele for the disease. When two heterozygotes are crossed in a Punnett square, the result is that 25% will be homozygous dominant (normal), 50% will be heterozygous carriers, and 25% will be homozygous recessive and will have cystic fibrosis.

8. **The correct answer is A.** Trypsin is a proteinase produced by the pancreas and secreted into the small intestine. It is involved in protein digestion, so if the levels were reduced, proteins would not be well digested. Amylase is the enzyme involved in carbohydrate digestion, and lipases are involved in the digestion of fats.

9. **The correct answer is D.** This question is simply asking about the function of mitochondria in the cell. Mitochondria are involved in aerobic respiration and are the site of the Krebs cycle and the electron transport chain. Aerobic cellular respiration produces large amounts of ATP. Therefore, the more mitochondria a cell has, the more ATP it can produce. Cells with higher ATP demands should have more mitochondria than cells with lower ATP demands.

10. **The correct answer is D.** Men pass on their genetic contribution to the next generation via sperm. Any mitochondria present in sperm typically do not enter the cell. The passage indicates that all mitochondria in a given cell are derived from those in the egg cell. Because a male does not pass on any of his mitochondria to the next generation, even if he has an mtDNA disease, he could never pass it on to his children. Only when the mtDNA of the egg cell is affected can the disease be passed on.

11. **The correct answer is B.** This question relies on some basic knowledge of endosymbiotic theory. Choice A suggests that this theory is supported because mitochondria are membrane bound. Since cells have many other membrane-bound organelles, this would not provide any compelling evidence for the mitochondria being unique. Choice C indicates that because mitochondria are found in multiple copies within a cell, this would be evidence to support endosymbiosis. Because other organelles are found in multiple copies, this would not be a plausible explanation. The best choice to support the idea that mitochondria were once free-living prokaryotic cells is that they have their own DNA. The passage explains that the mtDNA is circular, which corresponds to the typical DNA conformation in bacteria. Because mitochondria have their own DNA and it resembles that of prokaryotes, choice B would lend the best support to the endosymbiotic theory.

12. **The correct answer is** C. The question explains that mtDNA comes from a single source, which you know is the mother. In the nucleus of diploid cells, each gene is present in duplicate copies that can recombine during crossing over. Because mtDNA comes from a single source, recombination should not occur. The remaining choices listed such as transcription and translation should still be able to happen within the mitochondria. Any DNA is subject to spontaneous mutation, including the mtDNA.

13. **The correct answer is** A. Viagra works by increasing NO activity. The NOS enzyme is responsible for the conversion of L-arginine to L-citrulline. Something antagonistic to L-arginine would mean that less would be available to convert to L-citrulline and NO. Decreasing NOS activity would decrease NO. The passage explains that cGMP is needed to modulate the activity of NO. Decreasing cGMP would decrease NO activity. The PDE enzyme degrades cGMP, which in turn decreases NO activity. If the PDE enzyme were to be inhibited, cGMP could work longer and NO activity would increase.

14. **The correct answer is** C. Because you know that guanine is a nucleotide, it can be deduced that cyclic guanine monophosphate is some variant of a nucleotide.

15. **The correct answer is** B. Because NO is a gas with a half-life of just a few seconds, it seems impossible for NO to be in these supplements. The PDE enzyme would degrade cGMP and decrease the amount of NO produced. The best explanation is that the supplements contain the precursor to NO, which is L-arginine. Once ingested, the L-arginine could potentially be converted to L-citrulline and NO in the cells.

16. **The correct answer is** A. Nitroglycerin and erectile dysfunction drugs both have similar effects in that they are vasodilators, which increase blood flow to specific areas in the body. Taking both could dilate the vessels to a point where blood pressure drops critically low. With extreme hypotension, tissues and organs become oxygen-deprived.

17. **The correct answer is** A. Since the 3′ end of mRNA aligns with the 5′ end of DNA in transcription, the complementary base sequence of the mRNA, reading from the mRNA's 3′ end, will be G-U-A. Note that uracil is substituted for thymine in RNA. Since the 5′ end of tRNA aligns with the 3′ end of mRNA, the tRNA base sequence, from the tRNA's 5′ end, will be C-A-U. Except for the substitution of uracil, anti-codons are the same as the original DNA triplets they are translating.

18. **The correct answer is** C. Chain growth in DNA replication is initiated by a *primase* and is extended by a *DNA polymerase*. Thus the enzyme acting between Initiation → Elongation is *DNA polymerase*.

19. **The correct answer is** A. *Topoisomerases* are enzymes that cut one of the DNA strands so that it can begin to unwind and also serve to relieve pressure in the coil caused by its unwinding. Thus the enzyme acting between Double helix → Nicking of a strand is *topoisomerase*.

20. **The correct answer is** D. Abutting segments of unjoined DNA can be annealed by *ligases*. Thus the enzyme acting between Elongation → Closing of nicks is *DNA ligase*.

UNIT II

Molecules, Cells, and Organs

> **Foundational Concept:** Highly organized assemblies of molecules, cells, and organs interact to carry out the functions of living organisms.

Assemblies of Molecules, Cells, and Groups of Cells Within Multicellular Organisms

THE PLASMA MEMBRANE

The outer boundary of the cell is the **plasma membrane** (cell membrane). It forms a selectively permeable barrier between the cell and its external environment. The structure of the membrane itself allows for the selective passage of materials into and out of the cell through various mechanisms.

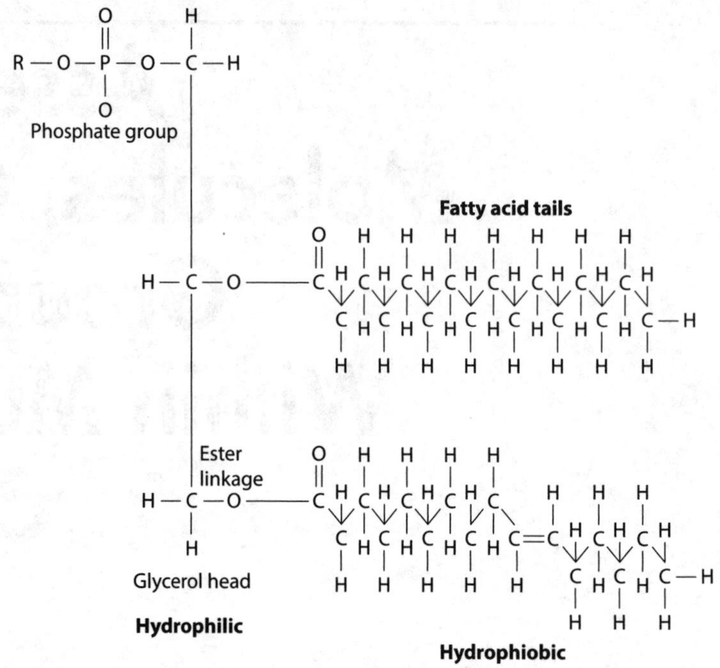

FIGURE 5-1 Phospholipid structure.

The plasma membrane is composed of a bilayer of phospholipids and proteins scattered within the bilayer. Phospholipids are unique molecules because they have polar (charged) and nonpolar (uncharged) regions. Figure 5-1 shows that the head of a phospholipid is composed of a glycerol and phosphate group (PO_4) that carries a charge and is hydrophilic. The tails of the phospholipid are fatty acids that are not charged and are hydrophobic. These fatty acids can be characterized as saturated or unsaturated depending on their structure. This is discussed in more detail in Chapter 4.

Phospholipids spontaneously arrange themselves in a bilayer in which the heads align themselves toward the inside and outside of the cell where water is located, and the fatty acid tails are sandwiched between the layers. Nonpolar molecules have an easier time crossing the bilayer than other types of molecules.

The Fluid Mosaic Model

In addition to the phospholipid bilayer, there are some other substances present in the plasma membrane. The **fluid mosaic model** seen in Figure 5-2 shows the basic membrane structure. Cholesterol, a steroid molecule, is found embedded within the interior of the membrane and its primary purpose is to regulate the fluidity of the membrane. Proteins are scattered within the bilayer, and they may serve multiple purposes such as membrane transport, enzymatic activity, cell adhesion, communication, as well as to serve as receptors for specific substances that may need to cross the membrane. Some proteins and lipids within the cell membrane contain carbohydrates on

99

CHAPTER 5:
Assemblies of
Molecules, Cells,
and Groups of Cells
Within Multicellular
Organisms

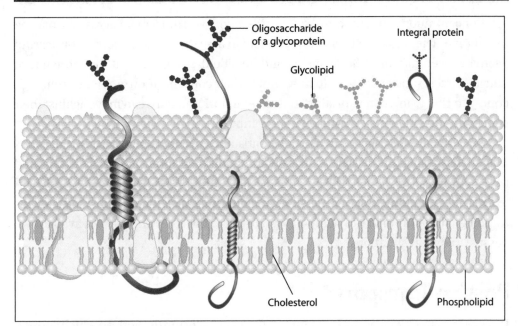

FIGURE 5-2 The fluid mosaic model.

the exterior surface. These glycoproteins and glycolipids often serve as identifying markers, or antigens, for the cell.

Membrane Dynamics

Within the plasma membrane, phospholipids display dynamic movement. This movement can be uncatalyzed or catalyzed. Uncatalyzed forms of movement include transbilayer diffusion where a phospholipid moves from one layer to another and lateral diffusion where the phospholipids move from side to side but stay on the same layer of the membrane. Catalyzed forms of diffusion use a protein catalyst to facilitate movement. Phospholipids can move from inner to outer or outer to inner layers using protein catalysts and ATP. There can also be coupled movement where one phospholipid moves from one layer to the other and another phospholipid moves in an opposite direction. This form of catalyzed movement requires a protein catalyst but does not require ATP.

MOVEMENT OF SOLUTES ACROSS MEMBRANES

There are a variety of ways that substances can cross the plasma membrane. The three main membrane transport methods are passive transport, active transport, and bulk transport. Passive transport occurs spontaneously without energy, active transport requires energy in the form of ATP, and bulk transport involves the transport of large items or large quantities of an item using specific mechanisms.

Concentration gradients are a key consideration with movement across the plasma membrane. The concentration gradient refers to a relative comparison of solutes and overall concentrations of fluids inside and outside the cell. Without the influence of outside forces, substances tend to move down their concentration gradient (from high concentration to low concentration) toward equilibrium. Items can move against their concentration gradient only with an energy input.

The direction in which transport of a substance occurs is regulated by the Gibbs free energy change. In passive transport, no additional input of energy is required ($\Delta G' = 0$) and all movement will be with the concentration gradient (moving from high to low concentration). In active transport mechanisms, movement against the concentration gradient (from low to high) may occur using the $\Delta G'$, which is not available in passive transport situations.

Passive Transport

Passive transport mechanisms include diffusion and osmosis, both of which move a substance from an area of high concentration to an area of low concentration. Diffusion and osmosis are spontaneous processes and do not require ATP.

DIFFUSION

Diffusion is defined as the movement of small solutes down their concentration gradients. In other words, dissolved particles move from whichever side of the membrane that has more of them to the side of the membrane that has less. Diffusion is a slow process by nature, but its rate can be influenced by temperature, the size of the molecule attempting to diffuse (large items are incapable of diffusion), and how large the concentration gradient is. Diffusion continues until equilibrium is met. Some small solutes move across the membrane through a carrier protein. When this occurs, the process is termed **facilitated diffusion**. All of the same normal rules of diffusion apply.

OSMOSIS

Osmosis is a very specific type of diffusion where the substance moving down its concentration gradient is water. As the concentration of solutes increases, the concentration of water decreases. Osmosis displays colligative properties in that the osmotic pressure depends on the concentration of solute present but not on the identity of the solute. In an attempt to have equally concentrated solutions both inside and outside the cell, osmosis occurs if the solute itself is unable to cross the cell membrane because its size is too large. Simply put, osmosis moves water from the side of the membrane that has more water (and less solute) to the side of the membrane that has less water (and more solute).

When the concentrations of solutes inside and outside the cell are equal, the solutions are termed **isotonic** and there is no net movement of water into or out of the cell.

101

CHAPTER 5:
Assemblies of
Molecules, Cells,
and Groups of Cells
Within Multicellular
Organisms

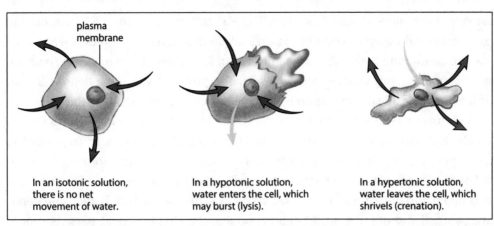

In an isotonic solution, there is no net movement of water.

In a hypotonic solution, water enters the cell, which may burst (lysis).

In a hypertonic solution, water leaves the cell, which shrivels (crenation).

FIGURE 5-3 Osmotic effects on animal cells. The arrows indicate the movement of water. In an isotonic solution, a cell neither gains nor loses water; in a hypertonic solution, the cell loses water; in a hypotonic solution, the cell gains water. *Source:* From Sylvia S. Mader, *Biology*, 8th ed., McGraw-Hill, 2004; reproduced with permission of The McGraw-Hill Companies.

In most situations, isotonic solutions are the goal for cells. A solution that has more water and less solute relative to what it is being compared to is termed **hypotonic**, while a solution that has less water and more solute relative to what it is being compared to is termed **hypertonic**. When cells are placed in hypertonic solutions, water leaves the cell via osmosis, which can cause cells to shrivel. Cells placed in hypotonic solutions gain water via osmosis and potentially swell and burst. The osmotic effects of each type of solution can be seen in Figure 5-3.

Active Transport

In contrast to passive transport, **active transport** is used to move solutes against their concentration gradient from the side of the membrane that has less solute to the side that has more. The solutes move via transport proteins in the membrane that act as pumps. Because this is in contrast to the spontaneous nature of passive transport, energy in the form of ATP must be invested to pump solutes against their concentration gradients. Individual items can be actively transported through protein pumps such as the proton pumps used during cellular respiration. There are also co-transporters that move more than one item at a time by active transport. Active transport mechanisms are essential to maintaining membrane potentials (charged states) within a variety of specialized cells within the body.

THE SODIUM-POTASSIUM PUMP AND MEMBRANE CHANNELS

The **sodium-potassium pump** is an example of a co-transporter used in neurons and will be discussed more extensively in Chapter 8. When neurons are not transmitting messages, their membranes are in resting potential. During resting potential, sodium-potassium (Na^+/K^+) pumps within the membrane are used to actively transport ions into and out of the axon. The Na^+/K^+ pumps bring 2 K^+ ions into the axon while sending out three Na^+ ions. This results in a high concentration of Na^+ outside the membrane and a high concentration of K^+ inside the membrane. There are also many negatively charged molecules such as proteins within the neuron so that ultimately the inside of the neuron is more negative than the outside of the neuron.

To transmit a message, the resting potential of the neuron must be disrupted and depolarized such that the inside of the cell becomes slightly less negative. Once the action potential has initiated, voltage gated channels in the membrane of the axon will open. Specifically, Na^+ channels open, allowing Na^+ to flow passively across the membrane into the axon in a local area. As soon as the Na^+ channels open and depolarize a small area of the axon, K^+ channels open, allowing K^+ to leak passively out of the axon. This restores the more negative charge within the axon, temporarily preventing the initiation of another action potential during a refractory period. The Na^+/K^+ pump can then be used to completely restore the resting potential by repolarization.

Bulk Transport

The methods for membrane transport described thus far are limited by the size of molecules and do not consider the movement of large items (or large quantities of an item) across the membrane. Endocytosis and exocytosis are used to move large items across the cell membrane and can be seen in Figure 5-4.

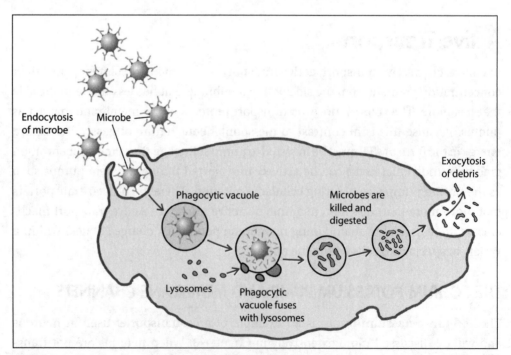

FIGURE 5-4 Endocytosis and exocytosis. Cells engulf large substances such as microbes via endocytosis and excrete large substances via exocytosis. *Source:* From Eldon D. Enger, Frederick C. Ross, and David B. Bailey, *Concepts in Biology*, 11th ed., McGraw-Hill, 2005; reproduced with permission of The McGraw-Hill Companies.

103

CHAPTER 5:
Assemblies of
Molecules, Cells,
and Groups of Cells
Within Multicellular
Organisms

ENDOCYTOSIS

Endocytosis is used to bring items into the cell. The membrane surrounds the item to form a vesicle that pinches off and moves into the cell. When liquids are moved into the cell this way, the process is termed **pinocytosis**. When large items, such as other cells, are brought into the cell, the process is termed **phagocytosis**. White blood cells are notorious for performing phagocytosis on items such as bacterial cells. Finally, there is receptor-mediated endocytosis, where the molecule to be moved into the cell must first bind to a cell membrane receptor before it can be transported.

EXOCYTOSIS

Exocytosis is used to transport molecules out of the cell. In this case, vesicles containing the substance to be transported move toward the cell membrane and fuse with the membrane. This releases the substance to the outside of the cell.

EUKARYOTIC CELL STRUCTURE AND FUNCTION

The cell is the basic unit of life. As a general rule, all cells are small in size in order to maintain a large surface area to volume ratio. Having a large surface area relative to a small volume allows cells to perform vital functions at a reasonably fast rate, which is necessary for survival. Cells that are too large have small surface area to volume ratios and have difficulties getting the nutrients that they need and expelling wastes in a timely manner.

There are two major categories of cells: **prokaryotic** and **eukaryotic**. Both prokaryotic and eukaryotic cells contain a variety of structures that are used to perform specific functions within the cell. There are some similarities between the two cell types, but there are also some significant differences. In this chapter, the focus will remain on eukaryotic cells, but prokaryotic cells will be revisited in Chapter 6. The following table depicts the major structural differences between prokaryotic and eukaryotic cells.

A Summary of Differences Between Eukaryotic and Prokaryotic Cells		
Characteristic	**Eukaryotic Cells**	**Prokaryotic Cells**
Cell size	Relatively larger	Relatively smaller
Presence of membrane-bound organelles	Present	Absent
Organization of genetic material	Linear pieces of DNA organized as chromosomes housed within the nucleus	A single loop of DNA floating in the cytoplasm
Oxygen requirements	Generally need oxygen to produce energy during cellular respiration	May not require oxygen to produce energy during cellular respiration

One primary factor that differentiates eukaryotic cells from prokaryotic cells is the presence of organelles. Organelles are membrane-bound compartments within the cell that have specialized functions. They help with cellular organization and ensure that specific reactions occurring in one organelle do not interfere with those occurring in another organelle.

There are many different structures and organelles that are found in eukaryotic cells, each with a specialized function to be discussed shortly. The structure of a typical eukaryotic cell can be seen in Figure 5-5. An overview of all major cellular components found in eukaryotic cells can be found in following table.

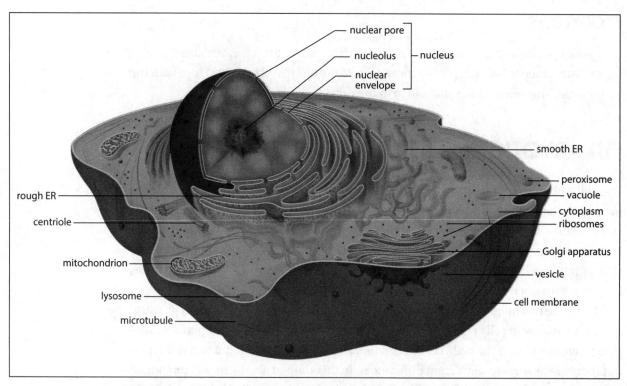

FIGURE 5-5 Animal cell structure. A typical animal cell contains a variety of structures and membrane-bound organelles. *Source:* From Sylvia S. Mader, *Biology*, 8th ed., McGraw-Hill, 2004; reproduced with permission of The McGraw-Hill Companies.

The Cytoplasm

The liquid portion of the cell is the **cytoplasm**, which consists of water, nutrients, ions, and wastes and can be the site of a variety of chemical reactions within the cell. The organelles and other structures of the cell are suspended within the cytoplasm.

The Nucleus

All eukaryotic cells contain a membrane-bound nucleus. The **nucleus** houses the genetic material of the cell in the form of chromosomes, which consist of deoxyribonucleic acid (DNA) associated with specialized proteins. The outer boundary of the

105

CHAPTER 5:
Assemblies of
Molecules, Cells,
and Groups of Cells
Within Multicellular
Organisms

Major Cell Structures and Their Functions	
Organelle or Structure	**Function**
Cytoplasm	Liquid portion of the cell in which organelles are suspended
Nucleus	Stores DNA of the cell
Nucleolus	Housed within the nucleus; makes rRNA used to produce ribosomes
Ribosomes	Involved in protein synthesis
Smooth endoplasmic reticulum	Produces lipids for the cell and is also involved in detoxification in liver cells
Rough endoplasmic reticulum	Produces and chemically modifies proteins
Golgi complex	Sorts contents from the endoplasmic reticulum and routes them to appropriate locations in the cell or marks them for secretion from the cell
Lysosomes	Vacuoles containing enzymes needed for cellular digestion and recycling
Peroxisomes	Vacuoles that digest fatty acids and amino acids; also breaks down the metabolic waste product hydrogen peroxide to water and oxygen
Mitochondria	Perform aerobic cellular respiration to produce ATP (energy) for the cell during aerobic cellular respiration
Cytoskeleton	Hollow microtubules are used for structural support, organelle movement, and for cell division.
	Microfilaments are used for cell movement.
	Intermediate filaments assist in structural support for the cell.
Cell wall	A rigid structure composed of cellulose on the outer surface of plant cells; provides structural support and prevents desiccation
Chloroplasts	Used for the process of photosynthesis in plants
Central vacuole	Used to store water, nutrients, and wastes in plants

nucleus is referred to as the nuclear membrane (also termed the *nuclear envelope*). It keeps the contents of the nucleus separate from the rest of the cell. The nuclear membrane has nuclear pores that allow certain substances to enter and exit the nucleus. Within the nucleus, there is a nucleolus. The job of the nucleolus is to make the **ribosomal ribonucleic acid** (rRNA) needed to produce ribosomes.

Ribosomes

Ribosomes can be found loose in the liquid cytoplasm of the cell (free ribosomes) or attached to the endoplasmic reticulum of the cell (bound ribosomes). Made from rRNA produced in the nucleolus and proteins, a ribosome consists of one large subunit and one small subunit that are assembled when protein synthesis is needed.

The Endomembrane System

The **endomembrane system** consists of several organelles that work together as a unit to synthesize and transport molecules within the cell. This endomembrane system consists of the smooth endoplasmic reticulum, rough endoplasmic reticulum, Golgi complex, lysosomes, peroxisomes, and vesicles that transport materials within the system.

ENDOPLASMIC RETICULUM

The **endoplasmic reticulum** (ER) is a folded network of double membrane-bound space that has the appearance of a maze. Some areas of the ER, known as the **rough ER**, contain bound ribosomes, whereas other areas, known as the smooth ER, do not. These two structures are connected, but their functions are distinct from each other.

In the **smooth ER**, the primary function is lipid synthesis. In certain types of eukaryotic cells (such as the liver), the smooth ER also plays a critical role in the production of detoxifying enzymes. The primary function of the rough ER, which has bound ribosomes, is related to protein synthesis. The ribosomes produce proteins that enter the rough ER where they are chemically modified and moved to the smooth ER.

The combined contents of the smooth ER and the rough ER are shipped by vesicles to the Golgi complex for sorting. Vesicles are tiny pieces of membrane that will break off and carry the contents of the ER throughout the endomembrane system.

GOLGI COMPLEX

Vesicles from the ER arrive at the **Golgi complex** (also called the Golgi apparatus) and deliver their contents, which include proteins and lipids. These molecules are further modified, repackaged, and tagged for their eventual destination. The contents of the Golgi complex leave via vesicles, with many of them moved to the plasma membrane for secretion out of the cell.

LYSOSOMES

Lysosomes are membrane-bound vacuoles (large sacs) that contain hydrolytic (digestive) enzymes used to break down any substances that enter the lysosomes. Cellular structures that are old, damaged, or unnecessary can be degraded in the lysosomes, as can substances taken into the cell by endocytosis. To function properly, the pH of the lysosomes must be acidic. If lysosomes rupture, the cell itself is destroyed. In some cases, cells purposefully rupture their lysosomes in an attempt to destroy themselves in a process known as apoptosis.

107

CHAPTER 5:
Assemblies of
Molecules, Cells,
and Groups of Cells
Within Multicellular
Organisms

PEROXISOMES

Peroxisomes are another type of vacuole found within the endomembrane system. They are capable of digesting fatty acids and amino acids. Enzymes within the peroxisomes degrade toxic hydrogen peroxide, a metabolic waste product, to water and oxygen gas. Peroxisomes also assist with the degradation of alcohol in the liver and kidney cells.

Mitochondria

Mitochondria are the organelles responsible for the production of energy in the cell. They perform aerobic cellular respiration that ultimately creates ATP, which is the preferred source of energy for cells. Because all cells require energy to survive, the process of cellular respiration is a vital one for the cell.

Mitochondria have some interesting and unusual features. They are bound by an inner and outer membrane, they contain their own DNA distinct from the nuclear DNA, and they can self-replicate. These unique features have led to the development of the **endosymbiotic theory**, which suggests that mitochondria are the evolutionary remnants of bacteria that were engulfed by other cells long ago in evolutionary time.

The Cytoskeleton

The **cytoskeleton** is composed of three types of fibers that exist within the cytoplasm of the cell. These fibers have a variety of functions, including structural support, maintenance of cell shape, and cell division.

Microtubules are responsible for structural support and provide tracks that allow for the movement of organelles within the cell. They are hollow fibers, made of the protein tubulin. A specialized grouping of microtubule is the **centriole**. A pair of centrioles is used within animal cells to assist with cell division. **Microfilaments** are made of the protein actin, which assists with cellular movement. Intermediate filaments provide structural support for the cell. These fibers vary in composition, depending on the cell type.

STRUCTURES THAT ALLOW FOR MOVEMENT

Certain types of animal cells contain additional structures, such as cilia and flagella, that allow for movement. **Cilia** are hairlike structures that move in synchronized motion on the surface of some cells. For example, cilia on the surface of cells lining the respiratory tract constantly move in an attempt to catch and remove bacteria and particles that may enter the respiratory tract. Some animal cells, such as sperm, contain a **flagellum**, which essentially acts as tails to allow for movement. Both cilia and flagella are composed of nine pairs of microtubules arranged circularly around a pair of microtubules. This is referred to as a $9 + 2$ arrangement. The sliding of microfilaments powered by ATP is what allows for the movement of these structures.

Cell Structures not Found in Animal Cells

Plant cells generally have all of the structures and organelles described to this point. However, there are a few additional structures that are unique to plant cells. These include a cell wall, chloroplasts, and a central vacuole.

The **cell wall** is composed of cellulose (fiber) and serves to protect the cell from its environment and desiccation. The chloroplasts within a plant cell contain the green pigment chlorophyll, which is used in the process of photosynthesis. **Chloroplasts** are similar to mitochondria in that they have their own DNA and replicate independently. Endosymbiotic theory is used to explain their existence in plants. Finally, plant cells contain a large central vacuole that serves as reserve storage for water, nutrients, and waste products. The **central vacuole** typically takes up the majority of space within a plant cell. Figure 5-6 illustrates the typical structure of a plant cell.

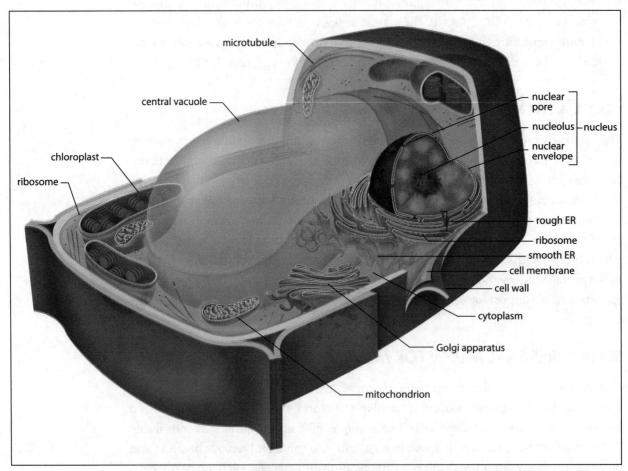

FIGURE 5-6 Plant cell structure. A typical plant cell contains structures and organelles similar to animal cells with the addition of chloroplasts, a cell wall, and a central vacuole. *Source:* From Sylvia S. Mader, *Biology*, 8th ed., McGraw-Hill, 2004; reproduced with permission of The McGraw-Hill Companies.

109

CHAPTER 5:
Assemblies of
Molecules, Cells,
and Groups of Cells
Within Multicellular
Organisms

CELLULAR ADHESION

Even though a cell is bound by its plasma membrane, it must be able to interact with the outside environment and other cells. Cellular junctions are connections between the membranes of cells that allow them to adhere to one another and to communicate with one another. These junctions occur in multiple forms: gap junctions, tight junctions, adherens junctions, and desmosomes.

In **gap junctions**, the cytoplasm of two or more cells connects directly. These connections serve as channels to allow for the rapid movement of substances between cells. One location where gap junctions are prominent is within the cells of cardiac muscle. **Tight junctions** are used to attach cells together, producing a leak-proof seal. This is critical in areas of the body where it would not be desirable to leak fluids. Tight junctions are common and are found in places such as the stomach lining, internal body cavities, and the outer surfaces of the body. **Adherens junctions** are used to attach cells in areas that need to stretch, such as the skin and bladder. **Desmosomes** are localized patches used to hold cells together within tissues. The major functions of cell junctions can be seen in the following table.

Cell Junctions	
Type	**Function**
Gap junctions	Used for rapid communication between cells via cytoplasmic connections
Tight junctions	Used to form tight, waterproof seals between cells
Adherens junctions	Used to form strong connections between cells that need to stretch
Desmosomes	Used to hold cells together in tissues such as the epithelia

TISSUES

A **tissue** is a group of similar type cells that perform specialized functions. Two or more tissue types associate with each other to form organs. There are four major tissue types found in animals: epithelial, connective, muscular, and nervous.

Epithelial Tissue

Epithelial tissues are generally found on surfaces of any part of the body in contact with the environment. The cells that form epithelial tissue occur in sheets or layers where one cell is directly connected to the next. A basement membrane of sticky polysaccharides and proteins made by the cells attaches the tissue to other underlying tissues.

Epithelial tissues are named according to the shape of their cells as well as the number of layers that compose the tissue. The cells that compose epithelial tissues come in the following shapes seen in Figure 5-7:

➤ **Squamous.** Flat cells.
➤ **Cuboidal.** Cube-shaped cells
➤ **Columnar.** Oblong-shaped cells

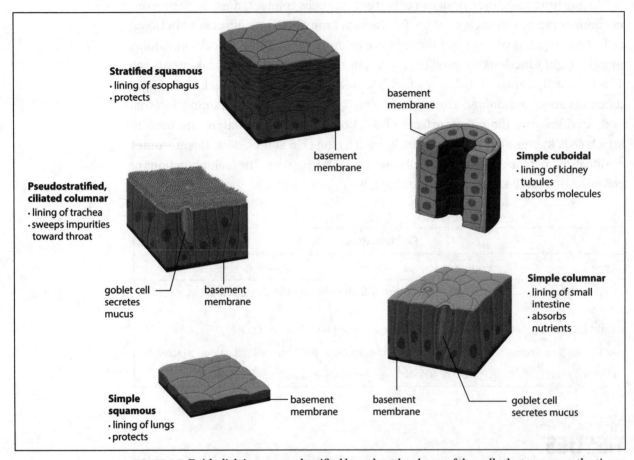

FIGURE 5-7 Epithelial tissues are classified based on the shape of the cells that compose the tissue and the number of layers found within the tissue. *Source:* From Sylvia S. Mader, *Biology*, 8th ed., McGraw-Hill, 2004; reproduced with permission of The McGraw-Hill Companies.

If there is a single layer of cells, the tissue is termed **simple**. If multiple layers of cells are present, the tissue is termed **stratified**. Epithelial tissue always has two names—one to indicate the cell shape and one to indicate the number of layers present.

There are multiple types of epithelial tissues that all have specific functions. Generally, cuboidal and columnar tissues are well suited to secreting products such as mucus or digestive enzymes and are usually found in simple form. They are also used for absorption in areas such as the digestive tract. Simple squamous epithelium is well

111

CHAPTER 5:
Assemblies of
Molecules, Cells,
and Groups of Cells
Within Multicellular
Organisms

suited to diffusion in places such as the alveoli (air sacs) of the lungs because it is so thin. Stratified squamous is used for structures such as skin, where entire layers of the tissue might be lost on a regular basis. Simple forms of epithelial cells that line closed spaces in the body, including body cavities, blood vessels, and lymphatic vessels, are termed **endothelium**. Most epithelial cells are replaced as often as they are shed.

Connective Tissue

Connective tissue comes in multiple varieties with very diverse functions. The common characteristic shared between all types of connective tissues is that they contain cells scattered within a nonliving matrix separated from surrounding tissues. The type of matrix varies from one type of connective tissue to the next, but generally it contains fibers such as collagen, elastic, and reticular fibers seen in Figure 5-8.

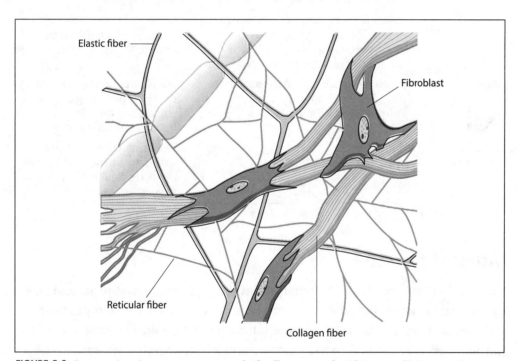

FIGURE 5-8 Connective tissues are composed of cells scattered within a nonliving matrix.

Fibroblasts are the primary cell type that produces matrix fibers. Collagen fibers have great strength, whereas elastic fibers have stretchability. Reticular fibers help attach one type of connective tissue to another type.

There are several types of connective tissue, including loose, dense, cartilage, bone, blood, and lymph. Each type of connective tissue is characterized by the specific cell types as well as the properties of the matrix. The characteristics of the major types of connective tissues can be seen in the following table.

Major Connective Tissue Types		
Tissue Type	**Characteristics**	**Functions**
Loose	Collagen and elastic fibers are abundant in the matrix to form a fairly loose consistency. Fibroblasts are the main cell types. Adipose tissue is a specialized form that stores fat for energy reserves and insulating properties.	Fills space in body cavities, attaches skin to underlying tissues, stores fat
Dense	Collagen fibers are abundant and tightly packed to provide tensile strength. Fibroblasts are the main cell type.	Tendons (attach muscles to bones) and ligaments (attach bone to bone)
Cartilage	Collagen fibers are embedded in a gel-like matrix. Chondrocytes are the major cell type.	Support of body structures such as ears, nose, trachea, and vertebrae
Bone	Collagen fibers are abundant within a rigid calcium phosphate matrix. Osteocytes, osteoblasts, and osteoclasts are the major cell types.	Structural support for the body, protection of internal organs, storage of calcium
Blood	Liquid matrix termed **plasma** Major cell types are red blood cells, white blood cells, and platelets.	Transports substances within the body, including oxygen and carbon dioxide, fights infection, blood clotting
Lymph	Liquid matrix Major cell type is white blood cells.	Fights infection, transports substances within the body, regulates fluid levels in other tissues

Muscular Tissue

There are three types of muscle found within the body: smooth, cardiac, and skeletal. All are composed of bundles of muscle cells, which all have the ability to contract. Each contains many mitochondria that produce the ATP required for contraction. The appearance of the muscle as well as its interaction with the nervous system determines the tissue type. The three muscle types seen in Figure 5-9 are as follows:

➤ **Smooth muscle** is under involuntary control by the nervous system. This means that it contracts with no conscious effort. Its appearance looks smooth, hence the name. Smooth muscle is found throughout the digestive tract, urinary tract, and reproductive system. It is also found in veins, where it helps blood move toward the heart.

➤ **Cardiac muscle** is found only in the heart and is also under involuntary control. It has a striated (striped) appearance when viewed microscopically. Any damage to the cardiac muscle, such as a heart attack, can have major, if not fatal, consequences.

113

CHAPTER 5:
Assemblies of
Molecules, Cells,
and Groups of Cells
Within Multicellular
Organisms

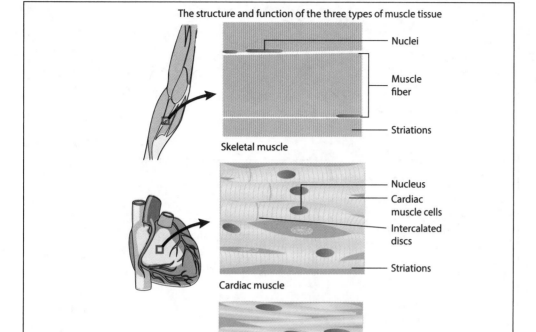

FIGURE 5-9 The three types of muscle.

➤ **Skeletal muscle** is under voluntary or conscious control. It has a striated appearance. Skeletal muscles are usually connected to bones and are used for movement.

Nervous Tissue

Nervous tissue is composed of two primary cell types: neurons and glial cells. **Neurons** have the ability to communicate with each other as well as with other cells in the body, while **glial cells** provide supporting functions to neurons. Mature neurons are unable to perform mitosis to replace themselves, which is one reason that neurological injuries and illnesses are so serious.

All neurons have a cell body that contains the nucleus and most of the cell's organelles. Projections reaching out from the cell body are dendrites and axons. **Dendrites** pick up messages and send them to the cell body. The cell body then processes the message and sends electrical impulses out through a long projection called the **axon**. In some cases, axons may be more than a meter in length. The axon terminates in synaptic knobs, which are extensions of the axon. The **synaptic knobs** can send messages to the dendrites of other neurons via neurotransmitters. The space between a synaptic knob of one neuron and the dendrite of another composes the synapse. The structure of a generalized neuron can be seen in Figure 5-10.

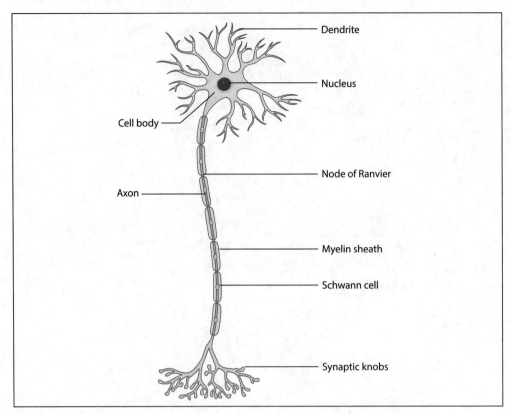

FIGURE 5-10 Neuron structure.

Many neurons have Schwann cells wrapped around their axons. These cells produce a hydrophobic lipoprotein called **myelin** that forms a sheath to insulate the axon and help impulses propagate at the fastest possible rate. The myelin sheath contains nodes of Ranvier that are gaps in the sheath. As impulses are sent down the length of the axon, they jump from node to node.

MEMBRANES

Membranes within the body are composed of an association of two tissue types. There are three major types of membranes: serous, mucous, and cutaneous.

➤ Serous membranes are made of epithelial and connective tissues and line internal body cavities and cover organs.

➤ Mucous membranes are also composed of epithelial and connective tissues. Their job is to secrete mucus onto surfaces of the body that are in contact with the outside environment such as the mouth, nose, trachea, and digestive tract.

➤ The cutaneous membrane covers the outer surface of the body and is also known as the skin. The upper layers of the skin are composed of epithelial and connective tissues.

Structure, Growth, Physiology, and Genetics of Prokaryotes and Viruses

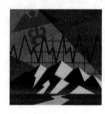

Read This Chapter to Learn About

➤ Cell Theory

➤ The Three Domains

➤ Viruses

➤ Subviral Particles

CELL THEORY

Eukaryotic cells were considered in Chapter 5 and prokaryotic cells will be discussed in this chapter. One foundational concept relating to cells is that of the **cell theory**. The cell theory proposed in the 1800s explains the relationship between cells and organisms. The primary tenets of the original cell theory proposed by Theodor Schwann and Matthias Schleiden include:

➤ All organisms are composed of one or more cells.

➤ The cell is the basic unit of structure, function, and organization in all organisms. Rudolf Virchow elaborated on the cell theory, adding the third tenet:

➤ All cells arise from preexisting cells.

Since the time the original cell theory was proposed, the original tenets have been elaborated on. Modern interpretations of the cell theory include the following additions to the original version:

> ➤ The cell contains hereditary information (DNA) that is passed on from cell to cell during cell division.
> ➤ All cells are basically the same in chemical composition and metabolic activities.
> ➤ All basic chemical and physiological functions are carried out inside the cells

THE THREE DOMAINS

There are three domains to which living organisms can be classified: Eukarya, Bacteria, and Archaea. All eukaryotic organisms classify in the domain Eukarya, leaving all prokaryotic cells to be classified as either Bacteria or Archaea. Although both of these domains share the characteristics of being single-celled, absorbing their nutrients, having a single loop of DNA, and lacking organelles, there are some differences between the two groups. Archaea used to be mistakenly classified as bacteria, but their molecular and cellular structures were found to be quite different. They have a unique cell wall, ribosomes, and membrane lipids. Archaea live in very diverse environments, and some species are termed **extremophiles** due to their extreme habitats such as polar ice caps, thermal vents, jet fuel, and others. Most Archaea species are anaerobes, and none are known to be pathogens.

Because of their medical and environmental significance, the focus of this chapter will be on bacteria.

Bacteria

Bacteria are extremely diverse. They may be classified according to the way they obtain nutrients from the environment or by their oxygen requirements. The following are the basic bacterial classifications:

> ➤ **Photoautotrophs.** These organisms produce their own nutrients through the process of photosynthesis, using carbon dioxide from the environment.
> ➤ **Photoheterotrophs.** These organisms perform photosynthesis but cannot use carbon dioxide from the environment. They extract carbon from a variety of other sources.
> ➤ **Chemoautotrophs.** These organisms get their energy from inorganic compounds, and their carbon needs are obtained from carbon dioxide.
> ➤ **Chemoheterotrophs.** These organisms obtain energy from inorganic substances, and their carbon is obtained from a variety of sources, excluding carbon dioxide. These organisms are further subdivided based on the source of carbon they use. Some species can extract carbon through parasitic or symbiotic interactions with a host or through the decomposition of other organisms.

117

CHAPTER 6:
Structure, Growth,
Physiology, and
Genetics of
Prokaryotes
and Viruses

Bacteria can also be classified based on their oxygen requirements, or lack thereof, for cellular respiration.

➤ **Obligate aerobes** always require oxygen for aerobic cellular respiration.

➤ **Obligate anaerobes** never need oxygen, generally do not divide, and in some cases, are killed by exposure to oxygen.

➤ **Facultative anaerobes** sometimes use oxygen and sometimes do not require oxygen for cellular respiration.

BACTERIAL STRUCTURE

As compared to eukaryotic cells, the structure of bacteria is less complex due to a lack of membrane-bound organelles. Figure 6-1 diagrams basic bacterial structure. Some structures such as the cytoplasm and ribosomes are common between eukaryotic and prokaryotic cells. However, many bacterial structures are unique as compared to eukaryotic structures. The table that follows shows the major structures present in bacterial cells as well as their functions.

Major Bacterial Structures	
Structure	**Function**
Plasma membrane	Outer boundary of the cell that displays selective permeability
Cytoplasm	Liquid portion of the cell where chemical reactions occur
Ribosomes	Site of protein synthesis
Chromosome	Contains the genes needed to provide instructions for protein synthesis in the cell. The bacterial chromosome consists of a single loop of DNA located in the nucleoid region of the cell.
Plasmids	Small, extra-chromosomal loops of DNA. Plasmids often contain genes to code for resistance to antibiotics.
Cell wall	Most bacteria have a cell wall that contains peptidoglycan. The cell wall is found on the outer surface of the cell membrane and typically occurs in one of two conformations that can be determined using the Gram-staining method. Gram-positive bacteria have a cell wall consisting of a single layer of peptidoglycan while Gram-negative bacteria have two layers: one layer of peptidoglycan and another layer of lipids in their cell wall.
Capsule and slime layers	A layer of sugars and proteins on the outer surface of some bacterial cells. It forms a sticky layer that can help the cell attach to surfaces.
Flagella	Bacteria may have a single flagellum, multiple flagella, or no flagella. Those with one or more flagella are motile as the flagella rotate to propel the cell. The bacterial flagella are different from eukaryotic flagella in structure. Bacteria flagella consist of the protein flagellin in a hollow, helical conformation that anchors into the cell membrane. A proton pump in the membrane provides power to rotate each flagellum.
Pili	Tiny proteins that cover the surface of some types of bacterial cells. They assist the cell in attaching to surfaces.
Spores	A few species of bacteria are capable of creating spores when environmental conditions are not favorable. When bacteria exist in spore form, they are capable of surviving adverse conditions for many years. When conditions become favorable, the spores germinate into the vegetative cell form.

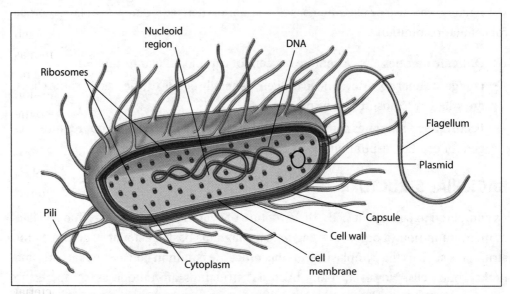

FIGURE 6-1 Bacterial structure. Bacterial cells lack membrane-bound organelles but have a variety of cell structures. *Source:* From George B. Johnson, *The Living World*, 3rd ed., McGraw-Hill, 2003; reproduced with permission of The McGraw-Hill Companies.

BACTERIAL MORPHOLOGY

Most bacteria have shapes that correspond to one of three typical conformations. These shapes and organization amongst cells can be used as diagnostic features. The shapes exhibited by most bacteria are as follows and can also be seen in Figure 6-2:

➤ **Cocci** are circular in shape. They may exist singly, in pairs (diplococci), in clusters (staphylococci), or in chains (streptococci).

➤ **Bacilli** are rod or oblong shaped. They may occur in chains.

➤ **Spirilli** have a spiral shape.

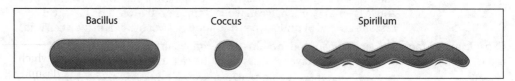

FIGURE 6-2 Bacteria come in a variety of shapes.

BACTERIAL REPRODUCTION

Bacteria lack the mitotic apparatus needed to perform mitosis, and because they only have a single chromosome, they really do not have a need for cell division as complex as mitosis. Bacteria do, however, have several ways of passing genetic material to other bacteria.

119

CHAPTER 6:
Structure, Growth,
Physiology, and
Genetics of
Prokaryotes
and Viruses

Binary Fission. Bacteria divide by the process of **binary fission**. It involves the replication of the single chromosome of DNA and the passing of a copy of the DNA to each of two daughter cells. This process can occur fairly quickly, in some cases as often as once every 20 minutes. Because bacteria are unicellular, creating a new cell means creating a new organism. This process is a type of asexual reproduction as each division produces genetically identical offspring. The only way to introduce variation into the population is by mutation, conjugation, or transformation.

In addition to their single chromosome, some bacteria may contain extra-chromosomal plasmids. It is possible for genetic information to be moved from plasmids to the chromosome and from the chromosome to plasmids. Transposons found in bacteria allow this sort of transfer. In addition to carrying genes for the transfer, transposons often carry genes for antibiotic resistance.

Conjugation. Some bacteria have another means of passing genetic material to other bacteria. During the process of **conjugation**, illustrated in Figure 6-3, a single bacterial cell may copy its plasmid and pass it to another cell. The most commonly studied type of plasmid to be passed is called the F plasmid or F factor (the *F* standing for *fertility*). In order to pass the plasmid to another cell, a physical connection must be established. This connection is referred to as the sex pilus, and it is made by the cell that contains the plasmid (the male, or F^+). The sex pilus connects to a cell lacking the plasmid (the female, or F^-) and serves as a bridge to pass a copy of the plasmid to the female. Once complete, both cells are male and contain the plasmid.

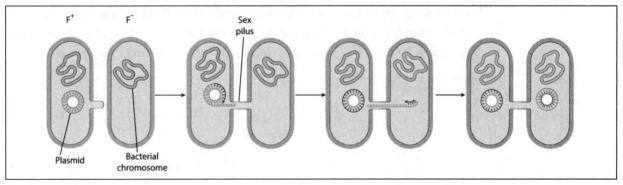

FIGURE 6-3 During conjugation, a bacterial cell containing a plasmid forms a sex pilus, which allows for the transfer of a copy of the plasmid to another bacterial cell that is lacking the plasmid. *Source:* From George B. Johnson, *The Living World*, 3rd ed., McGraw-Hill, 2003; reproduced with permission of The McGraw-Hill Companies.

Conjugation provides a rapid mechanism to pass plasmids within a population. Occasionally, plasmids become integrated into the chromosome, and when the plasmid is transferred via conjugation, some of the bacterial chromosome may be transferred as well.

Because many plasmids encode for resistance to antibiotics, rapid conjugation can quickly render an entire bacterial population resistant to a particular antibiotic under the right selective pressures. This has important medical significance in that an antibiotic is used to kill bacteria causing infections, and if the bacteria are resistant to that antibiotic, it is useless in stopping the infection. Some bacteria are resistant to multiple antibiotics as a result of having picked up several plasmids via conjugation.

Transformation. Another way that bacteria can pick up genetic variations is through **transformation**. Some bacteria are able to pick up DNA from their environment and incorporate it into their own chromosomal DNA. Bacteria that are able to pick up foreign DNA are termed *competent*. Although some bacteria are naturally competent, others can be coerced to develop competence by artificial means within the lab.

THE BACTERIAL GROWTH CYCLE

Bacteria follow a typical growth cycle, shown in Figure 6-4, which is limited by environmental factors as well as the amount of nutrients available. The following are the stages of the growth cycle:

➤ **Lag.** There is an initial lag in growth that occurs when a new population of bacteria begins to reproduce. This lag time is normally brief.

➤ **Logarithmic growth.** As bacteria begin to perform binary fission at a very rapid rate, logarithmic growth occurs. This can last for only a limited amount of time.

➤ **Stationary.** As the number of bacteria increase, resources decrease, and while some bacteria are still dividing, some are dying. This evens out the population count.

➤ **Decline (death).** As the population hits its maximum, the lack of nutrients along with a variety of wastes means that the population will begin to decline and more cells die than are being replaced by cell division. For the few species of bacteria that are capable of making spores, they would do so at this point in the growth cycle.

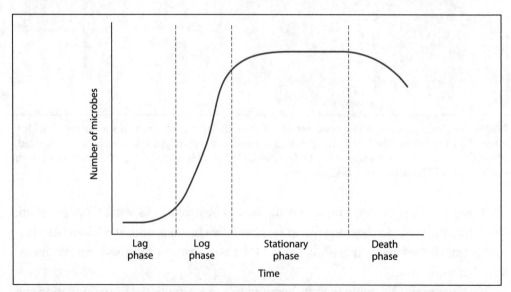

FIGURE 6-4 A growth curve of bacteria. Bacteria exhibit logarithmic growth until conditions are no longer ideal. At this point, a stationary phase occurs followed by a decline phase in which bacterial numbers decrease.

121

CHAPTER 6:
Structure, Growth,
Physiology, and
Genetics of
Prokaryotes
and Viruses

VIRUSES

Viruses are a unique biological entity in that they do not resemble typical cells. There is debate over whether viruses are living organisms at all because they are unable to reproduce without a host cell nor can they perform many of the duties associated with living organisms without the help of a host. Because viruses lack typical cell structures such as organelles, they are much smaller than any form of prokaryotic or eukaryotic cells.

Although some viruses contain more sophisticated structures, the only items required for a virus are a piece of genetic material, either DNA or RNA, and a protective protein coating for the genetic material. The viral genome can consist of only a few genes upward to a few hundred genes.

The Life Cycle of a Virus

Viruses are specific to the type of host cell that they infect. In order for a cell to be infected, it must have a receptor for the virus. If the receptor is absent, the cell cannot be infected by the virus. Although it seems odd that cells would evolve receptors for viruses, it is usually a case of mistaken identity. The viruses actually mimic another substance for which the cell has a legitimate need and thus has a receptor present. The process of viral infection is seen in Figure 6-5.

Once a virus binds to a receptor on the membrane of the host cell, the viral genetic material enters the host either by injecting itself across the cell membrane or by being taken in via endocytosis. At some point, the viral genes are transcribed and translated by the host cell. The nucleic acid of the virus is also replicated. Eventually new viruses are produced and released from the host cell. Because each virus contains a copy of the original genetic material, they should all be genetically identical. Mutations are the primary way to induce variation into the viral population.

TYPES OF VIRUSES

Viruses are categorized as animal viruses, plant viruses, or bacteriophages. They can be further categorized according to the type of nucleic acid they contain.

Animal Viruses. As the name implies, **animal viruses** are designed to infect the cells of various animals. Their genetic material may be DNA or RNA, depending on the virus. Animal viruses are usually categorized according to the type of DNA they possess, and whether the nucleic acid is single stranded or double stranded. Once the host cell takes in the DNA or RNA of the virus, the virus may immediately become active using the host cell machinery to transcribe and translate the viral genes. New viruses are assembled and released from the host cell by one of two methods: lysis of the host's cell membrane, which immediately kills the host cell, or by budding, where the new viruses are shipped out of the host cell via exocytosis. Budding does not immediately kill the host

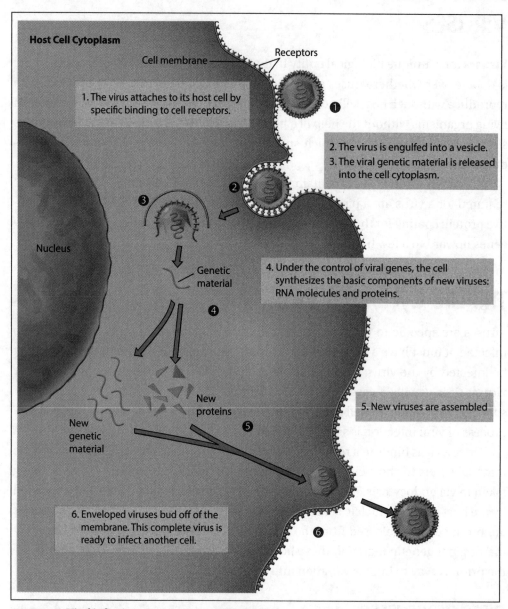

FIGURE 6-5 Viral infection. *Source:* From Marjorie Kelly Cowan and Kathleen Park Talaro, *Microbiology: A Systems Approach,* McGraw-Hill, 2004; reproduced with permission of The McGraw-Hill Companies.

cell, but it may eventually prove fatal to the host. Once the new viruses are released from the original host cell, they seek out new host cells to infect.

Alternatively, the virus may become latent, integrating itself into the chromosomes of the host cell, where it may stay for variable amounts of time. Eventually, the latent virus excises from the host chromosome and becomes active to produce and release new viruses. Some viruses are capable of alternating between active and latent forms multiple times. Infections caused by members of the herpes viruses family, such as cold sores and genital herpes, are notorious for alternating between active and latent forms.

Retroviruses. **Retroviruses** are a unique category of RNA viruses. The human immunodeficiency virus (HIV) was the first retrovirus to be discovered. The key characteristic

123

CHAPTER 6:
Structure, Growth,
Physiology, and
Genetics of
Prokaryotes
and Viruses

of retroviruses is that they enter the cell in RNA form that must be converted to DNA form. This is the opposite of the normal flow of information in the cell, which dictates that DNA produces RNA during transcription. The process of converting viral RNA backward into DNA is called reverse transcription and is achieved by an enzyme called reverse transcriptase.

This viral genome codes for reverse transcriptase. When the retrovirus enters the host cell, its RNA is immediately transcribed, and one result of this is the production of reverse transcriptase. The reverse transcriptase then produces a DNA copy of the viral genome. In the case of HIV, the DNA then integrates into the host cell's chromosomes (the host cell is $CD4^+$ T cells) and enters a latent phase that may last more than 10 years. When the viral DNA excises from the host chromosome, it becomes active and begins producing new viruses. When this happens on a mass scale, the death of host cells will signal the beginning of deterioration in the immune system that causes acquired immunodeficiency syndrome (AIDS).

BACTERIOPHAGES

Bacteriophages are DNA viruses that infect bacteria exclusively. They always inject their DNA into the host bacterial cell and then enter either a lytic cycle or a lysogenic cycle as seen in Figure 6-6. Bacteriophages can also transport parts of the bacterial genome to other cells.

The Lytic Cycle. In the **lytic cycle**, a bacteriophage immediately activates once in its host. New viruses are synthesized and leave the host cell via lysis, always killing their bacterial host. The new viruses then go out and infect new host cells.

The Lysogenic Cycle. The **lysogenic cycle** is a variation that some viruses use. After injecting DNA into their host, the viral DNA integrates into the bacterial chromosome. The viral DNA may stay integrated for variable lengths of time. Each time the bacterial cell divides by binary fission, the progeny receive a copy of the viral genome. Eventually, the viral DNA that has integrated into the chromosome excises and enters the lytic cycle, releasing new viruses and killing their host.

TRANSDUCTION

When new viruses are being packaged in a bacterial host, sometimes portions of the bacterial chromosome get packaged with the new viruses. When these viruses infect new bacterial hosts, not only do they deliver the viral genome but also some bacterial genes that can recombine with the new host's chromosome. This is the process of **transduction**.

SUBVIRAL PARTICLES

Prions are infectious agents that are composed solely of protein and contain no nucleic acid. The prions are products of a human gene that produces a misfolded prion protein

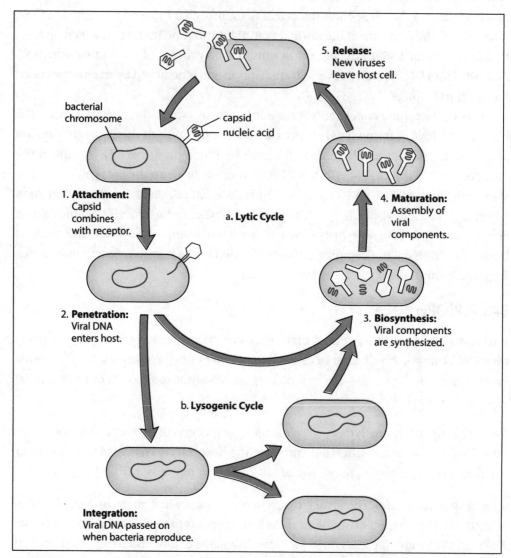

FIGURE 6-6 Bacteriophage life cycles. (a) In the lytic cycle, viral particles are released when the cell is lysed. (b) In the lysogenic cycle, viral DNA integrates into the host cell chromosome. The lysogenic cycle can be followed by the lytic cycle. *Source:* From Sylvia S. Mader, *Biology*, 8th ed., McGraw-Hill, 2004; reproduced with permission of The McGraw-Hill Companies.

called PrP. These prions act by inducing other normal proteins to convert to misfolded forms, which then convert additional proteins to prion form in a chain reaction. Prions can arise spontaneously or they can be acquired from the environment. They are best known for their association with Creutzfeldt–Jakob disease in humans, which causes a degenerative and fatal form of neurological encephalopathy.

Viroids are infectious agents that have similar structure to a virus but are smaller. They consist solely of a strand of RNA and lack a capsid or other proteins typically associated with viruses. Once a viroid is inside a host, the host cell's RNA polymerase replicates the viroid. The viroids appear to cause disease by altering gene regulation in the host. To date, viroids have been associated only with disease in plants.

Processes of Cell Division, Differentiation, and Specialization

MITOSIS

Mitosis is the process of normal cell division in eukaryotic cells. It occurs in most cells with the exception of gametes as well as mature nerve and muscle cells in animals. It begins with a single parent cell that replicates all components within the cell, divides the components into two piles, and then splits to form two genetically identical daughter cells. The most critical components for replication and division are the chromosomes, so particular care will be taken to ensure an equal distribution of chromosomes to each daughter cell.

Chromosomes

Chromosomes occur in homologous pairs as can be seen in the karyotype in Figure 7-1. For each pair of chromosomes found in an individual, one member of the pair came from the maternal parent and the other member of the pair came from the paternal parent. Recall the genetic inheritance of two alleles per trait—one allele per trait from each parent.

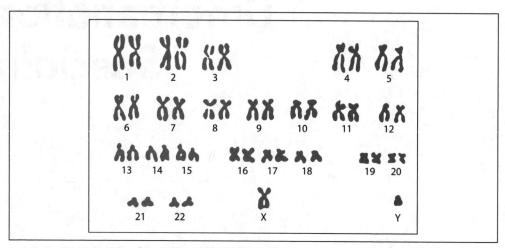

FIGURE 7-1 A karyotype. Chromosomes from a single cell are arranged in pairs to construct a karyotype. This karyotype is from a male. *Source:* From Eldon D. Enger, Frederick C. Ross, and David B. Bailey, *Concepts in Biology*, 11th ed., McGraw-Hill, 2005; reproduced with permission of The McGraw-Hill Companies.

The total number of chromosomes found in an individual is called the **diploid (2N) number**. When individuals reproduce, this number must be cut in half to produce **haploid (N) gametes**. The human diploid number is 46, and the human haploid number is 23. The process of mitosis begins with a diploid cell and ends with two identical diploid cells. In the process of meiosis, a diploid cell begins the process and produces four haploid gametes.

When a cell is not dividing, each chromosome exists in single copy called a chromatid. However, when the cell is preparing to divide, each chromosome must be replicated so that it contains two chromatids, sometimes called sister chromatids. Each chromosome has a compressed region called the centromere, and when the chromosomes replicate, the sister chromatids stay attached to each other at the centromere. Figure 7-2 shows the difference between an unreplicated and a replicated chromosome.

The Cell Cycle

Mitosis is used for the growth of organisms because it takes an increased number of cells for an organism to get bigger. When an individual has stopped growing, mitosis is only needed to replace cells that have died or been injured. For this reason, mitosis

127

CHAPTER 7:
Processes of
Cell Division,
Differentiation, and
Specialization

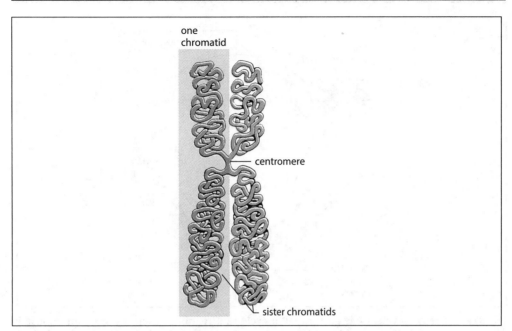

one chromatid

centromere

sister chromatids

FIGURE 7-2 Chromosome structure. A replicated chromosome consists of two sister chromatids attached to each other at the centromere. *Source:* From Sylvia S. Mader, *Biology*, 8th ed., McGraw-Hill, 2004; reproduced with permission of The McGraw-Hill Companies.

needs to be a regulated process that occurs only when new cells are needed. The **cell cycle** is used to regulate the process of cell division in each individual cell. A normal cell cycle has the following stages that can be seen in Figure 7-3:

➤ G_1. This is the first gap phase of the cell cycle. In this stage, the parent cell is growing larger, adding additional cytoplasm, and replicating organelles.

➤ **S.** During this phase of DNA synthesis, the chromosomes are all being replicated. Once this stage is complete, each chromosome consists of two sister chromatids connected at the centromere.

➤ G_2. This is the second gap phase. The cell continues to grow in size and make final preparations for cell division.

➤ **M.** During the **M phase**, mitosis actually occurs. The replicated chromosomes and other cellular components are divided to ensure that each daughter cell receives equal distributions. The division of the cytoplasm at the end of the M phase is referred to as cytokinesis.

The first three phases of the cell cycle, G_1, S, and G_2, are collectively called interphase. Interphase simply means preparation for cell division. The actual cell division occurs during the M phase of the cycle.

Some cells lose the ability to progress through the cell cycle and are thus unable to divide. Mature human nerve and muscle cells are an example. Cells without the ability to divide are considered to be in the G_0 phase of the cell cycle where division never resumes.

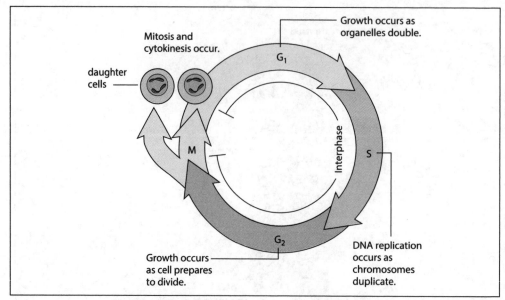

FIGURE 7-3 The cell cycle. Cells go through a cycle that regulates their division. Interphase is preparation for cell division and consists of the G_1, S, and G_2 phases of the cycle. The M phase is where the cells actually divide. *Source:* From Sylvia S. Mader, *Biology*, 8th ed., McGraw-Hill, 2004; reproduced with permission of The McGraw-Hill Companies.

M PHASE

The M phase of the cell cycle is subdivided into four stages: prophase, metaphase, anaphase, and telophase. The primary concern in these stages is alignment and splitting of sister chromatids to ensure that each daughter cell receives an equal contribution of chromosomes from the parent cell. A visual summary of the events of the M phase can be seen in Figure 7-4.

Prophase. Chromosomes are located in the nucleus. Prior to division, the chromosomes are not condensed and thus are not visible. Leaving the chromosomes in an uncondensed state makes it easier to copy the DNA but makes the chromosomes very stringy and fragile. Once the DNA is replicated, the chromosomes must condense so that they are not broken as they are divided up into the two daughter cells.

Another major event of **prophase** is a breakdown of the nuclear membrane releasing the chromosomes into the cytoplasm of the cell. The centrioles present in the cell replicate and move to opposite ends of the cell. Once they have migrated to the poles of the cell, they begin to produce a spindle apparatus consisting of spindle fibers that radiate outward forming asters. The spindle fibers are composed of microtubules that will ultimately attach to each chromosome at the kinetochore. The kinetochore appears at the centromere of each chromosome.

Metaphase. In **metaphase**, each chromosome is attached to a spindle fiber at the kinetochore. The chromosomes are aligned down the center of the cell at the metaphase plate.

129

CHAPTER 7:
Processes of
Cell Division,
Differentiation, and
Specialization

Anaphase. During **anaphase**, the centromere splits, allowing each chromatid to have its own centromere. At this point, the chromatids can be separated from each other and are pulled toward opposite poles of the cell separating the chromosomes into two distinct piles, one for each daughter cell.

Telophase. Now that the chromosomes have been divided into two groups, the spindle apparatus is no longer needed and disappears during **telophase**. A new nuclear membrane forms around each set of chromosomes, and the chromosomes uncoil back to their original state.

Finally, **cytokinesis** occurs where the cytoplasm is divided between the cells. A cleavage furrow forms, which pinches the cells apart from each other. The end result is two daughter cells ready to begin interphase of their cell cycles.

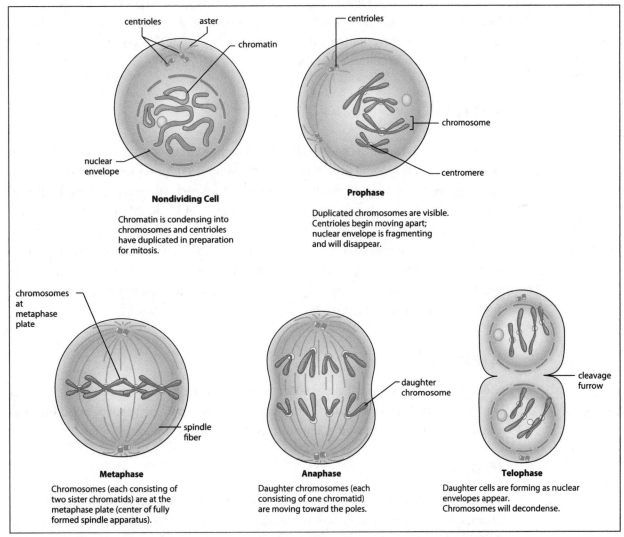

FIGURE 7-4 Mitosis consists of four phases: prophase, metaphase, anaphase, and telophase. *Source:* From Sylvia S. Mader, *Biology*, 8th ed., McGraw-Hill, 2004; reproduced with permission of The McGraw-Hill Companies.

Failure of Cell Cycle Regulatory Mechanisms

A normal cell divides about 50 times before its telomeres shorten to the point where the chromosome is risking damage on subsequent divisions. Once the telomeres shorten to a threshold point, **apoptosis** (programmed cell death) occurs in the cell. Some cells have the ability to bypass cell death and thus become immortal. This is a key characteristic of cancer cells.

Cancer develops by a failure of a variety of mechanisms used to regulate progression through the cell cycle. Checkpoints exist throughout the cycle to ensure that cell division does not occur unless necessary. When these checkpoints are bypassed, cell division happens continually, ultimately producing a mass of unnecessary cells termed a **tumor**. The genetic mechanisms of cancer were discussed previously in Chapter 2.

One of the biggest challenges to cancer treatment is finding a way to kill cancerous cells without killing healthy cells. Many cancer therapies target cells as they divide. Since cancer cells divide quickly, they can be damaged by these therapies. However, other cells in the body that are dividing are also damaged. This is the cause of many of the side effects related to cancer therapies.

MEIOSIS

Because mitosis produces genetically identical diploid daughter cells, it is not appropriate for sexual reproduction. If diploid cells were used for reproduction in humans, each egg would contain 46 chromosomes as would each sperm. This would result in embryos having 96 chromosomes. This number would double each generation if mitosis were used to produce gametes.

The process of **meiosis** begins with a diploid parent cell in the reproductive system that has completed interphase and then follows stages similar to mitosis, twice. The result is four haploid gametes that are genetically diverse. A summary of the events of meiosis can be seen in Figure 7-5.

Meiosis I

Meiosis I encompasses stages similar to mitosis with two major changes. The first involves genetic recombination between homologous pairs, and the second involves the alignment of chromosome pairs during metaphase of meiosis I.

PROPHASE I

During **prophase I** of meiosis, there are many similarities to prophase of mitosis. The chromosomes condense, the centrioles divide and move toward the poles of the cell, spindle fibers begin to form, and the nuclear membrane dissolves. The unique event seen in prophase I is crossing over, demonstrated in Figure 7-6.

131

CHAPTER 7:
Processes of
Cell Division,
Differentiation, and
Specialization

Homologous pairs of chromosomes associate and twist together in synapsis. This configuration consists of two replicated chromosomes, or a total of four chromatids, and is often called a **tetrad**. The synaptonemal complex assists in chromosome pairing, synapsis, and crossing over. At this point, crossing over can occur where pieces of one chromatid break off and exchange with another. Crossing over can occur in more than one location (double crossovers) and can unlink genes that were previously linked on the same chromosome. It is also an important source of genetic diversity, creating new combinations of alleles that were not seen previously.

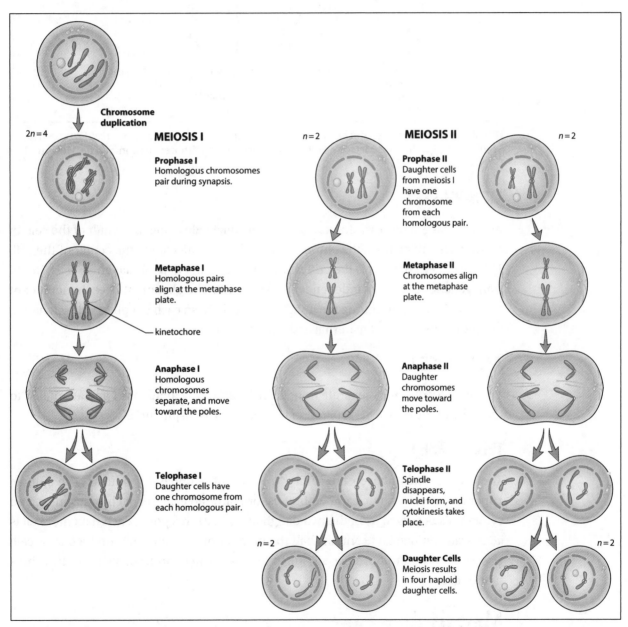

FIGURE 7-5 Meiosis consists of two rounds of cell division. *Source:* From Sylvia S. Mader, *Biology*, 8th ed., McGraw-Hill, 2004; reproduced with permission of The McGraw-Hill Companies.

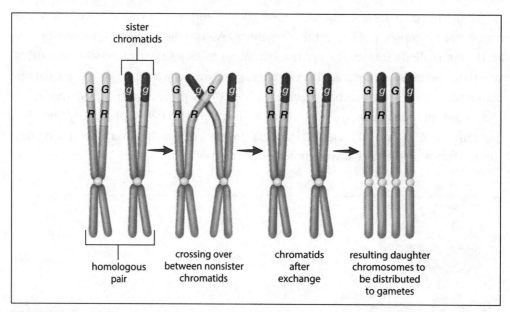

FIGURE 7-6 Crossing over during meiosis results in genetic diversity. *Source:* From Sylvia S. Mader, *Biology*, 8th ed., McGraw-Hill, 2004; reproduced with permission of The McGraw-Hill Companies.

METAPHASE I

In metaphase of mitosis, chromosomes align single file along the center of the cell. In **metaphase I** of meiosis, the chromosomes align as pairs along the center of the cell. This alignment of pairs is the critical factor in creating haploid daughter cells. Recall from genetics the law of independent assortment. The alignment of each member of the homologous pair during metaphase I is random, so each daughter cell will have a unique combination of maternal and paternal alleles.

ANAPHASE I

The homologous pairs separate from each other during **anaphase I** and are pulled to the poles of the cells. This separation is referred to as disjunction.

TELOPHASE I

The events of **telophase I** are similar to those of telophase of mitosis. The spindle apparatus dissolves, nuclear membranes form around each set of chromosomes, and cytokinesis occurs to form the two daughter cells. At this point, each daughter cell is genetically unique and contains half the number of chromosomes of the parent cell. However, these chromosomes are still in their replicated form, consisting of two chromatids each.

Meiosis II

Meiosis II is only necessary to split the chromatids present in the daughter cells produced during meiosis I. There is no interphase between meiosis I and II, because the chromosomes are already replicated. The events of meiosis II are as follows:

133

CHAPTER 7:
Processes of
Cell Division,
Differentiation, and
Specialization

➤ **Prophase II.** Centrioles replicate and move toward the poles of the cell, chromosomes condense, and the nuclear membrane dissolves.

➤ **Metaphase II.** Chromosomes align along the center of the cell.

➤ **Anaphase II.** Sister chromatids are separated and move toward the poles of the cell.

➤ **Telophase II.** Nuclear membranes re-form, and cytokinesis occurs to produce daughter cells.

At the end of meiosis II, there are four daughter cells. Each is haploid with a single copy of each chromosome. Each cell is genetically diverse as a result of crossing over and independent assortment.

GAMETOGENESIS

Meiosis results in four gametes. In men, all four of these gametes will become sperm. In women, only one of these gametes will become a functional oocyte that will be released once every 28 days during ovulation. If all four gametes became functional oocytes and were released each cycle, there would be the potential for four embryos. The three gametes that do not become functional oocytes in women are termed **polar bodies**. Some of the major differences between meiosis in men (spermatogenesis) and women (oogenesis) are described in the following table.

Differences Between Spermatogenesis and Oogenesis		
Characteristic	**Spermatogenesis**	**Oogenesis**
Time at which the process begins	At puberty	Before a female is born (during development)
Time at which the process ends	Never	At menopause
Time needed to complete meiosis	65–75 days	Many years
Number of gametes made	Unlimited numbers are possible.	The number of potential oocytes is set at birth in females.
Fates of the daughter cells	All four are sperm	One is the oocyte and the other three are polar bodies.
Age of the gametes	Not applicable— old sperm are degraded.	Women are born with a set number of follicles so that eggs are the same age as the woman.
Presence of arresting stages in meiosis	No	Yes. Meiosis I starts before birth and then arrests. Meiosis I resumes only after puberty. Only one cell is selected to complete meiosis I per month. Meiosis II only happens if fertilization occurs.

EMBRYOGENESIS

As the haploid nucleus of a sperm cell is contributed to an egg cell (also containing a haploid nucleus) during fertilization, the resulting cell is termed a *zygote*. The zygote begins cell division by mitosis. This produces a ball of identical cells that is the embryo. In humans, the first 8 weeks of development constitute embryonic development and all development after 8 weeks constitutes fetal development. The human gestation (development) period is 266 days, or about 9 months. These 9 months are divided into trimesters. Embryonic development is complete within the first trimester.

Fertilization

Sperm have the ability to survive about 48 hours in the female reproductive system, whereas an oocyte only survives about 24 hours. Sperm deposited prior to or right after ovulation are capable of fertilizing the egg, which should happen in the upper third of a fallopian tube. Whereas 200 to 500 million sperm are typically released during ejaculation, only about 200 will make it to the oocyte.

Secretions from the female system change the membrane composition of the sperm near its acrosome. This membrane instability causes the release of acrosomal contents. This allows the sperm to penetrate the corona radiata (outer layer) of the oocyte. Now the sperm must pass through the next layer of the oocyte, the zona pellucida. Then the first sperm to pass through the zona pellucida passes its nucleus into the oocyte. This causes a depolarization in the membrane of the oocyte, which makes it impenetrable to fertilization by other sperm. The nuclei of the oocyte and sperm fuse, creating the zygote.

Embryonic Development

About 1 day after fertilization, the zygote performs its first mitotic division, becoming an embryo. This initiates cleavage, which is the rapid cell division characteristic of early embryonic development. Within about 4 days, the embryo reaches the morula stage that consists of a ball of hollow cells. During early cleavage, the embryo may split into two, resulting in identical twins. By about 6 days, the center of the embryo hollows out and becomes fluid filled. The embryo is now termed a **blastula** or **blastocyst**.

The outer cells of the blastocyst are the trophoblast and aid in implantation and the development of extraembryonic membranes and the placenta. The inner cell mass of the blastocyst will continue development as the embryo and is the source of embryonic stem cells, which have the ability to differentiate into any cell type. Implantation of the embryo begins about one week after fertilization and completes by the second week. The events of early embryonic development can be seen in Figure 7-7.

The blastocyst produces a critical hormone that is important in the maintenance of pregnancy. **Human chorionic gonadotropin (HCG)** is the signal to the corpus luteum

135

CHAPTER 7:
Processes of
Cell Division,
Differentiation, and
Specialization

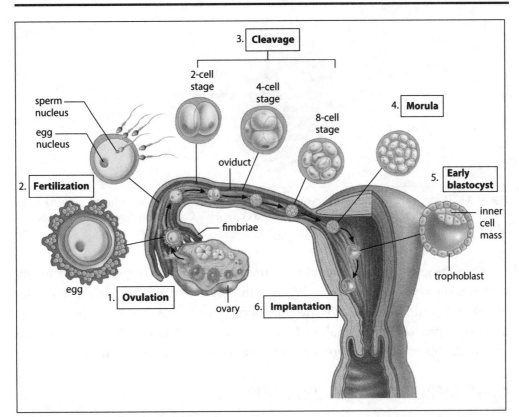

FIGURE 7-7 Early embryonic development. Fertilization occurs in the fallopian tube. The developing embryo moves down the tube to eventually implant in the endometrium of the uterus at the blastocyst stage of development. *Source:* From Sylvia S. Mader, *Biology,* 8th ed., McGraw-Hill, 2004; reproduced with permission of The McGraw-Hill Companies.

in the ovary to not degrade. Normally, the degradation of the corpus luteum causes a decline of estrogen and progesterone and triggers menstruation. At this point in development, menstruation would mean a loss of the embryo or spontaneous abortion. HCG ensures that the corpus luteum continues to secrete estrogen and progesterone so that menstruation is delayed.

The next event of embryonic development is the gastrula stage. During gastrulation, three primary germ layers are formed as the cells in the embryo shift into layers as seen in Figure 7-8. Once a cell enters a germ layer, its ability to differentiate into specific cell types is limited. The three germ layers and the fates of cells in these layers are as follows:

➤ **Ectoderm.** Cells in this layer express the genes needed to become skin cells and cells of the nervous system.

➤ **Mesoderm.** Cells in this layer express the genes needed to become muscles, bones, and most internal organs.

➤ **Endoderm.** Cells in this layer express the genes needed to become the lining of internal body cavities as well as the linings of the respiratory, digestive, urinary, and reproductive tracts.

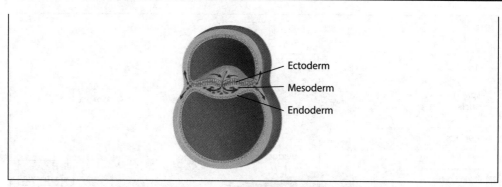

FIGURE 7-8 During gastrulation, embryonic cells shift into the primary germ layers. *Source:* From George B. Johnson, *The Living World*, 3rd ed., McGraw-Hill, 2003; reproduced with permission of The McGraw-Hill Companies.

Once the germ layers are complete, neuralization occurs to begin the development of the nervous system. Mesoderm cells form the notochord. Ectoderm above the notochord starts to thicken and folds inward to form neural folds that continue to deepen and fuse to produce a neural tube, which eventually develops into the central nervous system. At this point, a head and tail region have been established in the embryo.

GENE EXPRESSION IN EMBRYOGENESIS

Gene expression in embryos is regulated by a variety of factors. Gametes contain many epigenetic markers and when those gametes come together, the embryo inherits those markers. Through a process called reprogramming, most of the epigenetic markers inherited from the gametes are erased, although some of the markers remain. This reprogramming step is important because it allows the reprogrammed cells to have pluripotency, the potential to differentiate into any cell type, which is necessary during embryogenesis. These reprogrammed cells are referred to as embryonic stem cells. As embryogenesis progresses and cells differentiate, the cells begin to acquire new epigenetic markers. These epigenetic markers have considerable influence on further gene expression and differentiation.

As differentiation continues, certain cells can influence the gene expression of other cells in the process of induction via chemical messengers. Communication between cells is also used to establish positional information in the embryo that is critical to the formation of internal organs as well as the limbs. **Homeobox genes** produce proteins that are essential for guiding the development of the shape of the embryo. The proteins produced by the homeoboxes are transcription factors that serve to turn on specific genes within cells at specific times.

Induction helps ensure that the right structures occur in the right places. An additional process that is necessary during embryonic development is **apoptosis** of certain cells. While it seems odd to talk about cell death during development, it is necessary. For example, the separation of fingers and toes is the result of apoptosis of the cells that at one time joined the structures.

137

CHAPTER 7:
Processes of
Cell Division,
Differentiation, and
Specialization

The remainder of embryonic development deals with organogenesis and refining the shape of the embryo. Organ systems are developed on an as-needed basis with the most critical organs being produced first. By the fourth week, the heart is working and limbs are established. By the end of embryonic development (the eighth week), all major organs are established and most are functioning.

EXTRAEMBRYONIC MEMBRANES

While the embryo is in the process of implanting into the endometrium, four membranes will be formed outside of the embryo. They are as follows:

➤ The **amnion** surrounds the embryo in a fluid-filled sac, which serves a protective function and provides cushioning for the embryo and fetus.
➤ The **allantois** is a membrane that will ultimately form the umbilical cord, which is the connection between the embryo and the placenta (the organ that will deliver nutrients and oxygen and remove carbon dioxide and wastes).
➤ The **yolk sac** is where the first blood cells develop. In other species, it serves as a source of nutrients.
➤ The **chorion** will eventually become the embryo's side of the placenta.

THE PLACENTA

The **placenta** develops from the chorion and grows in size during development. It provides nutrients and oxygen to the embryo and removes wastes. Recall that fetal hemoglobin has a greater affinity for oxygen than adult hemoglobin. The placenta produces HCG, estrogen, and progesterone to maintain the pregnancy. It also produces the hormone relaxin to release the ligaments that attach the pubic bones to provide more space in the birth canal. It takes about 3 months for the placenta to fully develop.

Fetal Development

Fetal development is primarily a refinement of the organ systems that are already established during embryonic development. The fetus enlarges in size and the organ systems are refined, so that they are all functioning, or are capable of functioning at the end of gestation.

Birth

Labor is triggered by the hormone oxytocin that is produced by the posterior pituitary gland. Oxytocin causes contractions of the uterus, which intensify with time. Initially, the cervix must dilate, which can take hours. The amnion usually ruptures during the dilation stage. Once the cervix is dilated, contractions continue, which lead to expulsion of the baby. After the baby is delivered, the umbilical cord is clamped and cut, which severs the connection to the placenta. Finally, the placenta is delivered at the end of labor.

Unit II Minitest

20 Questions   **30 Minutes**

This minitest is designed to assess your mastery of the content in Chapters 5 through 7 of this volume. The questions have been designed to simulate actual MCAT questions in terms of format and degree of difficulty. They are based on the content categories associated with Foundational Concept 2, which is the theme of this unit. They are also designed to test the scientific inquiry and reasoning skills that the test makers have identified as essential for success in medical school.

In this test, most of the questions are based on short passages that typically describe a laboratory experiment, a research study, or some similar process. There are also some questions that are not based on passages.

Use this test to measure your readiness for the actual MCAT. Try to answer all of the questions within the specified time limit. If you run out of time, you will know that you need to work on improving your pacing.

Complete answer explanations are provided at the end of the minitest. Pay particular attention to the answers for questions you got wrong or skipped. If necessary, go back and review the corresponding chapters or text sections in this unit.

Now turn the page and begin the Unit II Minitest.

Directions: *Choose the best answer to each of the following questions. Questions 1–4 are not based on a passage.*

1. The DNA doubles and chromosomes replicate during which phase of the cycle cell?

   A. G_1 **B.** metaphase   **C.** S   **D.** G_2

2. When two solutions that differ in solute concentration are placed on either side of a semi-permeable membrane and osmosis is allowed to occur, which of the following will be observed?

   A. Water will move from an area of low solute concentration to an area of high solute concentration.

   B. The solute will move from the area of high concentration to an area of low concentration.

   C. There will be no net movement of water.

   D. Water will move from an area of high solute concentration to an area of low solute concentration.

3. A scientist discovers an unidentified unicellular organism. To identify it as eukaryotic, she must determine if it has

   A. ribosomes

   B. a cell membrane

   C. DNA

   D. mitochondria

4. Which of the following would help you identify an unknown cell type as connective?

   A. the ability to contract

   B. the presence of lots of cells arranged in sheets

   C. the presence of a basement membrane

   D. the presence of collagen fibers

Questions 5–8 are based on the following passage.

Passage I

The origin of eukaryotic organelles has been subject to speculation for many years. In particular, chloroplasts and mitochondria have some unusual features unlike the other organelles of the cell, which suggests they have had a unique history. The evidence collected as a result of the development of molecular research techniques provides an explanation for the origin of these organelles.

    The theory of endosymbiosis is used to explain the presence of organelles such as mitochondria and chloroplasts in modern-day eukaryotic cells. The theory suggests that small prokaryotic cells were at one time engulfed by larger prokaryotic cells. Once inside the larger cells, a symbiotic relationship developed. In the case of mitochondria, it has been speculated that the larger cell was likely anaerobic and ingested a smaller aerobic cell. Once inside, the aerobic cell was able to perform aerobic respiration to produce additional ATP for the host cell. To explain the evolution of chloroplasts, it has been suggested that cyanobacteria with the ability to photosynthesize were engulfed by a larger anaerobic prokaryotic cell. Support for this theory exists in the fact that both mitochondria and chloroplasts have double membranes, have their own genetic material that is different from typical eukaryotic chromosomal DNA, and have their own ribosomes.

5. According to the endosymbiotic theory presented in this passage, the original anaerobic cell that engulfed the smaller cell was likely to be performing _____ to produce ATP prior to entering a symbiotic relationship.
   A. glycolysis
   B. electron transport
   C. the Krebs cycle
   D. all of these

6. The genetic material of mitochondria and chloroplasts resemble that of modern-day bacteria as opposed to that of typical eukaryotic genetic material. This would mean which of the following?
   A. The DNA in these organelles exists in linear chromosome form.
   B. The DNA in these organelles exists in plasmid form.
   C. The DNA in these organelles exists in a single loop.
   D. The RNA in these organelles is single stranded.

7. Under normal circumstances, items engulfed by a eukaryotic cell might be broken down by which organelle?
   A. the lysosomes
   B. the smooth endoplasmic reticulum
   C. the Golgi apparatus
   D. the rough endoplasmic reticulum

8. Which of the following would lend additional evidence to the endosymbiotic theory?
   A. discovering a difference in the size of the subunits of the ribosomes inside the mitochondria and chloroplasts as compared to the rest of the cell
   B. finding that the inner membrane of the mitochondria and chloroplasts resembled that of modern bacteria
   C. finding plasmid DNA in the mitochondria and chloroplasts
   D. all of the above

Questions 9–12 are based on the following passage.

Passage II

In the early 1900s, it was noticed that cellular materials that passed from the tumors of chickens with cancer to chickens without cancer would eventually cause cancer to develop in the recipient chickens. In this case it appeared that the cancer was somehow "contagious," and it was suspected that viruses were somehow involved in this infectious type of cancer. Later, it was determined that certain viruses have the ability to genetically transform normal cells to a cancerous state by inserting into the chromosomes of their host cells. The virus that caused cancer was named the Rous sarcoma virus (RSV) after its founder. The RSV has only four genes. The *gag* gene codes for the capsid of the virus, the *env* gene codes for the envelope of the virus, the *pol* gene which codes for reverse transcriptase, and the *src* gene encodes for a tyrosine kinase.

Within normal cells, there are proto-oncogenes, which are involved in cell division and development. Since most cells are not reproducing all the time, proto-oncogenes tend to be expressed at low levels or not at all. If viral genetic material inserts into a proto-oncogene, it will be converted to an active oncogene, which stimulates excessive cell division, eventually leading to tumor development. Viruses with this ability are termed *oncogenic* viruses. While some viruses activate an oncogene by inserting their genetic material into a cellular proto-oncogene, some oncogenic viruses actually carry oncogenes into their hosts. Whether the virus inserts into a cellular proto-oncogene or it carries an oncogene into the cell, the end result is increased cell proliferation and changes in the cell, which can include lack of contact inhibition and immortality.

9. Oncogenic viruses are known to become latent as they enter into the host cell's chromosomes. Many oncogenic viruses are retroviruses. In order for a retrovirus to insert into the host cell's chromosomes, it must FIRST
   A. convert its RNA to DNA
   B. translate its RNA
   C. initiate transcription
   D. recombine with the host cell's chromosomes

10. Suppose a drug had been made to target the RSV. This drug attempts to prevent the packaging and release of the virus from its host cell. This drug would MOST likely target which of the RSV genes?
    A. *gag* and *env*
    B. *pol* and *src*
    C. *src* only
    D. *pol* only

11. It is known that some viruses carry activated oncogenes into their hosts. What is the BEST explanation for how a virus could acquire an oncogene?
    A. The virus spontaneously mutates.
    B. The virus acquires the oncogene via conjugation with another virus.
    C. The virus is transformed by DNA from another source.
    D. The virus acquired the oncogene from a previous host.

12. Once an oncogene is activated and a cell becomes cancerous, which of the following would be MOST likely to halt the excessive cell division associated with cancer?
    A. microtubule and mitotic disruption in dividing cells
    B. disruption of protein synthesis
    C. introduction of additional growth factors to the cell
    D. disruption of aerobic cellular respiration

Questions 13–16 are based on the following passage.

Passage III

Evolutionary theory predicts that given selective pressures, populations will evolve in certain ways. Antibiotic resistance that develops in bacteria is an excellent example of evolutionary selection in action. Spontaneous mutations in bacteria will happen in nature. Due to random chance, some of these mutations provide bacteria with the ability to survive in the presence of antibiotics that would normally kill them. These mutations can provide advantages to the bacteria such as the ability to degrade the antibiotics with enzymes, the ability to pump the antibiotic out of the cell, the ability to prevent the antibiotic from entering the cell, and by changing target molecules in the cell so that the antibiotic is unable to affect its target. Additionally, most antibiotic resistance genes can easily be passed from a resistant bacterium to a nonresistant bacterium via the process of conjugation. Transduction by viruses can also carry resistance genes from one bacterium to another. It becomes very easy for an entire bacterial population to become resistant to an antibiotic in a very short period of time.

Antibiotic resistance is a major public health concern because as bacteria develop resistance to certain antibiotics, those antibiotics are no longer capable of eliminating infections caused by resistant bacteria. Further, some bacteria are able to acquire mutations that provide them with resistance to multiple antibiotics. One such example is methicillin-resistant *Staphylococcus aureus* (MRSA). This type of bacteria can be carried asymptomatically by some people and passed to others where it will cause an infection. One of the most common places for MRSA to be spread is through hospitals. The problem with MRSA is that its multiple resistance leaves it susceptible to very few antibiotics. In fact, strains of MRSA are known to show resistance to nearly every antibiotic available.

13. Why would repeated use of antibiotics select for resistant strains of bacteria?
    A. The antibiotics would force the bacteria to mutate at a greater rate.
    B. The antibiotics would kill the susceptible bacteria, leaving only the resistant ones to multiply.
    C. The antibiotics would directly increase the rate of binary fission in resistant organisms.
    D. All of the above would be logical reasons that the repeated use of antibiotics selects for resistant bacteria.

14. Conjugation is one method bacteria use to pass their resistance genes to other bacteria. During conjugation, the genes transferred are typically located on
    A. the bacterial chromosome
    B. the ribosome
    C. the mRNA
    D. a plasmid

15. A variety of biotechnology techniques have been developed that allow for manipulated gene transfer. Often, antibiotic resistance genes are purposefully transferred along with the gene of interest. Why would this be important?

   A. to make sure that the transformed cells can survive in the presence of antibiotics

   B. to be able to use antibiotics as a marker to select between transformed and nontransformed cells

   C. the antibiotic resistance genes happen to be near the gene of interest being transferred

   D. to prevent infection of the transformed cells

16. When humans take antibiotics to treat infections, we rely on the fact that the antibiotics target the bacterial cells while leaving our own cells unharmed. What cell structure in bacteria is structurally different from eukaryotic cells and could potentially be a target of an antibiotic?

   A. the cell membrane

   B. the DNA nucleotides

   C. the ribosomes

   D. the cytoplasm

Questions 17–20 are not based on a passage.

17. Some human males have three sex chromosomes (XXY) and suffer from a genetic disease known as Klinefelter's syndrome. The symptoms include a failure to develop sexually and an impairment of intelligence. Klinefelter's syndrome is an example of a disease related to

   A. karyotype   **B.** point mutation

   C. homeostasis   **D.** bacterial origin

18. In humans, the number of tetrads formed during mitosis is

   A. 23   **B.** 46   **C.** 0   **D.** 4

19. The centromere, or primary constriction of the chromosome, contains rings of proteins that are intimately associated with a spindle fiber. These rings are called

   A. somites   **B.** centrioles

   C. asters   **D.** kinetochores

20. The two sets of chromosomes present in the cells of diploid organisms are derived from

   A. doubling of a haploid cell

   B. the contribution of one haploid set from each parent

   C. a reduction process within a tetraploid cell

   D. all of the above

This is the end of the Unit II Minitest.

Unit II Minitest Answers and Explanations

1. **The correct answer is** C. The majority of the cell cycle is spent in interphase which consists of three stages: G_1, S, and G_2. In the G_1 stage of interphase, the cell organelles are doubled and materials required for DNA synthesis are accumulated for the onset of cell division. The S stage of interphase is the stage of the cell cycle where the amount of DNA doubles with the replication of chromosomes. In the G_2 stage of interphase, which follows the synthesis of DNA, proteins required for the next cell division are synthesized. Metaphase is the stage in mitosis characterized by the precise lineup of the chromosomes along the equatorial plane.

2. **The correct answer is** A. Osmosis is a specialized form of diffusion, or passive transport. During osmosis, water always moves from the side of the membrane that has more water, to the side of the membrane that has less water. The only thing that moves by osmosis is water. This means that choice B can be eliminated because solutes are not moving by osmosis. If there is a concentration difference across the membrane, there will be water movement which eliminates choice C. When osmosis occurs, water moves from the side of the membrane that has more water to the side that has less water. This means that the side of the membrane with more water has less solute (and is therefore less concentrated) than the side of the membrane with less water and more solute (being more concentrated). Based on the choices provided, choice A is the most appropriate.

3. **The correct answer is** D. Prokaryotic and eukaryotic cells have several structures in common. In order to determine that a cell is eukaryotic, structures that are unique to eukaryotic cells must be identified. Ribosomes perform protein synthesis and can be found in all cells. The cell membrane is the outer boundary of the cell and is also found in all types or cells. DNA serves as the genetic material found in all cell types. Mitochondria (choice D) are true bound organelles that perform the process of cellular respiration. Because they are true organelles, they are found only in eukaryotic cells.

4. **The correct answer is** D. Connective tissues are characterized by cells scattered in a nonliving matrix. This matrix often consists of collagen fibers. Muscle has the ability to contract, while epithelial cells are characterized by cells arranged in sheets and a basement membrane.

5. **The correct answer is** A. A bacterial cell performing anaerobic respiration would perform a fermentation step following glycolysis. The Krebs cycle and electron transport chain are associated with aerobic cellular respiration.

6. **The correct answer is** C. This question is asking for a comparison between the organization of DNA in bacteria and eukaryotic cells. Eukaryotic DNA exists in multiple linear pieces termed *chromosomes*. Bacterial DNA consists of a single loop of DNA. While bacteria can have extrachromosomal DNA known as plasmids, this is not the case for all bacteria. While RNA is single stranded, it is not the primary genetic material of the cells and is only produced during transcription.

7. **The correct answer is A.** Once taken inside a cell, foreign items can be broken down in the lysosomes of the cell. The smooth endoplasmic reticulum is responsible for lipid synthesis, while the rough endoplasmic reticulum deals in protein labeling. The Golgi apparatus sorts and modifies contents from the endoplasmic reticulum.

8. **The correct answer is D.** All of the given choices would give support to the endosymbiotic theory. The subunit sizes of bacterial and eukaryotic ribosomes are known to be different. Bacterial cell membranes have some different properties as compared to their eukaryotic counterparts. Because plasmids are unique to bacteria, finding them in the chloroplasts or mitochondria would support the idea that these structures were once prokaryotic in nature.

9. **The correct answer is A.** Retroviruses are unique in that they enter their host as RNA but must convert themselves to DNA to enter the latent phase and insert into the host's chromosomes, which are also DNA. This is indicated by choice A. This conversion of RNA to DNA is carried out by the enzyme reverse transcriptase. The question is asking specifically about retroviruses, so choices B and C can be eliminated, as they are not unique to the retrovirus family. Choice D indicates that the retrovirus needs to recombine with the host chromosomes. Recombination implies genetic exchange between the two sources. Although the viral genetic material will insert into a proto-oncogene of the host, there will not be an exchange of DNA.

10. **The correct answer is A.** The passage describes the function of the four genes found in RSV. Packaging of viruses for release involves the viral envelope and capsid, which implicates the *gag* gene and the *env* gene. The *pol* gene codes for reverse transcriptase, which converts viral RNA to DNA and is not needed for the packaging viruses. The *src* gene encodes for tyrosine kinase. Kinases phosphorylate other molecules, which would not be part of the viral packaging process.

11. **The correct answer is D.** Oncogenes develop when a proto-oncogene activates. In order for a virus to carry an oncogene into its host, that virus must be derived from a virus that picked up the gene from a former host cell. Spontaneous mutation alone could not account for a virus acquiring an entire proto-oncogene, which eliminates choice A. Viruses do not conjugate, so choice B can be eliminated as well. Transformation occurs when a cell incorporates foreign DNA from its environment into its own genome. This occurs with bacteria but not viruses, meaning that choice C can also be eliminated. This leaves transduction as the only choice. When a virus excises from the host chromosome, it can take with it genes from the host's chromosome. A virus could feasibly acquire an activated oncogene when excising from its host, and this gene could be transferred to a new host.

12. **The correct answer is A.** This question is essentially asking how a cancerous cell could have its cell division halted. Because cancer is characterized by uncontrolled mitosis, the best way to halt the cancer would be to halt mitosis. Disrupting protein synthesis, or aerobic cellular respiration, would not directly affect cell division, so these choices can be eliminated. Introducing additional growth factors to the cell would only increase the rate of cell division, which is the opposite of what this question is asking. The only feasible choice would be to interfere with the microtubules (spindle fibers) and halt mitosis.

13. **The correct answer is B.** For this question, the best strategy is to find the most logical sounding answer. Choice A suggests that antibiotics cause the mutation rate to increase. You have no evidence to support this assertion; therefore this choice should be eliminated. Choice C suggests that antibiotics increase the rate of reproduction in bacteria. Again, you have no evidence to support this. Choice D can be eliminated since other choices have already been found incorrect. This leaves choice B as your answer. The antibiotics will kill all but the resistant bacteria, leaving them to multiply and lead to a new generation of resistant bacteria.

14. **The correct answer is D.** This question is asking about a basic knowledge of bacterial conjugation. During conjugation, a bacterial cell copies a plasmid and transfers that plasmid to a recipient that is lacking the plasmid. Because the question tells you that the resistance genes are often passed by conjugation and you know conjugation passes plasmids, then you can assume that the resistance genes are located on plasmids.

15. **The correct answer is B.** This question requires you to locate the most logical explanation as to why antibiotic genes are often purposefully transferred along with a gene of interest in biotechnology procedures. Because the question does not provide information on what type of cells are being transformed, don't assume anything. Choice A suggests that you need resistance genes transferred so the cells can survive in the presence of antibiotics. If the cells transformed are not bacterial, they would survive anyway, as antibiotics would target and kill only bacteria. Choice C suggests that the antibiotic genes are transferred out of convenience because they happen to be near the gene of interest. If the gene of interest is not coming from bacteria, then there could not be any antibiotic resistance genes nearby. Choice D really doesn't offer much in the way of logic, suggesting that antibiotic resistance would be necessary to prevent infection in transformed cells. The only logical explanation is choice B. In order to determine if a cell was transformed with the gene of interest or not, antibiotics could be added. The transformed cells that picked up the gene of interest would also pick up the antibiotic resistance marker and would grow in the presence of antibiotics. The nontransformed cells would not be resistant to the antibiotics and would be killed.

16. **The correct answer is** C. Of the choices listed, only the ribosomes are structurally different between prokaryotic and eukaryotic cells. While both eukaryotic and prokaryotic ribosomes have a small and large subunit, the sizes of these subunits are different in prokaryotic cells.

17. **The correct answer is** A. The karyotype is the characteristic morphology of a species' chromosome set. The normal karyotype for humans consists of 23 pairs of chromosomes. The twenty-third pair constitutes the sex chromosomes, which consist of a pair of X chromosomes in the female or an X and Y chromosome in the male. In Klinefelter's syndrome, males exhibit an altered karyotype in that they possess a third X chromosome.

18. **The correct answer is** C. Mitosis is the process during which chromosomes are distributed evenly to two new cells that arise from the parent cell undergoing division. Tetrads, or the formation of four new cells, do not occur during mitosis. Thus the number of tetrads formed during mitosis is 0.

19. **The correct answer is** D. During the S phase of interphase before mitosis proper, each chromosome will have replicated. The two chromosomal strands or chromatids are identical in their genetic material and are joined at a constricted region called the centromere. Within the centromere are one or more rings of protein known as kinetochores, which play a significant role in the attachment of the spindle fibers to the chromosomes.

20. **The correct answer is** B. Diploid organisms have two sets of 23 chromosomes, with one (haploid) set provided by each parent.

UNIT III

Systems of Tissues and Organs

Foundational Concept: Complex systems of tissues and organs sense the internal and external environments of multicellular organisms and, through integrated functioning, maintain a stable internal environment within an ever-changing external environment.

Structure and Function of the Nervous and Endocrine Systems and Ways in Which These Systems Coordinate the Organ Systems

THE NERVOUS SYSTEM

The nervous system has the daunting task of coordinating all the body's activities. The **central nervous system (CNS)** is composed of the brain and spinal cord, and the **peripheral nervous system (PNS)** is composed of all nervous tissue located outside of the brain and spinal cord. Nerves are the primary structures within the PNS. In order to understand the functioning of the CNS and PNS, it is necessary to look at the detailed function of neurons, the basic units of function within the nervous system.

The Neuron

Neurons perform the critical function of transmitting messages throughout the body. There are several types of neurons: sensory, motor, and interneurons. **Sensory (afferent) neurons** exist in the PNS, pick up sensory impulses, and direct their messages toward the CNS. **Motor (efferent) neurons** exist in the PNS and direct their messages away from the CNS to peripheral parts of the body. **Interneurons**, which transfer messages, are found only in the CNS.

While neurons perform the critical function of transmitting messages throughout the body, there are also a large number of glial cells present in the nervous system. Glial cells provide support to neurons and, unlike mature neurons, are capable of mitosis.

The basic structure of a neuron can be seen in Figure 8-1. The major structures within the neuron are as follows:

➤ **Dendrites.** Projections that pick up incoming messages

➤ **Cell body.** Processes messages and contains the nucleus and other typical cell organelles

➤ **Axon.** Projections that carry electrical messages down their length

➤ **Synaptic knobs.** Extensions at the ends of an axon that send electrical impulses converted to chemical messages in the form of neurotransmitters to other neurons

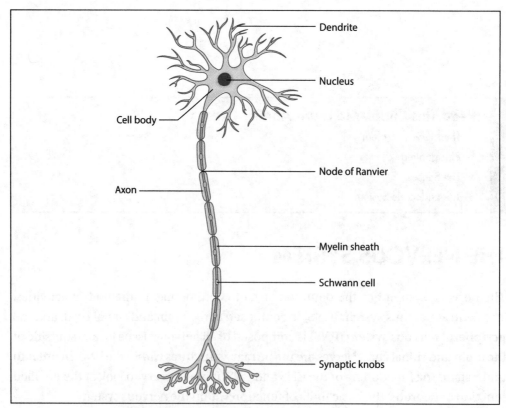

FIGURE 8-1 Neuron structure.

153

CHAPTER 8:
Structure and
Function of the
Nervous and
Endocrine Systems
and Ways in Which
These Systems
Coordinate the
Organ Systems

➤ **Myelin sheath.** Covering, produced by Schwann cells (specialized glial cells), that surrounds the axon of some neurons; gaps between the myelin are called nodes of Ranvier

➤ **Synapse.** The space between the synaptic knob of one neuron and the dendrite of another neuron

Basic Function of a Neuron

Neurons send messages in the form of electrical impulses throughout the body. They do this through a complex series of processes involving changes from a resting potential to an action potential and communication via neurotransmitters.

RESTING POTENTIAL

In order to understand how neurons generate electrical impulses to send messages, it is necessary to understand the state of the neurons when they are not generating electrical impulses. This is termed the **resting potential** of the neurons. It requires the maintenance of an unequal balance of ions on either side of the membrane to keep the membrane polarized. To maintain the resting potential, a great deal of ATP is required.

During resting potential, sodium-potassium (Na^+/K^+) pumps within the membrane of the axon are used to actively transport ions into and out of the axon. The Na^+/K^+ pumps bring 2 K^+ ions into the axon while sending out 3 Na^+ ions. This results in a high concentration of Na^+ outside the membrane and a high concentration of K^+ inside the membrane. There are also many negatively charged molecules such as proteins within the neuron so that ultimately the inside of the neuron is more negative than the outside of the neuron. The resting potential is about -70 mV. Figure 8-2 shows the resting potential in a neuron.

ACTION POTENTIAL

To transmit a message, the resting potential of the neuron must be disrupted and depolarized such that the inside of the cell becomes slightly less negative. For this **action potential** to occur, there is a threshold voltage that must be achieved to initiate the action potential, which is about -50 mV. Once the action potential has initiated, voltage gated channels in the membrane of the axon open. Specifically, Na^+ channels open, allowing Na^+ to flow passively across the membrane into the axon in a local area. This local flow of Na^+ causes the next Na^+ channel to open. This continues down the length of the axon toward the synaptic knobs like a wave as seen in Figure 8-3.

Although the speed of the axon potential varies depending on the axon diameter and whether the axon is myelinated or not, its strength cannot. Action potentials are an all-or-nothing event. If the threshold voltage is not hit, the action potential does not happen. If the threshold value is achieved or exceeded, the action potential occurs with the same electrical charge of about $+35$ mV each time.

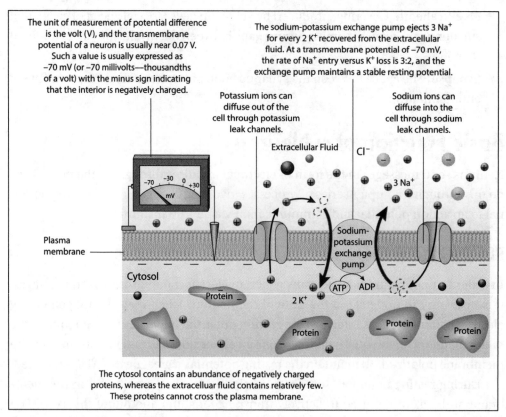

The unit of measurement of potential difference is the volt (V), and the transmembrane potential of a neuron is usually near 0.07 V. Such a value is usually expressed as –70 mV (or –70 millivolts—thousandths of a volt) with the minus sign indicating that the interior is negatively charged.

The sodium-potassium exchange pump ejects 3 Na⁺ for every 2 K⁺ recovered from the extracellular fluid. At a transmembrane potential of –70 mV, the rate of Na⁺ entry versus K⁺ loss is 3:2, and the exchange pump maintains a stable resting potential.

Potassium ions can diffuse out of the cell through potassium leak channels.

Sodium ions can diffuse into the cell through sodium leak channels.

The cytosol contains an abundance of negatively charged proteins, whereas the extracelluar fluid contains relatively few. These proteins cannot cross the plasma membrane.

FIGURE 8-2 Resting potential. During resting potential, the sodium-potassium pumps maintain an unequal balance of ions inside and outside the axon.

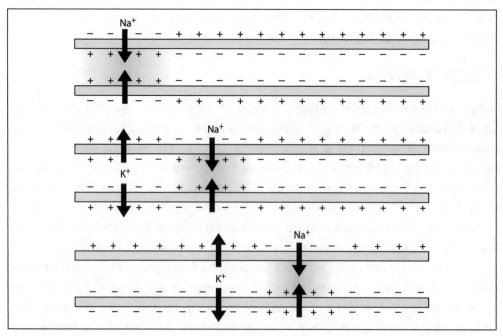

FIGURE 8-3 During the action potential, Na⁺ enters the neuron, causing depolarization.

155

CHAPTER 8:
Structure and
Function of the
Nervous and
Endocrine Systems
and Ways in Which
These Systems
Coordinate the
Organ Systems

In myelinated neurons, the voltage gated ion channels are only permeable to ions at the nodes of Ranvier. This allows for the action potential to jump from one node to the next in the process of salutatory conduction.

As soon as the Na^+ channels open and depolarize a small area of the axon, K^+ channels open, allowing K^+ to leak passively out of the axon. This restores the more negative charge within the axon, temporarily preventing the initiation of another action potential during a refractory period. The Na^+/K^+ pump can then be used to completely restore the resting potential by repolarization. By the time an action potential reaches the end of an axon, the rest of the axon is already repolarized.

Communication Between Neurons

More than 50 types of **neurotransmitters** have been identified in humans, each with very diverse functions. Each neuron specializes in specific types of neurotransmitters and contains vesicles full of them within their synaptic knobs. When an action potential reaches the synaptic knobs, the vesicles containing neurotransmitters fuse with the membrane by exocytosis and release their contents to the synapse. This neurotransmitter release requires calcium to occur. The neuron that releases the neurotransmitter is termed the **presynaptic neuron** and the neuron that responds to the neurotransmitter is termed the **postsynaptic neuron**. The neurotransmitter will bind to the receptors on the postsynaptic neurons.

The nature of the receptor determines the response in the postsynaptic neuron. In some cases, the binding of the neurotransmitter to a receptor initiates an excitatory response in which some sodium channels open in an attempt to hit the threshold value to generate an action potential in the postsynaptic neuron. This is a graded response in that the more neurotransmitter binding to receptors in the synapse, the more sodium that leaks into the postsynaptic neuron, which increases the odds of an action potential occurring. In other cases, the binding of the neurotransmitter to a receptor will initiate an inhibitory response that discourages the generation of an action potential in the postsynaptic neuron. This usually occurs by the addition of chloride ions (Cl^-) to the interior of the axon, making it more negative and less likely that the threshold value needed for an action potential will be generated.

A single neuron may receive messages in the form of neurotransmitters from multiple other neurons. In some cases, a neuron can receive excitatory and inhibitory signals at the same time. The response of this neuron is all or nothing, either an action potential occurs or it does not. If the excitatory signals outweigh the inhibitory signals, an action potential occurs. If the inhibitory signals outweigh the excitatory signals, an action potential does not occur.

Once a neurotransmitter has been released into the synapse and has interacted with a receptor, it must be cleared from the synapse to avoid sending repeated messages. Depending on the type of neurotransmitter, removal may be via reuptake, where the neurotransmitters are taken back into the presynpatic neuron, or by enzymatic degradation of the neurotransmitter in the synapse.

The Central Nervous System

The central nervous system (CNS) is composed of the brain and spinal cord. The brain and spinal cord both consist of many neurons and supporting glial cells. White matter within the brain and spinal cord consists of myelinated axons. Gray matter consists of clusters of cell bodies of neurons.

Cranial bones and vertebrae protect the CNS, as do protective membranes called the **meninges**. There are three meninges (dura mater, arachnoid, and pia mater). Between two of the meninges and within cavities of the brain, there is **cerebrospinal fluid**. This fluid has several critical functions such as providing nutrients and removing wastes as well as providing cushioning and support for the brain. Cerebrospinal fluid is made by the brain and is eventually reabsorbed by the blood.

The **blood–brain barrier** is another mechanism of protection for the brain. While the name implies that the blood–brain barrier is a structure, it is not. It is a mechanism that selects for components in the blood that are allowed to circulate into the brain via brain capillaries. This selection is based on a unique membrane permeability that allows for the easy passage of most lipid soluble molecules, while preventing other molecules from entering the brain tissue. The benefits of the blood–brain barrier are that it protects the brain from substances in the blood that might cause damage

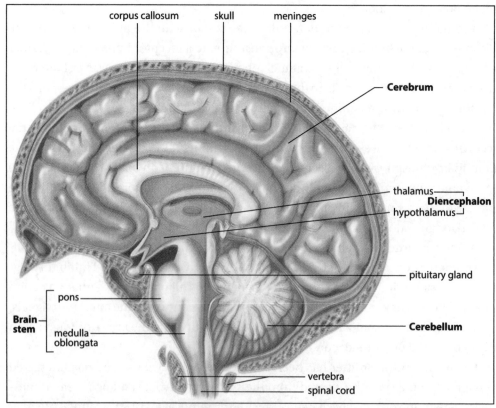

FIGURE 8-4 Brain structure. The cerebrum of the brain is divided into right and left hemispheres connected by the corpus callosum. *Source:* From Sylvia S. Mader, *Biology*, 8th ed., McGraw-Hill, 2004; reproduced with permission of The McGraw-Hill Companies.

157

CHAPTER 8:
Structure and
Function of the
Nervous and
Endocrine Systems
and Ways in Which
These Systems
Coordinate the
Organ Systems

and it maintains a consistent environment for the brain, which is not very tolerant of fluctuations.

STRUCTURE AND FUNCTION OF THE BRAIN

The brain is the central command center of the nervous system. It processes conscious thought and sensory information, it coordinates motor activities of skeletal muscle and other organ systems within the body, and it maintains vital functions such as heart rate and ventilation.

The brain is divided into the **cerebrum**, **cerebellum**, **brain stem**, and **diencephalon** as seen in Figure 8-4. The cerebrum in particular has extremely diverse functions. The right and left hemispheres process information in different ways. The right side of the brain tends to specialize in spatial and pattern perception, while the left side of the brain tends to specialize in analytical processing and language. The connection of the two hemispheres via the corpus callosum is essential to integrating the functions of both sides of the brain.

Integration of functions of the brain is also accomplished via the **limbic system**. Complex activities such as mood and emotions, as well as memory, cannot be achieved in a single area of the brain. Instead, several areas of the brain must interact. The limbic system, a tract of neurons that connects several areas of the brain, including the cerebrum, hypothalamus, and medulla, and areas associated with the sense of smell, provides for this interaction. Within the limbic system, the hippocampus helps convert short-term memories to long-term memories.

The functions of each of the parts of the brain can be seen in the following table:

Major Structures of the Brain and Their Functions	
Structure	**Function**
Cerebrum	The cerebrum is the largest portion of the brain and is divided into right and left hemispheres as well as into four lobes (frontal, parietal, occipital, and temporal). Within the cerebrum there are specific areas for each of the senses, motor coordination, and association areas. All thought processes, memory, learning, and intelligence are regulated via the cerebrum. The cerebral cortex is the outer tissue of the cerebrum.
Cerebellum	The cerebellum is located at the base of the brain. It is responsible for sensory-motor coordination for complex muscle movement patterns and balance.
Brain stem	The brain stem is composed of several structures and ultimately connects the brain to the spinal cord. The **pons** connects the spinal cord and cerebellum to the cerebrum and diencephalon. The **medulla oblongata** (or medulla) has reflex centers for vital functions such as the regulation of breathing, heart rate, and blood pressure. Damage to the medulla is usually fatal. Messages entering the brain from the spinal cord must pass through the medulla.

(Continued)

Major Structures of the Brain and Their Functions	
Structure	**Function**
	The **reticular activating system (RAS)** is a tract of neurons that runs through the medulla into the cerebrum. It acts as a filter to prevent the processing of repetitive stimuli. The RAS is also an activating center for the cerebrum. When the RAS is not activated, sleep occurs.

Diencephelon	The diencephalon is composed of two different structures.
	   The **hypothalamus** is used to regulate the activity of the pituitary gland in the endocrine system. In addition, the hypothalamus regulates conditions such as thirst, hunger, sex drive, and temperature.
	   The **thalamus** is located adjacent to the hypothalamus and serves as a relay center for sensory information entering the cerebrum. It routes incoming information to the appropriate parts of the cerebrum.

The Spinal Cord and Reflex Actions

The spinal cord serves as a shuttle for messages going toward and away from the brain. It also acts as a reflex center, having the ability to process certain incoming messages and provide an autonomic response without processing by the brain. Spinal reflexes are important because they are faster than sending a message to the brain for processing.

The **reflex arc** seen in Figure 8-5 is a set of neurons that consists of a receptor, a sensory neuron, an interneuron, a motor neuron, and an effector. It involves both the CNS and the PNS. The receptor transmits a message to a sensory neuron, which routes the message to an interneuron located in the spinal cord. The interneuron processes the message in the cord and sends a response out through the motor neuron. The motor neuron passes the message to an effector, which can carry out the appropriate response.

The Peripheral Nervous System

The **peripheral nervous system (PNS)** is composed of pairs of nerves that are bundles of axons. There are 12 pairs of **cranial nerves** branching off the brain stem and 31 pairs of **spinal nerves** branching off the spinal cord. Some nerves are composed of only sensory neurons, others of only motor neurons, and others of a combination of sensory and motor neurons. The nerves that exist in the PNS are categorized into one of two divisions: the somatic nervous system or the autonomic nervous system.

The **somatic nervous system** controls conscious functions within the body such as sensory perception and voluntary movement due to innervation of skeletal muscle. The **autonomic nervous** system controls the activity of involuntary functions within the body to maintain homeostasis. The autonomic nervous system is further subdivided into the sympathetic and parasympathetic branches. Both branches innervate most internal organs. The sympathetic branch is regulated by the neurotransmitters

159

CHAPTER 8:
Structure and
Function of the
Nervous and
Endocrine Systems
and Ways in Which
These Systems
Coordinate the
Organ Systems

epinephrine (adrenaline) and norepinephrine (noradrenaline). When activated, the sympathetic branch produces the **fight-or-flight response** in which heart rate increases, ventilation increases, blood pressure increases, and digestion decreases. These responses prepare the body for immediate action.

The **parasympathetic branch** is antagonistic to the sympathetic branch and is the default system used for relaxation. Generally, it decreases heart rate, decreases ventilation rate, decreases blood pressure, and increases digestion. The neurotransmitter **acetylcholine** is the primary regulator of this system.

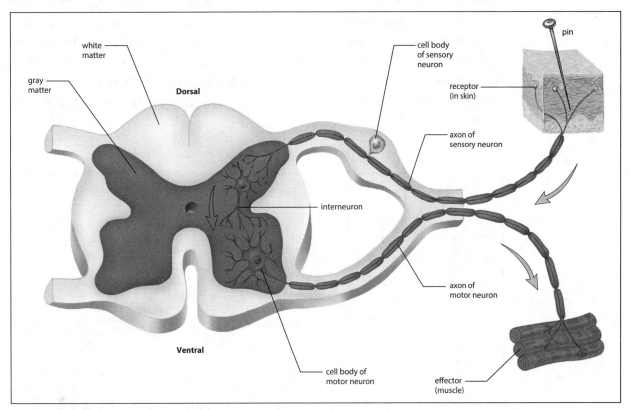

FIGURE 8-5 A reflex arc. A stimulus is carried by a sensory neuron to interneurons located in the spinal cord, which relays messages to motor neurons. *Source:* From Sylvia S. Mader, *Biology*, 8th ed., McGraw-Hill, 2004; reproduced with permission of The McGraw-Hill Companies.

BIOSIGNALING

There are many mechanisms by which **biosignaling** is achieved. Gated ion channels have already been exemplified in action and resting potentials. Another means for biosignaling is the use of **G protein–coupled receptors**. These transmembrane receptors are able to sense various molecules, such as hormones, growth factors, and neurotransmitters, to activate signal transduction pathways within cells. They essentially allow cells to gather information from their environment and to act on that information by changing cell functioning.

Each type of G protein–coupled receptors displays high levels of specificity to unique signals. Humans are thought to have as many as 1,000 different types of G protein–coupled receptors, each specific to a unique signal. The G protein–coupled receptors are single polypeptides embedded within the plasma membrane of a cell with portions looping inside and outside of the cell. Signaling molecules bind at the extracellular loops. The structure of G protein–coupled receptors has been highly conserved over evolutionary time.

When G protein–coupled receptors interact with a signaling molecule, it initiates a conformational change in the receptor. This triggers an interaction between the receptor and G proteins in the plasma membrane. G proteins are named as such because they have the ability to bind to guanosine triphosphate (GTP) and guanosine diphosphate (GDP). When G proteins are active, they can interact with other membrane proteins via signal transduction, ultimately relaying messages in the cell, typically by the use of second messenger systems. A simplified diagram of this process can be seen in Figure 8-6.

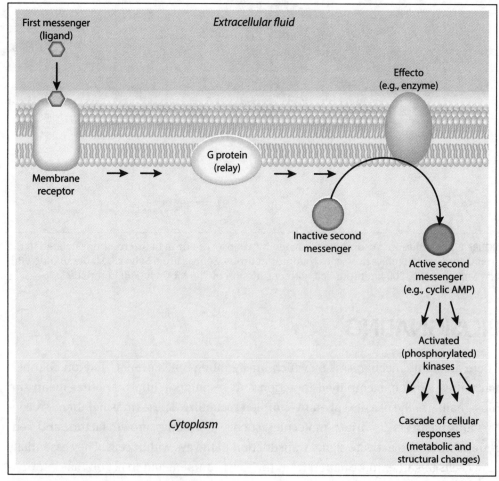

FIGURE 8-6 G protein–coupled receptors.

161

CHAPTER 8:
Structure and
Function of the
Nervous and
Endocrine Systems
and Ways in Which
These Systems
Coordinate the
Organ Systems

A common target of activated G proteins is adenylyl cyclase that catalyzes the synthesis of cyclic adenosine monophosphate (cAMP) from ATP. In humans, cAMP is involved in signaling in many systems of the body, including the nervous and endocrine systems. The enzyme phospholipase C also serves as a target for activated G proteins. This enzyme is involved in the synthesis of the second messengers diacylglycerol (DAG) and inositol triphosphate (IP3) from phosphatidylinositol in plasma membranes. These second messengers are important in various responses through the body, including the blood-clotting pathways.

THE SENSES

Sensory receptors located throughout the body are able to communicate with the nervous system, ultimately allowing for the perception of sensory information via the senses. There are various types of sensory receptors that differ based on the stimulus to which they are sensitive. Typical sensory receptors in the body, as well as the stimulus they are sensitive to, are seen in the following table.

Sensory Receptors and Their Stimuli		
Receptor	**Stimulus Detected**	**Functions or Senses**
Chemoreceptors	Chemicals	Gustation (taste) and olfaction (smell)
Thermoreceptors	Temperature	Monitoring body temperature
Photoreceptors	Light	Vision
Mechanoreceptors	Pressure	Tactile perception in the skin, proprioception (sense of body awareness), hearing, and equilibrium
Pain receptors	Pressure and chemicals	Conveys messages to the CNS concerning tissue damage

Receptor Potential

Each sensory receptor is sensitive to a particular stimulus. The intensity of the stimulus is conveyed by a graded receptor potential. The greater the stimulus, the larger the receptor potential will be. When the receptor potential hits the threshold level, an action potential is generated. Over time, most sensory receptors stop responding to repeated stimuli in the process of sensory adaptation so that action potentials are no longer generated and you are no longer aware of the stimulus.

The Special Senses

The special senses of the body include taste, smell, hearing, balance (equilibrium), and vision. The receptors for each of the special senses are located within the head in specialized structures.

TASTE

The sense of taste relies upon chemoreceptors located within taste buds on the tongue and, to a lesser degree, in other parts of the mouth. Five primary sensations can be perceived by the receptors of the tongue. These include sweet, sour, salty, bitter, and umami. These can be stimulated independently or in combinations to produce the perception of a variety of tastes. Different regions of the tongue have different sensitivities to particular tastes. In addition to information provided by chemoreceptors located within the taste buds, a large portion of the perception of taste is actually dependent on the sense of smell.

SMELL

The chemoreceptors for olfaction (smell) are located in small patches in the top of each nasal cavity and are covered in mucus. When chemicals from the air dissolve in mucus, they stimulate the receptors. The message from the receptor eventually makes its way to the cerebrum as well as to the limbic system. Unlike the chemoreceptors in the mouth, those in the nose are sensitive to about 1,000 different chemicals. Combinations of signals from several receptors allow people to perceive more than 10,000 different scents.

HEARING AND EQUILIBRIUM

The structures of the ear seen in Figure 8-7 are responsible for the sense of hearing as well as the sense of balance or equilibrium. Mechanoreceptors in the ear are sensitive to pressure and sound waves that enter the outer ear. The structures of the outer ear consist of the **pinna**, which funnels sound waves toward the **auditory canal**. Once in the auditory canal, sound waves need to travel to the middle ear.

The middle ear contains the **tympanic membrane** (eardrum), which produces vibrations in response to sound waves. Three bones (ossicles) in the middle ear (the malleus, incus, and stapes) amplify the signal as it moves toward the inner ear.

The inner ear consists of a variety of structures. The amplified signals from the ossicles will reach the **cochlea**. Inside the cochlea exists the **organ of Corti**, which contains specialized mechanoreceptors called hair cells that contain fluid with small "hairs" on the surface. When the fluid in the hair cells vibrates, the hairs send a message that is transduced into action potentials. These action potentials travel via the auditory nerve to the cerebrum for processing.

The **vestibular apparatus** within the inner ear is used to maintain a sense of equilibrium. Within the vestibular apparatus, semicircular canals of the inner ear contain hair cells filled with fluid. This fluid moves during motion of the head, changing the positioning of the hairs within the cell. The hair cells then send a message to the cerebrum for processing regarding the positioning of the head. The vestibular apparatus also contains the vestibule, which helps in the perception of balance when the head and body are not moving.

CHAPTER 8:
Structure and
Function of the
Nervous and
Endocrine Systems
and Ways in Which
These Systems
Coordinate the
Organ Systems

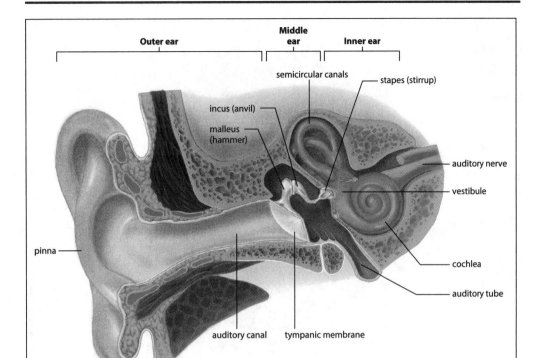

FIGURE 8-7 Ear structure. The outer ear collects sound waves, which then pass to the middle ear, where the sound waves are amplified. The inner ear is responsible for both hearing and equilibrium. *Source:* From Sylvia S. Mader, *Biology*, 8th ed., McGraw-Hill, 2004; reproduced with permission of The McGraw-Hill Companies.

VISION

The eyes are responsible for vision and contain two types of photoreceptors that are sensitive to different forms of light. The **rods** are used for night vision and black-and-white vision, while the **cones** are used for color vision. Cones come in three varieties and are sensitive to red, blue, or green light.

The eye has three layers. The outer layer is the **sclera** or the white of the eye. The middle layer of the eye is the **choroid**, which is used to supply oxygen and nutrients to other tissues of the eye. The inner layer of the eye is the **retina**, which contains photoreceptors and is connected to the optic nerve.

Light waves enter the eye through the transparent cornea, which protects the underlying lens of the eye seen in Figure 8-8. As light enters the cornea, it moves through the **pupil**. The diameter of the pupil can be adjusted by the **iris** that surrounds it. The lens focuses the light into an image on the **retina** located at the back of the eye. The rods and cones convert the image into patterns, which are sent to the cerebrum for processing via the **optic nerves**. The area where the optic nerve leaves the retina is lacking in photoreceptors and is commonly referred to as the blind spot.

The shape of pigments located in the rods and cones is modified when a stimulus is received. These modified pigments change the membrane permeability, resulting in a receptor potential that will ultimately produce an action potential that can be

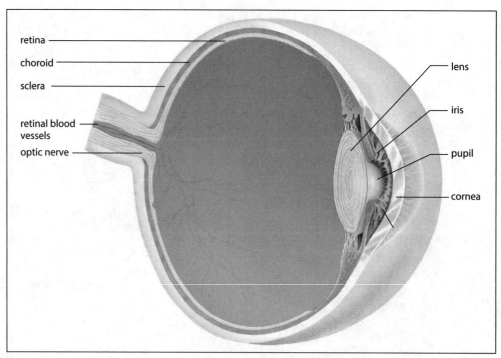

FIGURE 8-8 Eye structure. The photoreceptors for vision are located in the retina on the inner layer of the eye. *Source:* From Sylvia S. Mader, *Biology*, 8th ed., McGraw-Hill, 2004; reproduced with permission of The McGraw-Hill Companies.

transported by the optic nerves. Retinol is a pigment found in rods and cones, which binds to the protein opsin. Rods and each kind of cone all have a different form of opsin that can be distinguished from each other. The specific opsin found in rods is rhodopsin. Modification of any type of opsin results in stimulation of the receptor and a message being sent to the cerebrum for processing.

THE ENDOCRINE SYSTEM

To maintain homeostasis in the body, it is necessary to regulate the functioning of specific targets within the body. The endocrine system functions in this regulation. It is made up of endocrine glands located throughout the body. These glands secrete hormones that function to achieve this regulation.

Endocrine Glands

As stated previously, **endocrine glands** secrete hormones into the bloodstream. Some endocrine structures also have the ability to serve exocrine functions as well. An **exocrine gland** secretes its products onto a surface, into a body cavity, or within organs. The pancreas is an example of a gland with endocrine and exocrine functions.

165

CHAPTER 8:
Structure and
Function of the
Nervous and
Endocrine Systems
and Ways in Which
These Systems
Coordinate the
Organ Systems

Its ability to secrete the hormones insulin and glucagon into the blood qualifies it as an endocrine gland, while its ability to secrete digestive enzymes into the small intestine also qualifies it as an exocrine gland.

The endocrine system is composed of endocrine glands located throughout the body. There are some glands that specialize at endocrine function, while others have multiple functions, at least one of which is the secretion of hormones. The major endocrine glands can be seen in Figure 8-9.

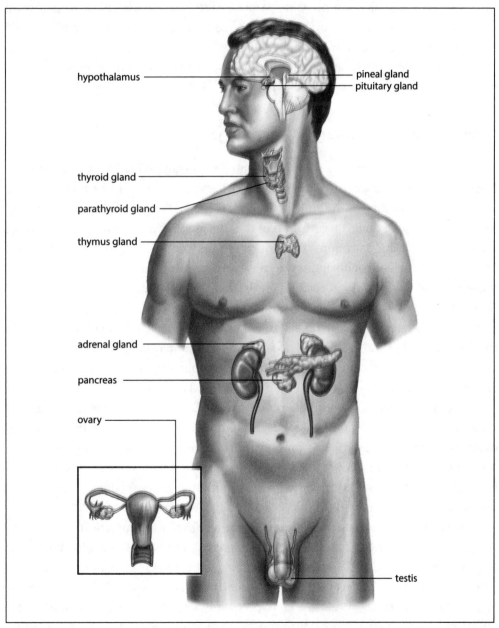

FIGURE 8-9 The endocrine system. Anatomic location of major endocrine structures of the body. *Source:* From Sylvia S. Mader, *Biology,* 8th ed., McGraw-Hill, 2004; reproduced with permission of The McGraw-Hill Companies.

Hormones

A hormone is a chemical messenger secreted into the bloodstream that travels to a specific target in the body and changes the functioning of that target. The target can be individual cells, tissues, or entire organs.

There are two major categories of hormones: **steroids** (lipid-soluble) and nonsteroids (water-soluble, peptide). Steroid hormones are derivatives of the lipid cholesterol and are produced from terpenoid precursors, whereas nonsteroid hormones are made of either modified amino acids or small proteins. The target cell receptors for steroid hormones exist in the cytoplasm of the cell, while the receptors for nonsteroid hormones exist on the cell membrane of the cell.

Hormone secretion is regulated by several mechanisms, and the different types of hormones function in different ways in the cell.

REGULATION OF HORMONE SECRETION

The secretion of hormones is usually regulated via **negative feedback mechanisms**. During negative feedback, the response of the endocrine system or a target is the opposite of a stimulus. For example, if the level of a specific hormone gets particularly high (the stimulus), then the secretion of that hormone will be reduced (opposite of the stimulus). Additionally, some conditions such as low blood calcium (the stimulus) may trigger the release of hormones to cause an opposite response (the breakdown of bone tissue to increase blood calcium levels). It is not uncommon to see antagonistic hormones—two hormones with opposing functions, such as a hormone to raise blood sugar and another to lower blood sugar. Being able to adjust a particular situation in the body from high and low ends is necessary to maintain **homeostasis**. Failure of the endocrine system to maintain homeostasis can lead to conditions such as diabetes, hyper- or hypothyroidism, growth abnormalities, and many others.

Although not nearly as common as negative feedback mechanisms, **positive feedback mechanisms** do exist. In this case, the stimulus causes actions in the body (regulated by hormones) that further amplify that stimulus, moving the body away from homeostasis. While this may sound like a bad thing, it is necessary in some cases, such as childbirth, where one hormone amplifies another. Positive feedback mechanisms are short lived, and eventually homeostasis is returned via lack of stimulus.

The nervous system can override endocrine feedback mechanisms in some cases. When the body is extremely stressed or experiencing trauma, the nervous system can exert control over the endocrine system to make adjustments to help the body cope with the situation. The hypothalamus in the brain is the main link between the endocrine and nervous systems. The hypothalamus monitors body conditions and makes changes when it deems appropriate. It produces regulatory hormones that influence glands such as the pituitary, which, in turn, regulates other glands in the endocrine system.

167

CHAPTER 8:
Structure and
Function of the
Nervous and
Endocrine Systems
and Ways in Which
These Systems
Coordinate the
Organ Systems

Hormone Specificity

Because hormones travel through the bloodstream, they encounter countless potential targets as they circulate. The specificity of hormones is based on their interaction with a receptor on the target cells. Only cells that have a receptor for a specific hormone will be affected by that hormone. Once a hormone binds to the receptor, the cells functioning will be changed in some way. These changes can involve gene expression, chemical reactions, membrane changes, metabolism, and so forth. Because the hormones must travel through the blood, it is a relatively slow process.

Mechanisms of Action of Hormones

As stated earlier, the two types of hormones differ in their chemical composition, receptor sites, and mechanisms of action. The target cell receptors for steroid hormones exist in the cytoplasm of the cell, while the receptors for nonsteroid hormones exist on the cell membrane of the cell. These differences affect the mechanism of action of the two types of hormones.

STEROID HORMONE MECHANISM OF ACTION

Steroids are derivatives of cholesterol, which are lipid soluble and can easily cross the plasma membrane. Once inside a cell, the steroid locates and binds to a cytoplasmic receptor. The steroid-receptor complex moves into the nucleus and interacts with DNA to cause activation of certain genes. This serves as the signal to initiate transcription and translation so that a new protein is expressed by the cell. This new protein will in some way change how the cell is functioning. A summary of steroid hormone action can be seen in Figure 8-10.

PEPTIDE HORMONE MECHANISM OF ACTION

Peptide hormones are composed of amino acid derivatives or small proteins and do not cross the plasma membrane. They recognize a receptor on the plasma membrane surface. The hormone itself is termed a **first messenger**, since it will never enter the cell and only triggers a series of events within the cell, many of which are moderated by G proteins found in the plasma membrane. The binding of the hormone to the receptor initiates a series of reactions in the cell, which ultimately lead to the production of a second messenger molecule within the cell. A common second messenger of nonsteroid hormones is **cyclic adenosine monophosphate (cAMP)**. Cyclic AMP is a derivative of ATP. The second messenger changes the function of the target cell by altering enzymatic activities and cellular reactions. A summary of nonsteroid hormone action can be seen in Figure 8-11.

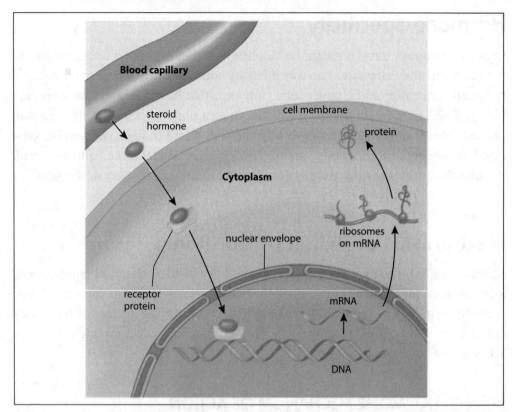

FIGURE 8-10 Steroid hormone mechanism of action. Steroid hormones act only on the cells in which they find their receptors in the cytoplasm of the cell. *Source:* From Sylvia S. Mader, *Biology*, 8th ed., McGraw-Hill, 2004; reproduced with permission of The McGraw-Hill Companies.

Other Chemical Messengers

In addition to steroid and nonsteroid hormones, there is another category of chemical messengers—the **prostaglandins**. These are lipid-based molecules released from cell membranes, not from endocrine glands. Prostaglandins function as a sort of local hormone involved in functions as diverse as regulation of body temperature, blood clotting, the inflammatory response, and menstrual cramping caused by uterine contractions.

Major Endocrine Glands and Their Products

The major endocrine glands of the body include the hypothalamus, pituitary gland (separated into the anterior lobe and posterior lobe), pineal gland, thyroid gland, parathyroid glands, and adrenal glands. Some organs within the body also have endocrine functions and these include the thymus gland, ovaries, testes, pancreas, heart, placenta, kidneys, stomach, and small intestine.

169

CHAPTER 8:
Structure and
Function of the
Nervous and
Endocrine Systems
and Ways in Which
These Systems
Coordinate the
Organ Systems

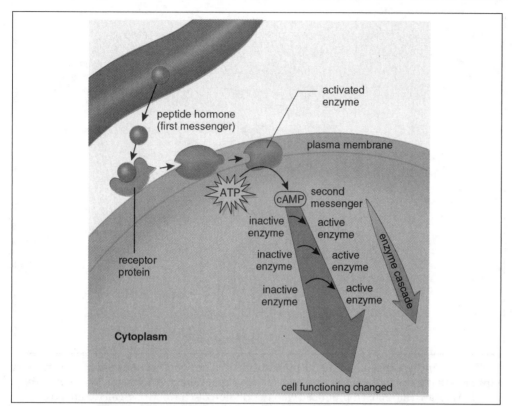

FIGURE 8-11 Nonsteroid hormone mechanism of action. Nonsteroid (peptide) hormones serve as first messengers and find their receptors on the cell membrane of the cell. *Source:* From Sylvia S. Mader, *Biology*, 8th ed., McGraw-Hill, 2004; reproduced with permission of The McGraw-Hill Companies.

The **hypothalamus** and **pituitary gland** have a unique relationship based on their proximity to each other in the brain seen in Figure 8-12. The pituitary gland secretes many hormones; some of these hormones influence the secretion of hormones from other endocrine glands. The regulatory hormones made by the hypothalamus control the secretion of hormones from the anterior pituitary. The hypothalamus produces releasing hormones that stimulate the release of anterior pituitary hormones as well as inhibiting hormones, which inhibit the release of hormones from the anterior pituitary. The hypothalamus also makes antidiuretic hormone and oxytocin, but both are stored and released from the posterior pituitary.

The following table lists the major hormones and the glands that produce them. Unless marked with an asterisk, each of these hormones is a nonsteroid.

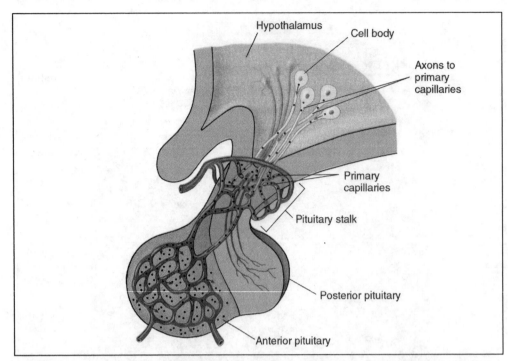

FIGURE 8-12 The hypothalamus and the pituitary gland. The hypothalamus produces regulatory hormones that travel to the pituitary gland. *Source:* From George B. Johnson, *The Living World,* 3rd ed., McGraw-Hill, 2003; reproduced with permission of The McGraw-Hill Companies.

Endocrine Structures and the Hormones That They Make (*Steroid Hormones)	
Endocrine Structure	**Hormones Made and Function**
Anterior pituitary	**Follicle-stimulating hormone (FSH):** in women, FSH stimulates the secretion of estrogen in the ovaries and assists in egg production via meiosis; in men, FSH has a role in sperm production.
	Luteinizing hormone (LH): in women, LH stimulates the production of estrogen and progesterone by the ovaries and causes ovulation; in men, LH is involved in testosterone secretion from the testes.
	Thyroid-stimulating hormone (TSH): stimulates the thyroid gland
	Growth hormone (GH): stimulates growth of muscle, bone, and cartilage
	Prolactin (PRL): stimulates the production of milk
	Adrenocorticotropic hormone (ACTH): stimulates the cortex of the adrenal glands
	Endorphins: act on the nervous system to reduce the perception of pain
Posterior pituitary (these hormones are made by the hypothalamus but are released by the posterior pituitary)	**Antidiuretic hormone (ADH):** allows for water retention by the kidneys and decreases urine volume; also known as vasopressin
	Oxytocin (OT): causes uterine contractions during childbirth; also stimulates milk ejection

171

CHAPTER 8:
Structure and
Function of the
Nervous and
Endocrine Systems
and Ways in Which
These Systems
Coordinate the
Organ Systems

Endocrine Structure	Hormones Made and Function
Pineal gland	**Melatonin:** influences patterned behaviors such as sleep, fertility, and aging
Thyroid gland	**Thyroid hormone (TH):** regulates metabolism throughout the body; also acts on the reproductive, nervous, muscular, and skeletal systems to promote normal functioning; T3 and T4 require iodine to function properly **Calcitonin (CT):** influences osteoblasts, which build bone in response to high blood calcium levels; ultimately lowers blood calcium levels
Parathyroid glands	**Parathyroid hormone (PTH):** influences osteoclasts, which break down bone in response to low blood calcium levels; this ultimately increases blood calcium levels; PTH is antagonist to CT
Adrenal medulla (inner portion of the adrenals)	**Epinephrine:** released in response to stress; causes fight-or-flight response; also known as adrenaline **Norepinephrine:** released in response to stress; causes fight-or-flight response; also known as noradrenaline

Adrenal cortex (outer portion of the adrenals)	**Glucocorticoids*:** help cells convert fats and proteins into molecules that can be used in cellular respiration to make ATP; high levels inhibit the inflammatory response of the immune system; examples are cortisol and cortisone
	    Mineralocorticoids*: increase sodium retention by the kidneys and potassium excretion; an example is aldosterone
	    Gonadocorticoids*: secreted in small amounts; examples are androgens and estrogens

Thymus	**Thymopoietin:** stimulates the maturation of certain white blood cells involved with the immune system (T cells); decreases with age as the thymus gland atrophies **Thymosin:** stimulates the maturation of certain white blood cells involved with the immune system; decreases with age as the thymus gland shrivels
Ovaries	**Estrogen*:** involved in the development of female secondary sex characteristics as well as follicle development and pregnancy **Progesterone*:** involved in uterine preparation and pregnancy
Testes	**Testosterone*:** a type of androgen needed for the production of sperm as well as for the development and maintenance of male secondary sex characteristics
Pancreas	**Insulin:** decreases blood sugar after meals by allowing glucose to enter cells to be used for cellular respiration; a lack of insulin or lack of response by cell receptors to insulin is the cause of diabetes mellitus; made by the beta islet cells **Glucagon:** increases blood sugar levels between meals by allowing for the breakdown of glycogen; antagonistic to insulin; made by the alpha islet cells
Heart	**Atrial natriuretic peptide (ANP):** made by the heart to lower blood pressure

(*Continued*)

Endocrine Structure	Hormones Made and Function
Kidneys	**Renin/angiotensin:** Used to regulate blood pressure by altering the amount of water retained by the kidneys **Erythropoietin (EPO):** stimulates the production of red blood cells from stem cells in the red bone marrow
Stomach	**Gastrin:** released when food enters the stomach; causes the secretion of gastric juice needed to begin the digestion of proteins
Small intestine	**Cholecystokinin (CCK):** stimulates the release of pancreatic digestive enzymes to the small intestine; also stimulates the release of bile from the gallbladder to the small intestine **Secretin:** stimulates the release of fluids from the pancreas and bile that are high in bicarbonate to neutralize the acids from the stomach
Placenta (temporary organ during pregnancy)	**Human chorionic gonadotropin (HCG):** signals the retention of the lining of the uterus (endometrium) during pregnancy **Relaxin:** used to release ligaments attaching the pubic bones to allow for more space during childbirth **Estrogen:** needed to maintain pregnancy **Progesterone:** needed to maintain pregnancy

Structure and Integrative Functions of the Main Organ Systems

INTEGUMENTARY SYSTEM

The **integumentary system**, or skin, is composed of a variety of specialized tissue types to meet its diverse functions. The skin has also been described as a membrane but, because it is made of two or more tissue types, it also qualifies as an organ. The skin serves as a protective barricade against abrasion and infection, it conserves water, eliminates wastes, synthesizes vitamin D, regulates temperature to maintain homeostasis, and relays sensory information to the central nervous system.

Structure of the Skin

The structure of the skin can be seen in Figure 9-1. There are two layers within the skin, each of which is composed of a variety of tissue types. In addition, there is an underlying layer, which provides support to the skin.

EPIDERMIS

The **epidermis** is a thin layer found on the surface of the body. It is composed of five layers of stratified squamous epithelial tissue, which is connected to the dermis via a basement membrane. Cells in the bottom (basal) layer of the epidermis constantly divide by mitosis to provide enough skin cells to replace those lost due to shedding. An overgrowth of epidermal cells causes calluses. Because the epidermis only contains epithelial tissues, there are no blood vessels present to provide O_2 and nutrients. These items must be provided from the dermis via diffusion.

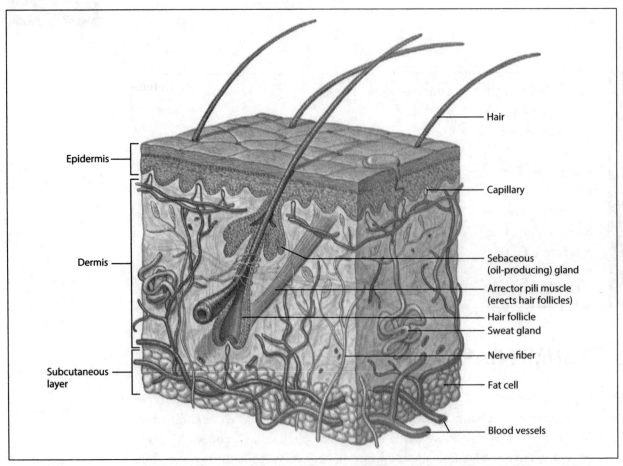

FIGURE 9-1 The skin is composed of a variety of tissue types and contains accessory structures in the form of glands, follicles, and hair. *Source:* From George B. Johnson, *The Living World*, 3rd ed., McGraw-Hill, 2003; reproduced with permission of The McGraw-Hill Companies.

175

CHAPTER 9:
Structure and
Integrative Functions
of the Main
Organ Systems

As cells move upward in the epidermis, they die due to lack of O_2 and nutrients. They are also filled with the waterproofing protein called keratin. The cells near the top of the epidermis are dead, keratinized cells that are relatively impenetrable to water. Nails are a specialized structure containing highly keratinized cells growing from a nail bed. They are used for protection at the ends of the extremities.

In the bottom layers of the epidermis, melanocytes are present. These cells make the protein melanin, which protects the cells from UV damage and provides the skin with pigmentation. Those with more melanin, and thus darker skin, have better protection against UV damage to the skin.

DERMIS

The **dermis** is much thicker than the epidermis. Its primary function is to support the epidermis and anchor it to deeper tissues. The main tissue type is relatively dense connective tissue containing collagen and elastic fibers. There is a good blood supply as well as many sensory neurons located within the dermis. There are also accessory structures found within the dermis:

➤ **Hair follicles and hair.** Hair follicles allow for the growth of hair. Hair itself is composed of dead, keratinized epidermal cells that are pushed up and out of the follicle. In mammals, hair is used to help regulate body temperature. Since humans lack significant amounts of hair on most of their body, it does not help with temperature regulation. Each hair follicle has attached to it a small arrector pili muscle, which can adjust the positioning of the hair follicle. In animals with a lot of hair, this raises the hair to help provide insulation around the body to conserve heat. In humans, the contraction of these muscles causes goosebumps. Since muscle contractions generate heat, the shivering that occurs due to rapid muscle contractions, including the arrector pili muscles, is a way to generate heat when the body is cold.

➤ **Sweat glands.** Sweat glands are used for dual purposes, including the cooling of the body by the evaporative action of water on the skin's surface, as well as the excretion of waste products such as urea and electrolytes in small concentrations. Some sweat glands secrete directly to the skin's surface, while others secrete into hair follicles. Sweat glands are under the control of the nervous system.

➤ **Sebaceous glands.** Each hair follicle is associated with a sebaceous (oil) gland. These glands secrete a fluid called sebum into the follicles to lubricate the follicle and the skin. In individuals that excrete excess sebum, bacteria may accumulate in the follicles, resulting in the inflammation characteristic of acne.

SUBCUTANEOUS LAYER

The subcutaneous layer is also known as the **hypodermis**, and it has the job of supporting the skin. It contains a large proportion of loose connective tissue as well as an excellent blood supply. The subcutaneous layer anchors the skin to tissues and muscle deeper within the body. It also serves as an insulator that helps with thermoregulation in the body due to the presence of adipose tissue also known as subcutaneous fat.

Because blood is warmer than body temperature, the patterns of circulation in the surface capillaries of the dermis and subcutaneous layer can be used to conserve or release heat as needed. During **vasoconstriction**, blood vessels constrict, keeping blood and heat near the body's core. During **vasodilation**, the blood vessels dilate, allowing some of the heat from the blood to escape through the surface of the skin.

MUSCULAR SYSTEM

Muscles provide structural support, help maintain body posture, regulate openings into the body, assist in thermoregulation via contractions (shivering) that generate heat, and contract to help move blood in the veins toward the heart, thus assisting in peripheral circulation. In Chapter 5, three types of muscle tissue were introduced. Skeletal muscle and cardiac muscle are striated, whereas smooth muscle is not. Cardiac and smooth muscle are involuntary, whereas skeletal muscle is under voluntary control.

Skeletal Muscle

Skeletal muscles are responsible for voluntary movement. The cells in skeletal muscle have multiple nuclei as the result of the fusing of multiple cells. The muscle cells also contain high levels of mitochondria to provide ATP needed for contraction and the protein myoglobin that acts as an O_2 reserve for muscles.

The fibers of skeletal muscle can be classified as fast-twitch or slow-twitch fibers. **Fast-twitch fibers** are designed for a fast rate of contraction, but they lack stamina and fatigue easily because their primary energy source is anaerobic cellular respiration. They have less myoglobin and mitochondria than slow-twitch cells. The **slow-twitch fibers** contain more mitochondria and more myoglobin, giving them longer endurance as they obtain most of their ATP from aerobic cellular respiration.

STRUCTURAL ORGANIZATION OF SKELETAL MUSCLE

Muscles are a bundle of muscle cells held together by connective tissue as seen in Figure 9-2. The muscle cells have **sarcoplasm** (cytoplasm), a modified endoplasmic reticulum called the **sarcoplasmic reticulum**, and a plasma membrane called the **sarcolemma**, which interacts with the nervous system via the **transverse tubule system** (T tubule). This system provides channels for ion flow through the muscle and has anchor points for sarcomeres.

Within the muscle cells are bundles of muscle fibers called **myofibrils** made of the proteins actin, troponin, tropomyosin, and myosin. **Actin fibers** have a thin diameter and associate with the proteins **troponin** and **tropomyosin** to produce thin

177

CHAPTER 9:
Structure and
Integrative Functions
of the Main
Organ Systems

filaments. **Myosin** fibers have a thick diameter with protruding heads and are called thick filaments.

In skeletal muscles, the actin and myosin fibers overlap each other in highly organized, repeating units called sarcomeres. The overlapping of the fibers is what causes striation of the muscle. The shortening of sarcomeres is what causes muscle contraction. The structure of a sarcomere can be seen in Figure 9-3.

The major regions of the sarcomere are as follows:

➤ **M line.** Marks the center of the sarcomere

➤ **Z line.** Separates one saromere from the next

➤ **H zone.** Area where only thick filaments are present; shortens during contraction

➤ **I band.** Area where only thin filaments are present; shortens during contraction

➤ **A band.** Area where thick and thin filaments overlap

Sliding Filament Model. Muscle tissues have regions where the sarcolemma is in contact (via a synapse) with the synaptic knobs of a motor neuron from the somatic

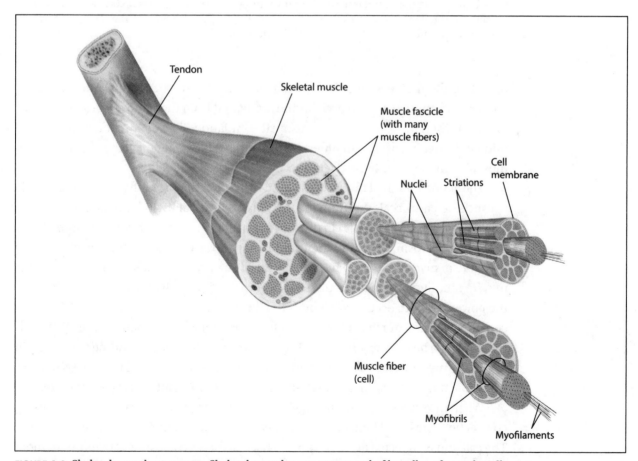

FIGURE 9-2 Skeletal muscle structure. Skeletal muscles are composed of bundles of muscle cells or fibers. Each fiber is composed of myofibrils, which are in turn composed of myofilaments. *Source:* From George B. Johnson, *The Living World*, 3rd ed., McGraw-Hill, 2003; reproduced with permission of The McGraw-Hill Companies.

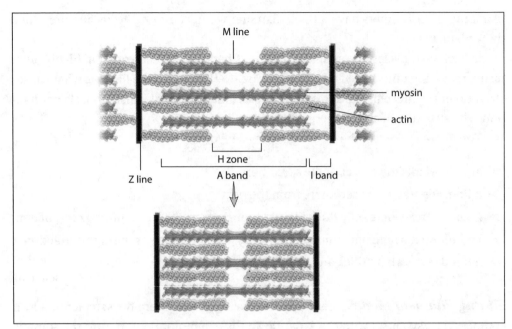

FIGURE 9-3 Sarcomere structure. Shortening of the sarcomere occurs when actin filaments move toward the center of the sarcomere. This shortening of the sarcomere is responsible for skeletal muscle contraction. *Source:* From Sylvia S. Mader, *Biology,* 8th ed., McGraw-Hill, 2004; reproduced with permission of The McGraw-Hill Companies.

branch of the peripheral nervous system. This area is the **neuromuscular junction**. A neurotransmitter called **acetylcholine** is released from the motor neuron and binds to receptors on the sarcolemma, causing the initiation of an action potential that will initiate shortening of the sarcomeres. The muscle fibers influenced by a single neuromuscular junction are termed a **motor unit**.

The action potential that occurs based on stimulation from the motor neuron will cause the release of calcium from the sarcoplasmic reticulum into the sarcoplasm. The calcium binds to the troponin in the thin filaments. This causes a conformational shift in the tropomyosin protein in the thin filament. This change in shape allows for the exposure of myosin binding sites on the actin. The myosin heads can now bind to the myosin binding sites on the actin, forming cross-bridges. Hydrolysis of ATP allows for the power stroke to occur, which pulls the thin filaments toward the center of the sarcomere. The release of the myosin heads from the actin occurs when another ATP binds to the myosin heads. Calcium is used again to expose the myosin binding sites on actin so that the myosin heads can bind and the power stroke can occur. The process repeats, each time pulling the thin filaments closer in toward the center of the sarcomere.

When the sarcolemma is no longer stimulated by the motor neuron, the process of contraction ends. ATP binds to myosin heads, causing them to dissociate from actin. The calcium is collected and transported back to the sarcoplasmic reticulum. Without calcium, the myosin binding sites are blocked by troponin and tropomyosin, and the sarcomere will return to its original length.

179

CHAPTER 9:
Structure and
Integrative Functions
of the Main
Organ Systems

Smooth Muscle

Smooth muscle can be found in multiple parts of the body, including the bladder, digestive tract, reproductive tracts, and surrounding blood vessels. Each cell in smooth muscle contains a single nucleus, as opposed to the multiple nuclei found in skeletal muscle. Smooth muscle contains actin and myosin, but it is not organized as sarcomeres, which is why smooth muscle lacks striations. The actin and myosin slide over each other. This sliding is regulated by calcium and requires energy provided by ATP.

The autonomic branch of the peripheral nervous system innervates smooth muscles via sympathetic and parasympathetic stimulation to produce involuntary contractions. The sympathetic response generally uses the neurotransmitters epinephrine (adrenaline) and norepinephrine (noradrenaline) to prepare the body for physical activity. The parasympathetic response, on the other hand, responds to acetylcholine and is used to return the body and muscles to a relaxation state. Smooth muscle can perform myogenic activity, meaning it can also contract without stimulation from the nervous system.

Cardiac Muscle

Cardiac muscle is only found in the myocardium of the heart. It is striated due to the presence of sarcomeres (which require calcium and ATP for contraction, just as in skeletal muscle) but is not multinucleated like skeletal muscle. A typical cardiac muscle cell has one, or possibly two, nuclei. Cardiac muscle is innervated by the autonomic branch of the peripheral nervous system. Like smooth muscle, it can also perform myogenic activity, contracting without stimulation from the nervous system.

SKELETAL SYSTEM

Skeletons can exist as **exoskeletons** found on the exterior of the body or **endoskeletons** found on the interior of the body. The disadvantage of an exoskeleton (found in many arthropods) is that it does not grow with the organism, making it necessary to shed the skeleton and produce a new one to accommodate growth. An endoskeleton is found in vertebrates, including fish, birds, and mammals.

The human endoskeleton, seen in Figure 9-4, is made of bone and associated cartilage. It is divided into two major parts: the axial skeleton and the appendicular skeleton. The **axial skeleton** is composed of the skull, vertebral column, sternum, and rib cage. The pelvic and shoulder girdles and limbs in the body are part of the **appendicular skeleton**.

The skeleton is used for protection of internal organs, support, storage of calcium and phosphates, production of blood cells, and movement. The skeleton itself is composed of bones and associated cartilage.

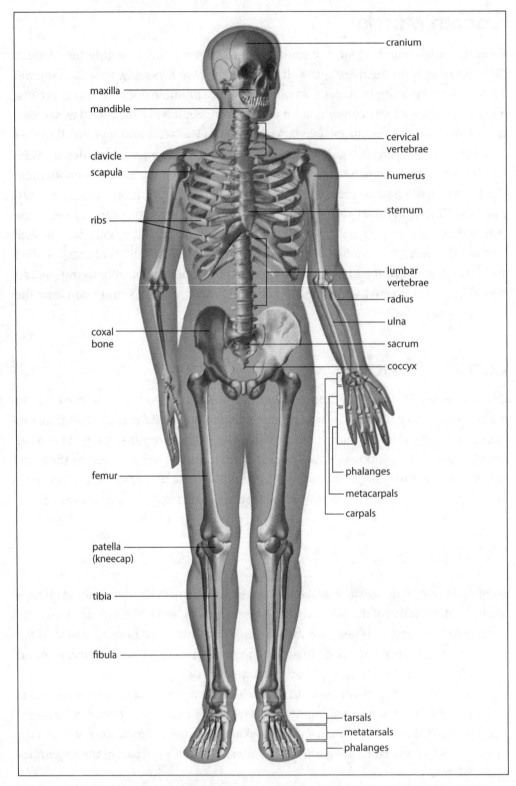

FIGURE 9-4 The human skeleton. The axial skeleton is composed of the skull, vertebral column, sternum, and ribs. The remaining bones in the body are part of the appendicular skeleton. *Source:* From Sylvia S. Mader, *Biology*, 8th ed., McGraw-Hill, 2004; reproduced with permission of The McGraw-Hill Companies.

181

CHAPTER 9:
Structure and
Integrative Functions
of the Main
Organ Systems

Cartilage Structure

Cartilage is a connective tissue. The matrix is termed **chondrin** and the primary cell type is the **chondrocyte**. During embryonic development, the skeleton begins as cartilage. During the developmental period, much of the cartilage is subject to **ossification**, where it is turned into bone by a calcification process. Only a small amount of cartilage remains in the adult skeleton, because most of it has been converted to bone. The primary areas where cartilage is found in the adult skeleton are the nose, ears, discs between vertebrae, rib cage, joints, and trachea. Cartilage is unique in that it contains no blood vessels, nor is it innervated.

Bone Structure

Bone tissue is found as compact bone and spongy bone. **Compact bone** is very dense, whereas **spongy bone** is less dense and contains marrow cavities. Within marrow cavities, there is yellow and red bone marrow. **Red bone marrow** contains the hematopoietic stem cells that differentiate into red blood cells, white blood cells, and platelets. **Yellow bone marrow** is primarily a reserve for adipose (fat) tissue.

Long bones within the body have a characteristic structure, as seen in Figure 9-5. The ends of the bone are typically covered in cartilage and are termed the **epiphyses**. The ends are made primarily of spongy bone covered in a thin layer of compact bone. The shaft of the bone, the **diaphysis**, is made of compact bone surrounding a marrow cavity. The **epiphyseal plate** is a disc of cartilage that separates the diaphysis from each epiphysis, and this is where bone lengthening and growth occur. The **periosteum** surrounds the bone in a fibrous sheath and acts as a site for the attachment of muscles via tendons.

The microscopic structure of bone consists of the **matrix**, which is found within **osteons** seen in Figure 9-6. Within each osteon, there is a **Haversian canal** that contains blood vessels, nerves, and lymphatic vessels. The canal is surrounded by lamellae, which are concentric circles of hard matrix. Within the matrix of the **lamellae**, there are small spaces called **lacunae**, where mature bone cells reside. Small bridges of **canaliculi** connect the lacunae within an osteon and merge into the Haversian canal in order to distribute nutrients and wastes.

Bone Cells

Within the bone, there are three major cell types: osteocytes, osteoblasts, and osteoclasts. The **osteocytes** are found within the lacunae of osteons. They are mature bone cells involved in the maintenance of bone tissue. Osteoblasts and ostoeclasts are found within bone tissue as well and are immature cells. Both are involved in the constant process of breaking down and building bone known as bone remodeling. **Osteoblasts** build bone by producing components of the matrix, whereas osteoclasts break down

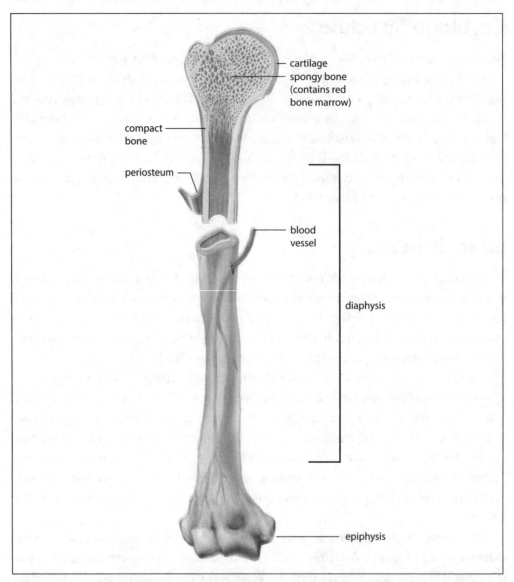

FIGURE 9-5 Long-bone structure. Spongy bone tissue contains red bone marrow and is located at the ends of long bones. The hollow marrow cavity located in the shaft of the bone contains yellow bone marrow. *Source:* From Sylvia S. Mader, *Biology*, 8th ed., McGraw-Hill, 2004; reproduced with permission of The McGraw-Hill Companies.

bone in the process of bone reabsorption. Eventually, osteoblasts and osteoclasts become trapped within matrix of bone tissue and become osteocytes. **Osteoblasts** are also responsible for bone growth and ossification during development. Ideally, the levels of matrix break down and building will be in equilibrium once growth is complete.

The hormone **calcitonin** from the thyroid gland and **parathyroid hormone** from the parathyroid glands are responsible for the process of bone remodeling. When blood calcium levels are high, calcium is stored in the matrix, thus building bone. When blood calcium levels are low, calcium is released from the matrix by breaking down bone

183

CHAPTER 9:
Structure and
Integrative Functions
of the Main
Organ Systems

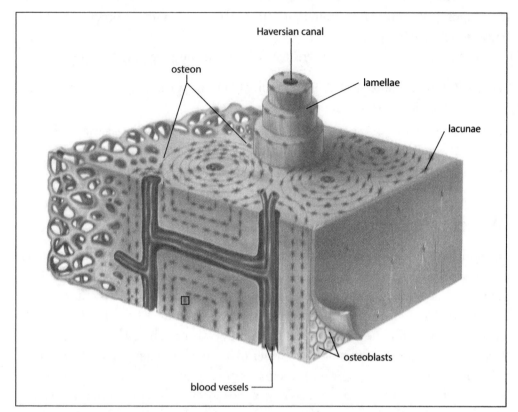

FIGURE 9-6 Bone tissue structure. *Source:* From Sylvia S. Mader, *Biology*, 8th ed., McGraw-Hill, 2004; reproduced with permission of The McGraw-Hill Companies.

tissues. The levels of blood calcium must be carefully regulated, as calcium is needed for muscle contraction, nervous system communication, and other functions.

Joints

Joints are areas where two bones meet and are composed of connective tissues.

Immovable joints such as those involved with skull bones do not move at all. **Partially movable joints** have some degree of flexibility, such as the vertebrae in the spinal column. **Synovial joints**, such as the hip or knee, have a much larger range of motion and have a fluid-filled joint cavity. **Ligaments** are made of dense connective tissue and attach one bone to another within a synovial joint.

CIRCULATORY SYSTEM

The **circulatory system** in humans consists of a four-chambered heart to pump blood and a series of vessels needed to transport blood in the body. **Blood** is a connective tissue used to deliver O_2, nutrients, water, hormones, and ions to all the cells of the body. It is also used to pick up the CO_2 and wastes produced by cells and to move these to the appropriate areas for elimination. Further, it assists in thermoregulation in the body as well as fighting infectious agents.

The circulatory system is closely linked to the following organ systems in the body:

➤ **Respiratory system.** For the elimination of CO_2, the pickup of O_2, and assistance regulating blood pH

➤ **Urinary system.** For the filtration of blood, removal of nitrogenous wastes, regulation of blood volume and pressure, and regulation of blood pH

➤ **Digestive system.** For the pickup of nutrients to be distributed to the body

Blood

The critical functions of the circulatory system are achieved by blood, which is transported through the system. Blood consists of a liquid matrix, plasma, and formed elements or cells. Humans contain between 4 and 6 liters of blood, and this entire volume can be circulated through the body in less than one minute. The pH of blood is 7.4 (slightly basic), and the temperature is slightly warmer than body temperature. Because the temperature of blood is warmer than the body, changing patterns of circulation can help distribute heat to where it is needed in the body. **Vasoconstriction** decreases the diameter of vessels, keeping blood closer to the core to warm the body, whereas **vasodilation** increases the diameter of the vessels, allowing them to release heat toward the surface of the skin to cool the body.

PLASMA

Plasma is the liquid portion of the blood, and it occupies approximately 55% of the total volume of blood. The primary component of plasma is water. In order to adjust the volume of blood in the body, the water levels of plasma can be altered. This is one role for the kidneys, which can retain or release water via urine to adjust the blood volume. An increase in blood volume increases blood pressure, while a decrease in blood volume decreases blood pressure.

In addition to water, plasma also contains nutrients, cellular waste products, respiratory gases, ions, hormones, and proteins. There are three classes of plasma proteins produced by the liver: immunoglobulins, albumins, and fibrinogen. **Immunoglobulins** are primarily used in the immune response, **albumins** are used to transport certain molecules within the blood, and **fibrinogen** is an inactive form of one protein needed to clot blood.

FORMED ELEMENTS

The formed elements, or cells, of the blood are all derived from **hematopoietic stem cells** in the bone marrow. The three types of cells found in the blood are erythrocytes (red blood cells), **leukocytes** (white blood cells), and **thrombocytes** (platelets), all seen in Figure 9-7.

185

CHAPTER 9:
Structure and
Integrative Functions
of the Main
Organ Systems

The **hematocrit value** of blood is a relative comparison of cell volume to plasma volume. The percentage of blood occupied by cells is considered the hematocrit value and is generally about 45. Because red blood cells are by far the most abundant blood cell, hematocrit values are primarily influenced by red blood cells.

Erythrocytes. **Erythrocytes** are the most abundant type of blood cell. As they mature from hematopoietic stem cells in the bone marrow due to the influence of the hormone **erythropoietin (EPO)**, they do something odd in that they lose their organelles. Without organelles, these cells are unable to perform aerobic cellular respiration and they cannot perform mitosis to replace themselves. These cells live only about 120 days, at which point they are destroyed by the liver and spleen. The end product of red blood cells' hemoglobin breakdown is **bilirubin**, which is ultimately excreted into the small intestine via bile from the liver.

In order to make new red blood cells, more hematopoietic stem cells in the bone marrow must be coerced to differentiate into red blood cells by the hormone EPO. Red blood cells also have an unusual biconcave disc shape that provides them with increased surface area and the ability to be flexible as they move through small vessels.

Transport of Gases. The critical component of erythrocytes is the protein **hemoglobin**. Each erythrocyte contains about 250 million hemoglobin molecules. Functional hemoglobin consists of four protein chains, each wrapped around an iron (heme) core.

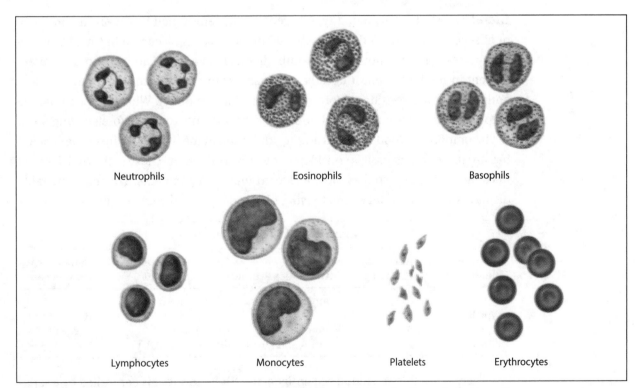

Neutrophils   Eosinophils   Basophils

Lymphocytes   Monocytes   Platelets   Erythrocytes

FIGURE 9-7 A comparison of blood cell types: red blood cells, white blood cells, and platelets all have different structures and functions. *Source:* From Eldon D. Enger, Frederick C. Ross, and David B. Bailey, *Concepts in Biology*, 11th ed., McGraw-Hill, 2005; reproduced with permission of The McGraw-Hill Companies.

A molecule of hemoglobin is capable of carrying four molecules of O_2. In total, a single red blood cell can carry about a billion O_2 molecules. The affinity of hemoglobin for O_2 is good; however, fetal hemoglobin has a higher affinity for O_2 than does adult hemoglobin. Further, the respiratory poison carbon monoxide (CO) has a much greater affinity for hemoglobin than does O_2. Carbon monoxide binds to hemoglobin at the expense of O_2, ultimately starving the cells of O_2.

As hemoglobin binds to one O_2 molecule, a conformational change in the shape of hemoglobin occurs to allow for the loading of the next three O_2 molecules. The same process occurs during the unloading of O_2. Once O_2 is unloaded in the capillary beds of the body, some of the CO_2 produced by the cells is carried by hemoglobin. CO_2 also combines with water to produce carbonic acid, which dissociates into hydrogen ions and bicarbonate ions. The hemoglobin carries the hydrogen ions whereas the bicarbonate ions are carried by plasma. The **Bohr effect** states that increasing concentrations of hydrogen ions (which decrease blood pH) and increasing concentrations of CO_2 will decrease hemoglobin's affinity for O_2. This allows for O_2 to unload from hemoglobin into tissues of the body, such as muscle, when CO_2 levels are high in tissues. In the lungs, a high level of O_2 encourages the dissociation of hydrogen ions from hemoglobin and these hydrogen ions will join with bicarbonate ions in the plasma to form CO_2 and water. The CO_2 is then exhaled. The enzyme carbonic anhydrase catalyzes the formation and disassociation of carbonic acid.

Blood Type. The ABO blood type is genetically determined based on the presence or absence of specific antigens on the red blood cells, as discussed in Chapter 3. The immune system does not produce antibodies against any self antigens (ones that are present in the body), but it does have the ability to produce antibodies against any antigens that are considered foreign (absent from the body). When an incompatible blood transfusion occurs, the antibodies in the recipient attack the foreign antigens of the incompatible blood type, causing agglutination of the blood. Because type O blood has no surface antigens, it is considered the universal donor. Those with type AB blood make no antibodies, so they are considered universal recipients. The following table displays some important characteristics of blood types and compatibilities.

Blood Types and Compatibilities				
Blood Type	Antigens Present	Antibodies Produced	Can Donate to Types	Can Receive from Types
Type A	A	anti-B	A, AB	A, O
Type B	B	anti-A	B, AB	B, O
Type AB	A and B	none	AB	A, B, AB, O
Type O	none	anti-A and anti-B	A, B, AB, O	O

There is another red blood cell antigen, the **Rh factor**, that is controlled by a separate gene. If the Rh factor is present, this is considered Rh^+ and no antibodies are made against the Rh factor. If the Rh factor is absent, this is considered Rh^- and anti-Rh antibodies can be made. Those that are Rh^+ can receive blood matched for ABO type

187

CHAPTER 9:
Structure and
Integrative Functions
of the Main
Organ Systems

that is Rh$^+$ or Rh$^-$. Those who are Rh$^-$ can only receive blood matched by ABO type and that is also Rh$^-$.

Leukocytes. **Leukocytes**, or white blood cells, are a diverse collection of cells, all of which are derived from stem cells in the red bone marrow and function throughout the body. They are found in much lower levels than red blood cells; however, the white blood cell level can fluctuate greatly, particularly when a person is fighting infection. Details of the specific types of white blood cells will be discussed later in this chapter with the immune system.

White blood cells can be categorized in the following manner and are distinguished based on their microscopic appearance:

➤ **Granulocytes** have cytoplasm with a granular appearance. These cells include **neutrophils**, **basophils**, and **eosinophils**. Neutrophils are used to perform phagocytosis. Basophils are involved in inflammation and allergies. Eosinophils are involved in dealing with parasitic infections.

➤ **Agranulocytes** have cytoplasm that does not have a grainy appearance. They include **monocytes**, which mature into **macrophages**, and **lymphocytes**, which are further subdivided into **T cells** and **B cells**. Monocytes and macrophages perform phagocytosis, whereas lymphocytes function in the adaptive defenses of the immune system.

Thrombocytes. **Thrombocytes**, or **platelets**, are fragments of bone marrow cells called megakaryocytes. Platelets live only 10 to 12 days once mature, so they are replaced often. During injury to blood vessels, a complex series of reactions is initiated, which ultimately converts the inactive plasma protein fibrinogen to fibrin. The platelets release **thromboplastin**, which converts the inactive plasma protein prothrombin to the active form, thrombin. **Thrombin** then converts fibrinogen to fibrin. **Fibrin** forms a meshwork around the injury that serves to trap other cells to form a clot. The process of blood clotting requires multiple plasma proteins as well as calcium and vitamin K.

Blood Vessels

Blood flow progresses in unidirectional loops as seen in Figure 9-8. One loop is the **systemic circuit**, which moves blood from the heart throughout the body and back to the heart. The other loop is the **pulmonary circuit**, which moves blood from the heart to the lungs and back to the heart. The blood flows in these loops through a series of vessels, the major ones being arteries and veins.

ARTERIES AND VEINS

Arteries are large blood vessels leaving the heart. The arteries have thick walls and are very elastic to accommodate blood pressure. As arteries leave the heart, they branch into smaller vessels called **arterioles**, which become more and more narrow, eventually forming the **capillaries**, which are the smallest vessels. Capillary beds are the site of gas exchange within tissues and are so small that red blood cells have to line up single file to pass through them. In the capillary beds O_2 is releases and CO_2 is picked up.

Once the gases have been exchanged, the capillaries become wider in diameter and become **venules**, which head back toward the heart. The venules become larger veins that ultimately merge into the heart. **Veins** are not as thick walled as arteries, because they do not have to deal with the forces exerted by blood pressure. Although blood pressure pushes blood through arteries and arterioles, the movement of blood in venules and veins is facilitated by smooth muscles that contract to push the blood along and by valves that close to prevent backflow of blood. Vasoconstriction and

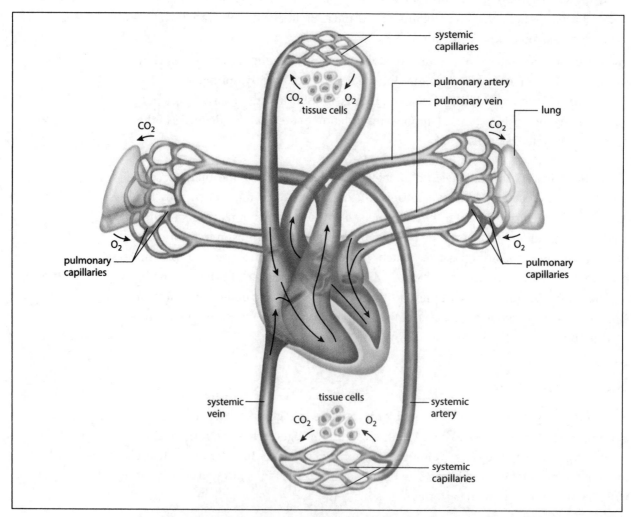

FIGURE 9-8 Blood flow through the body. The right side of the heart pumps blood to the lungs, where external respiration occurs, whereas the left side of the heart pumps blood to the body, where internal respiration occurs. *Source:* From Sylvia S. Mader, *Biology*, 8th ed., McGraw-Hill, 2004; reproduced with permission of The McGraw-Hill Companies.

189

CHAPTER 9:
Structure and
Integrative Functions
of the Main
Organ Systems

vasodilation of arteries serves as a means of regulating blood flow, blood pressure, and temperature.

The arteries of the systemic circuit branch off the left side of the heart and carry oxygenated blood to the capillaries of the body where gas exchange occurs. Deoxygenated blood returns to the right side of the heart via systemic veins. The pulmonary circuit involves pulmonary arteries that branch off the right side of the heart and carry deoxygenated blood toward the lungs. The pulmonary capillaries allow for gas exchange with the **alveoli** (air sacs) of the lungs. The newly oxygenated blood now moves back toward the left side of the heart via pulmonary veins.

CAPILLARY BEDS

A **capillary bed** is a collection of capillaries all branching off a single arteriole that serves a specific location in the body. The blood entering the systemic capillary bed is oxygenated and high in nutrients. As blood moves through the capillary bed, O_2 and nutrients diffuse out into tissues and CO_2 and wastes diffuse in. After this has happened, the capillaries merge into a venule, which carries the deoxygenated blood back toward the heart. In pulmonary circulation, deoxygenated blood enters the pulmonary capillary bed, where CO_2 diffuses out and O_2 diffuses in, causing oxygenation of the blood. **Precapillary sphincters** guard the entrance to the capillary beds.

The movement of materials into and out of the capillaries is based on pressure. Hydrostratic pressure on the arteriole end of the capillary bed pushes fluid containing O_2 and nutrients out of the capillaries. Most of the water that is pushed out must be reclaimed on the venule end of the capillary bed. Because the solute concentration in the capillaries is higher than the fluids surrounding them, osmosis draws the water back into the capillaries at the venule end of the capillary bed as CO_2 and wastes diffuse in. Any excess water that is not reclaimed will be returned to circulation by the lymphatic system. Some materials may enter or exit the capillaries via endocytosis or exocytosis.

Structure of the Heart

The structure of the heart can be seen in Figure 9-9. The **myometrium** is the cardiac muscle of the heart. Tissues other than muscle compose supporting structures such as valves and chamber linings. The right and left sides of the heart have very distinct functions and are kept separate from each other by the **septum**, which is a thick barricade between the two sides of the heart. Each side of the heart has two chambers. The upper chamber is the atrium and the lower chamber is the **ventricle**. The atrium and ventricle are separated by **atrioventricular (AV)** valves. **Semilunar valves** regulate the flow of blood out of the ventricles. A fluid-filled sac called the **pericardium** surrounds the entire heart.

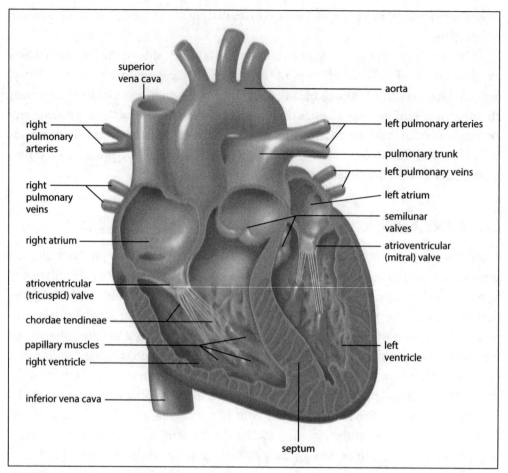

FIGURE 9-9 Heart structure. The venae cavae carries deoxygenated blood into the right side of the heart. The aorta carries oxygenated blood out of the left side of the heart. *Source:* From Sylvia S. Mader, *Biology,* 8th ed., McGraw-Hill, 2004; reproduced with permission of The McGraw-Hill Companies.

Blood Flow Through the Heart

Blood essentially flows in two loops, or circuits, within the body. The right side of the heart receives deoxygenated blood from the body and pumps this blood to the lungs to be oxygenated. The right side is considered the pulmonary circuit. The left side of the heart receives oxygenated blood from the lungs and pumps it to the body. This is the systemic circuit.

PULMONARY CIRCUIT

The pulmonary circuit begins when veins within the body eventually merge into the venae cavae, which lie on the dorsal wall of the thoracic and abdominal cavities. The **superior vena cava** comes from the head and neck, whereas the **inferior vena cava** comes from the lower extremities. These vessels carry deoxygenated blood and merge into the right atrium of the heart. As the atrium contracts, blood passes through an

AV valve (the tricuspid valve) into the right ventricle. As the ventricle contracts, blood passes through a semilunar valve (the pulmonary semilunar valve) into the pulmonary arteries. The **pulmonary arteries** carry blood to the lungs and are the only arteries in the body that do not carry oxygenated blood. They branch into capillaries that surround the alveoli (air sacs) in the lungs. Once gas exchange has occurred, pulmonary veins carry the oxygenated blood toward the left side of the heart into the systemic circuit. The pulmonary veins in the body are the only veins to carry oxygenated blood.

SYSTEMIC CIRCUIT

The oxygenated blood carried by the **pulmonary veins** enters the heart through the left atrium. As the atrium contracts (in sync with contraction of the right atrium), blood is pushed through another AV valve (the bicuspid valve) to the left ventricle. When the ventricle contracts (also in sync with the right ventricle), the blood is pushed into the aorta via a semilunar valve (the aortic semilunar valve). The **aorta** is the largest artery in the body, running along the dorsal wall of the body next to the inferior vena cava. The aorta splits into arteries, arterioles, and eventually capillaries where the blood is once again deoxygenated and must be pushed back to the right side of the heart to begin the process all over again.

The first branches off the aorta are the **coronary arteries**, which serve to provide circulation to the surface of the heart. Blockage of the coronary arteries can stop blood flow to the cardiac muscle, causing death of the cardiac muscle, which is characteristic of a heart attack. After blood flows through the coronary arteries, deoxygenated blood is returned to the right side of the heart by coronary veins.

Cardiac Cycle and Regulation of Heart Rate

During the cardiac cycle, the events of a single heartbeat, two contractions occur. First, the two atria contract simultaneously, pushing blood into the ventricles. Next, the two ventricles contract (systole), pushing blood out of the heart. A brief resting period (diastole) will occur to allow the two atria to refill with blood and then the cycle begins again. An **electrocardiogram (ECG)** can be used to visualize the electrical currents that are generated by the heart during the cardiac cycle.

Cardiac muscle is involuntary and has the ability to contract on its own without stimulation from the nervous system. The impulses that generate heart contraction are spread through the conducting system of the heart as seen in Figure 9-10. The **sinoatrial (SA) node**, also known as the pacemaker, is a bundle of conducting cells in the top of the right atrium that initiates contractions. The SA node sends electrical impulses through the two atria, causing them to contract. The impulse arrives at the **atrioventricular (AV) node** and then is spread through the **bundle of His** and through **Purkinje fibers** in the walls of the ventricles, causing ventricular contraction.

Although the SA node generates its own rate of contraction at an average of 70 contractions per minute, the heart is innervated by the autonomic nervous system, which

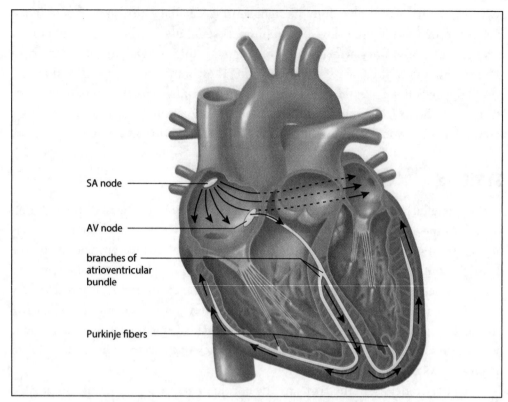

FIGURE 9-10 Conducting system of the heart. The SA node located in the right atrium serves as the pacemaker of the heart. *Source:* From Sylvia S. Mader, *Biology*, 8th ed., McGraw-Hill, 2004; reproduced with permission of The McGraw-Hill Companies.

can adjust the rate of contraction. The sympathetic branch of the autonomic nervous system can increase the rate of contraction, whereas the parasympathetic branch can decrease the rate of contraction. The medulla oblongata in the brain monitors conditions such as blood pH level (which is an indicator of CO_2 and O_2 levels) and signals adjustments in the heart rate as appropriate for the situation.

Blood Pressure

Blood pressure is a measurement of the force that blood exerts on the walls of a blood vessel. Typically it is measured within arteries. The pressure has to be enough to overcome the peripheral resistance of the arteries and arterioles. It is expressed with two values: a systolic pressure and a diastolic pressure. The systolic pressure is the higher value and is the pressure exerted on arteries as the ventricles contract. The diastolic pressure is the lower value and is a measurement of pressure on the arteries during ventricular relaxation. The primary means of regulation of blood pressure is by regulation of blood volume through the kidneys. The higher the blood volume, the higher the blood pressure is. A **sphygmomanometer** is used to measure blood pressure.

193

CHAPTER 9:
Structure and
Integrative Functions
of the Main
Organ Systems

RESPIRATORY SYSTEM

The respiratory system has the primary job of providing the body with O_2 and eliminating CO_2. Pulmonary arteries, which are low in O_2 and high in CO_2, come off the right side of the heart and carry deoxygenated blood to the lungs. These arteries branch off into capillaries surrounding the alveoli in the lungs. CO_2 diffuses from the pulmonary capillaries into the alveoli to be exhaled. O_2 that enters the lungs is distributed to hemoglobin in the erythrocytes within the capillaries. The newly oxygenated blood travels via pulmonary veins back to the left side of the heart, from which it is distributed throughout the body.

In addition to oxygenating blood, the respiratory structures are responsible for pH regulation, vocal communication, the sense of smell, and protection from infectious agents and particles.

Structure of the Respiratory System

The respiratory system is essentially a series of tubes that conducts air into the alveoli located in the lung tissues. The major structures of the system can be seen in Figure 9-11.

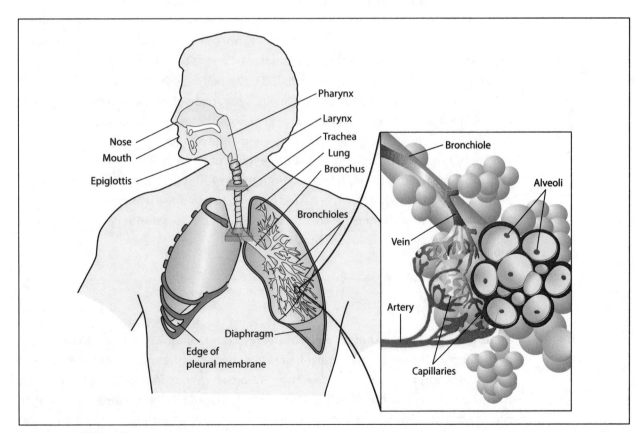

FIGURE 9-11 The respiratory system.

Air is inhaled through the nose or mouth. Because the respiratory system is an open system, it is particularly vulnerable to infection. In the nose and pharynx (back of the throat), air is warmed to body temperature, moisturized so that gas exchange can occur, and filtered. Both areas are covered with a mucus membrane that helps prevent desiccation of the tissues and collects particles and microbes that may enter the system. The nose is particularly well suited to filtration because it has cilia and hair to help trap substances that enter the respiratory system. Although filtration in the nose and pharynx does not catch all particles and microbes, it catches many of them. The nose has the additional function of olfaction.

Air that passes through the nose or mouth moves into the **pharynx**, where there are two passageways: the **esophagus** and the **larynx**. During breathing, air flows through the glottis, which is the opening of the larynx. The larynx is the voice box; it is made of cartilage and has vocal cords that vibrate, producing sound. Unless a person is swallowing, the esophagus is closed off and the glottis is open. However, if a person is swallowing, a small piece of cartilage called the **epiglottis** covers the glottis and stops food from entering the larynx.

As air flows through the larynx, it eventually makes its way into the trachea and the lower respiratory tract. The trachea is supported by C-shaped rings of cartilage. The interior surface of the trachea is covered with mucus and cilia to further trap any particles or microbes that may not have been caught in the nose or pharynx.

The trachea branches off toward the left and right into **bronchi**. The two bronchi branch into smaller and smaller tubes called **bronchioles**. Smooth muscles surrounding the bronchioles can adjust their diameter to meet O_2 demands. The bronchioles terminate in tiny air sacs called the **alveoli**. The alveoli are numerous to provide a large amount of surface area for gas exchange. They are made of simple **squamous epithelium** that allows for easy gas exchange with the capillaries that surround them.

The lungs are a collection of resilient tissue, encompassing the bronchioles and alveoli. In humans, the right lung has three lobes of tissue, whereas the left lung has only two lobes. A fluid-filled pleural membrane surrounds each lung. A surfactant fluid produced by the tissues decreases surface tension in the lungs, which keeps the alveoli inflated, preventing them from collapsing. Without surfactant to relieve surface tension, the lungs are unable to function.

Ventilation

Gas exchange within the lungs results from pressure gradients. To get air into the lungs, the volume of the chest cavity must increase to decrease pressure in the chest cavity. This allows air to flow from an area of more pressure (outside the body) to an area with less pressure (the chest cavity). This is the process of **inhalation** (or inspiration). It occurs when the diaphragm, the thin muscle that separates the thoracic cavity from the abdominal cavity, contracts and pushes down, as seen in Figure 9-12. The intercostal

195

CHAPTER 9:
Structure and
Integrative Functions
of the Main
Organ Systems

muscles of the rib cage also assist in inhalation by contracting to help move the rib cage up and out. When the diaphragm and intercostal muscles relax, the volume of the chest cavity decreases, which results in a higher level of pressure inside the chest cavity as compared to outside. This forces air to leave the lungs by the process of **exhalation** (expiration).

The control of ventilation rate is by the medulla oblongata of the brain. The diaphragm is innervated and neurally connected to the area of the medulla that controls breathing. The **inspiratory neurons** are active, causing contraction of the diaphragm, followed by a period of inactivity that allows for relaxation of the diaphragm and exhalation. In a relaxed state, the diaphragm is stimulated between 12 and 15 times per minute. During times of increased O_2 demand and excessive CO_2 production, this rate can increase significantly. Although it might be expected that O_2 levels are the primary influence on breathing rate, it turns out that the primary trigger is the CO_2 level, which is monitored by chemoreceptors located in the brain and in certain large blood vessels. As CO_2 levels increase, the pH decreases (due to carbonic acid), and the breathing rate increases to eliminate the excess CO_2. This, in turn, increases the O_2 levels.

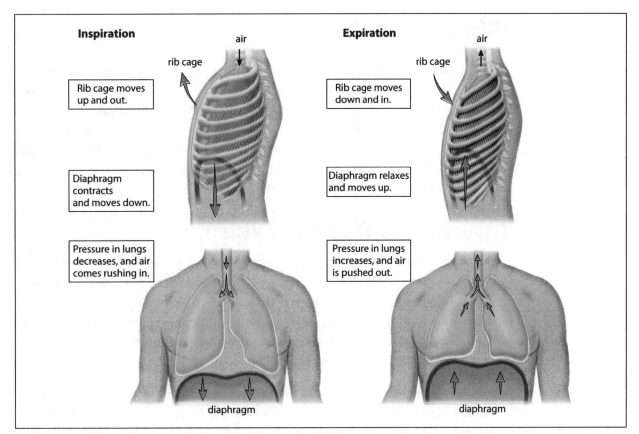

FIGURE 9-12 Ventilation. Contraction of the diaphragm allows for inspiration, whereas relaxation of the diaphragm allows for exhalation. *Source:* From Sylvia S. Mader, *Biology*, 8th ed., McGraw-Hill, 2004; reproduced with permission of The McGraw-Hill Companies.

GAS EXCHANGE

The concentration of gases can be measured as partial pressures. After an inhalation, the amount of O_2 or partial pressure of O_2 in the alveoli is greater than the amount of O_2 or partial pressure in the capillaries surrounding the alveoli. Gases flow from an area of high concentration (partial pressure) to an area of low concentration (partial pressure), so O_2 moves from the alveoli into the capillaries and there binds to hemoglobin. Further, immediately following inhalation, CO_2 levels are low in the alveoli and high in the capillaries. **Diffusion** moves the CO_2 into the alveoli where it can be exhaled. At this point, the blood in the pulmonary capillaries is oxygenated and ready to move back to the left side of the heart via pulmonary veins.

The role of CO_2 exchange is important in the maintenance of acid–base balance within the body. When CO_2 interacts with water, it forms carbonic acid. The carbonic acid is converted to bicarbonate ions and hydrogen ions, as described with the circulatory system. The bicarbonate ions help buffer pH in the body. When the pH of the body becomes too acidic, the reaction can be reversed. The bicarbonate and hydrogen ions join together to produce carbonic acid, which is then converted to water and CO_2. The CO_2 is exhaled in order to adjust pH.

DIGESTIVE SYSTEM

The digestive system is designed to extract nutrients from food and eliminate wastes. The three primary components of the diet that require digestion are **carbohydrates**, **proteins**, and **fats**. The digestive system has the following functions: mechanical digestion of food achieved by chewing, chemical digestion of food achieved by assorted digestive enzymes, absorption of nutrients into the bloodstream, and the elimination of waste products. The **gastrointestinal tract**, seen in Figure 9-13, is set up as a series of modified tubes to keep food and digestive enzymes sequestered from the body.

Tissues of the Digestive System

The contents of the system need to be kept away from the rest of the body for two major reasons. First, any contact of the digestive enzymes with the rest of the body could actually result in the digestion of self tissues. Second, the digestive system is an open system where infectious organisms can enter. To make sure that the components of the digestive system are kept separate from the rest of the body, the digestive tubes are composed of four tissue layers as follows:

➤ The **mucosa layer** is a mucus membrane that actually comes in contact with food. It serves as a lubricant and provides protection from desiccation, abrasion, and digestive enzymes. The mucosa lacks blood vessels and nerve endings.

➤ The **submucosa layer** is below the mucosa. It contains blood vessels, lymphatic vessels, and nerve endings. Its primary function is to support the mucosa and to transport materials to the bloodstream.

197

CHAPTER 9:
Structure and
Integrative Functions
of the Main
Organ Systems

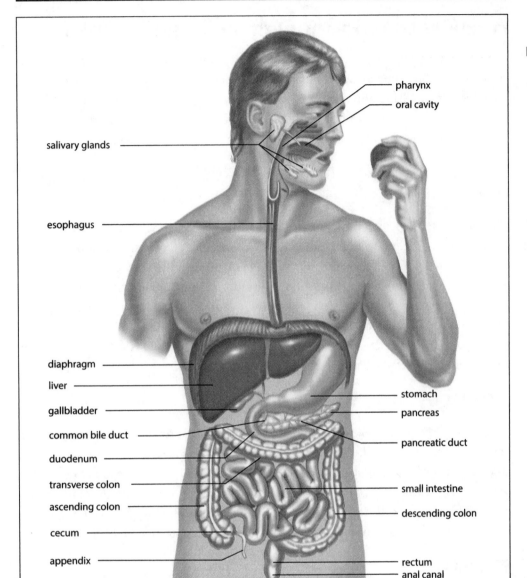

FIGURE 9-13 The digestive system. The digestive system includes the gastrointestinal tract as well as the accessory structures of the liver and pancreas. *Source:* From Sylvia S. Mader, *Biology*, 8th ed., McGraw-Hill, 2004; reproduced with permission of The McGraw-Hill Companies.

➤ The **muscularis layer** is composed of two layers of smooth muscle that run in opposing directions. The nerve endings in the submucosa serve to stimulate the muscularis layer to produce contractions that propel food through the system. The muscular contractions are termed **peristalsis**.

➤ The **serosa** is a thin connective tissue layer that is found on the surface of the digestive tubing. Its purpose is to reduce friction with other surfaces in contact with the gastrointestinal (GI) tract.

Pathway of Food Through the Digestive Tract

Food enters the digestive tract at the oral cavity. From there, it moves to the esophagus and then the stomach. Small bits of the stomach contents are released to the small intestine. The small intestine completes digestion with assistance from secretions from the liver and pancreas, and is the site where nutrients are absorbed into the bloodstream. Finally, the waste products of digestion are solidified in the large intestine and are released.

ORAL CAVITY

As food is ingested and enters the mouth, three sets of salivary glands begin to secrete saliva. The **teeth** are responsible for mechanical digestion of food by breaking it into smaller pieces by chewing. As **saliva** mixes with the chewed food, chemical (enzymatic) digestion begins. In addition to its lubricating function, saliva contains the digestive enzyme **amylase**, which begins the chemical breakdown of carbohydrates such as starch. Because food does not stay in the mouth for long, amylase rarely gets to complete its job in the oral cavity. During chewing, the food is rolled into a **bolus** (small ball) by the tongue and is ready to be swallowed.

ESOPHAGUS

As food is ready to be swallowed, it must pass by the pharynx. Recall that the pharynx has two openings: one to the larynx and one to the esophagus. Normally, the esophagus is closed during breathing so that air passes through the larynx. When food touches the pharynx, a reflex action occurs that pushes the epiglottis over to cover the glottis of the larynx. This allows for the bolus to proceed down the esophagus. Once in the esophagus, muscular contractions will force the food toward the stomach by peristalsis.

STOMACH

The stomach is a relatively small, curved organ when empty, but is capable of great expansion when full of food due to the presence of many folds in the interior lining of the stomach. The stomach is unique in that it has a very acidic environment, and its secretions must be retained in the stomach. Tightly closing muscular sphincters guard the top and bottom of the stomach, making sure secretions stay in the stomach.

The **cardiac sphincter** opens to allow the bolus to enter the stomach. Once food is inside the stomach, it is mixed with gastric juice for the purpose of liquefying the food as well as initiating the chemical digestion of proteins. The hormone **gastrin** signals the gastric glands of the stomach to begin producing gastric juice as well as to start churning.

Gastric juice is composed of a mixture of mucus to protect the stomach lining from being digested; pepsinogen, which is an inactive form of the enzyme that digests protein; and hydrochloric acid, which is needed to activate the pepsinogen to its active

199

CHAPTER 9:
Structure and
Integrative Functions
of the Main
Organ Systems

form called pepsin. The hydrochloric acid secreted in the stomach provides an overall pH of 1 to 2, which is highly acidic. Normally a pH this low would denature enzymes, but pepsin is unusual in that it is inactive except at a low pH. The low pH of the stomach is also helpful in killing most, but not all, infectious agents that may have entered the digestive tract with food.

After food mixes with gastric juice, the resulting liquid is called **chyme**. The chyme leaves the stomach in small bursts as the pyloric sphincter opens. Depending on the size and nutritional content of the meal, it takes on average about 4 hours for the stomach to empty its contents into the small intestine. Strangely, the only items that are absorbed into the bloodstream directly from the stomach are alcohol and aspirin.

SMALL INTESTINE

The small intestine is a tube of approximately 6 meters in length. Its primary job is to complete the chemical digestion of food and to absorb the nutrients into the bloodstream. The small intestine relies on secretions from the liver and pancreas to complete chemical digestion. As the pyloric sphincter of the stomach opens, small amounts of chyme enter the top region of the small intestine, which is termed the **duodenum**. The acidity from gastric juice must be neutralized. This is achieved by the secretion of sodium bicarbonate from the pancreas into the small intestine. In addition to receiving secretions made from the pancreas, the duodenum also receives secretions from the liver. These secretions help with chemical digestion, which occurs in the middle region of the small intestine termed the **jejunum** and the lower end of the small intestine termed the **ileum**.

Liver and Gallbladder. The **liver** is composed of several lobes of tissue and is one of the larger organs in the body. The liver has numerous functions within the body. In the case of the digestive system, the liver produces **bile**, which is a fat emulsifier. Although bile is not an enzyme, it helps break fats into smaller pieces so they are more susceptible to digestion by enzymes secreted from the pancreas. Bile contains water, cholesterol, bile pigments, bile salts, and some ions. Bile from the liver is stored in the **gallbladder**, a small structure on the underside of the liver. As food enters the small intestine, the hormones secretin and cholecystokinin (CCK) signal for the release of bile to the small intestine via the common bile duct.

The liver has some additional functions within the digestive system. Following the absorption of nutrients in the small intestine, blood from the capillaries in the small intestine will travel directly to the liver via the hepatic portal vein. Once in the liver, the glucose levels of the blood will be regulated. When blood glucose levels increase, the liver will store the excess as glycogen under the influence of insulin. When blood sugar levels are low, the liver will break down glycogen to release glucose under the influence of glucagon. The liver will also package lipids in lipoproteins to allow them to travel throughout the body. The smooth endoplasmic reticulum within the liver cells produces enzymes to detoxify certain harmful substances. The liver also stores vitamins A, E, D, and K (the fat-soluble vitamins). After these functions occur in the liver, blood reenters general circulation.

Pancreas. The **pancreas** secretes pancreatic juice into the small intestine via the pancreatic duct. Although the pancreas has cells involved in endocrine functions (producing insulin and glucagon), it also has exocrine cells that produce pancreatic juice. Signaled by the hormones secretin and CCK, the pancreas secretes pancreatic juice when food enters the small intestine. Pancreatic juice contains the following substances:

➤ **Bicarbonate ions.** Act as a neutralizer of stomach acid
➤ **Amylase.** Completes carbohydrate (starch) digestion that began in the oral cavity to release glucose
➤ **Proteinase.** Completes protein digestion that was started in the stomach to release amino acids. There are three specific proteinases found in pancreatic juice: trypsin, chymotrypsin, and carboxypeptidase.
➤ **Lipase.** Breaks down fats to fatty acids and glycerol
➤ **Nuclease.** Breaks down DNA and RNA to nucleotides

Absorption of Nutrients. Once the bile and pancreatic juice are mixed with the contents of the small intestine, chemical digestion is nearly complete. Although the pancreatic enzymes are most essential to chemical digestion, a few additional enzymes are needed. These enzymes are made by the small intestine and include

➤ **Maltase.** Breaks down the disaccharide maltose to glucose
➤ **Sucrase.** Breaks down the disaccharide sucrose to glucose and fructose
➤ **Lactase.** Breaks down the disaccharide lactose to glucose and galactose
➤ **Aminopeptidase.** Breaks down small pieces of proteins to amino acids

Once food has been exposed to the secretions of the pancreas, liver, and small intestine, chemical digestion is complete. Then the nutrients must be absorbed and the wastes eliminated. It can take anywhere from 3 to 10 hours for nutrients to be absorbed from the small intestine.

The small intestine has an internal anatomy with a tremendous surface area, making it well suited for absorption, as seen in Figure 9-14. The **mucosa** in the small intestine is folded into **villi**, which form the brush border. The villi are then further folded into microscopic **microvilli**. Within each villus, there are capillaries and a lacteal (a lymphatic capillary). Nutrients such as glucose and other simple sugars, amino acids, vitamins, and minerals diffuse into the capillaries within each villus. From there they are carried into the blood circulation. The products of fat digestion take another route. The fat products are assembled into a triglyceride and packaged in a special coating, including cholesterol, which creates a **chylomicron**. These structures cannot diffuse into

201

CHAPTER 9:
Structure and
Integrative Functions
of the Main
Organ Systems

capillaries, so they enter the lacteals. The lymphatic fluids deliver the chylomicrons to the bloodstream at the thoracic duct, which is a merger between the two systems.

LARGE INTESTINE

Now that the nutrients have been absorbed into the bloodstream, the remnants of digestion have made their way to the **large intestine**. Now water must be reclaimed by the body to solidify the waste products. These waste products are stored by the large intestine and released at the appropriate time. In addition, the large intestine contains a large and diverse population of normal flora or harmless resident microbes, all of which are part of the microbiome. Members of the microbiome are responsible for the synthesis of certain vitamins that the body needs. Additionally, certain changes to the microbiome are linked to various diseased states within the body.

The large intestine has a much larger girth than the small intestine, but its length is reduced. The large intestine is about 1.5 meters long. There are four regions within the large intestine:

➤ The **cecum** is a small area where the large intestine connects with the small intestine on the right side of the body. There is an outgrowth of this area that constitutes

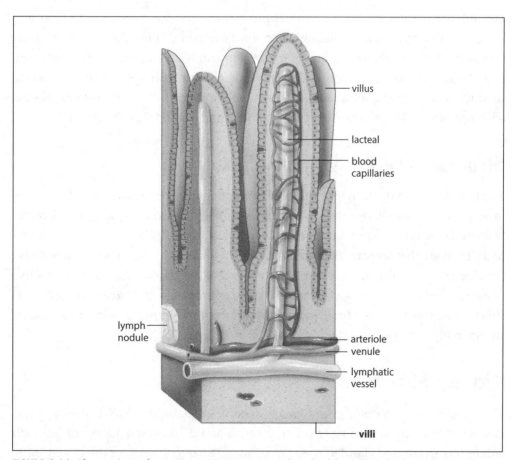

FIGURE 9-14 Absorption of nutrients. Nutrients are absorbed by villi, which are located in the small intestine. *Source:* From Sylvia S. Mader, *Biology*, 8th ed., McGraw-Hill, 2004; reproduced with permission of The McGraw-Hill Companies.

the appendix. The **appendix** has nothing to do with digestion, but it happens to be located within the digestive system. The appendix is a vestigial structure thought to play a noncrucial role in the lymphatic system.

➤ The **colon** constitutes the majority of the large intestine. The ascending colon moves up the right side, the transverse colon moves horizontally across the abdomen, and the descending colon runs down the left side of the body. The primary role of the colon is water absorption in order to solidify the feces. Vitamin absorption can also occur in the colon. It can take up to 24 hours for materials to pass through the colon.

➤ The **rectum** is the ultimate destination for feces in the large intestine. Stretching of this area stimulates nerves and initiates the defecation reflex.

➤ The **anal canal** receives the contents of the rectum for elimination. There are two sphincters regulating exit from the anal canal. The first internal sphincter operates involuntarily, and the second external sphincter is under voluntary control.

URINARY SYSTEM

The urinary system consists of the kidneys that produce urine, and supporting structures that store and eliminate urine from the body. The **kidneys** are the main excretory organs of the body; however, the skin can also act as an excretory organ. In addition to producing urine as a means of eliminating nitrogenous cellular waste products, the urinary system also regulates blood pressure by adjusting blood volume, adjusting blood pH, and regulating the osmotic concentrations of the blood.

Structures of the Urinary System

The two kidneys of the urinary system filter blood to produce urine. The urine moves toward the bladder via two **ureters**, which are tubes that connect each kidney to the bladder. Once urine moves into the bladder, it is stored until it eventually leaves the body through the **urethra**. The anatomy of the urethra is different in males and females. In males, the urethra is relatively long and is shared with the reproductive system so that sperm can move through it when appropriate. In females, the urethra is shorter, and it is only used for urine passage. The structures of the urinary system are shown in Figure 9-15.

Kidney Structure

The kidneys are located along the dorsal surface of the abdominal wall, above the waist, and are secured by several layers of connective tissue, including a layer of fat. Each kidney has an **adrenal gland** located on top of it. The outer region of the kidney is the **renal cortex**, the middle portion is the **renal medulla**, and the inner portion is the **renal pelvis**, as shown in Figure 9-16.

203

CHAPTER 9:
Structure and
Integrative Functions
of the Main
Organ Systems

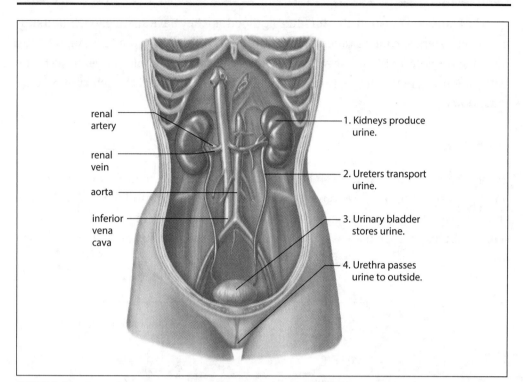

FIGURE 9-15 The urinary system. The kidneys produce urine, which is carried to the bladder by the ureters, where it is eliminated from the system. *Source:* From Sylvia S. Mader, *Biology*, 8th ed., McGraw-Hill, 2004; reproduced with permission of The McGraw-Hill Companies.

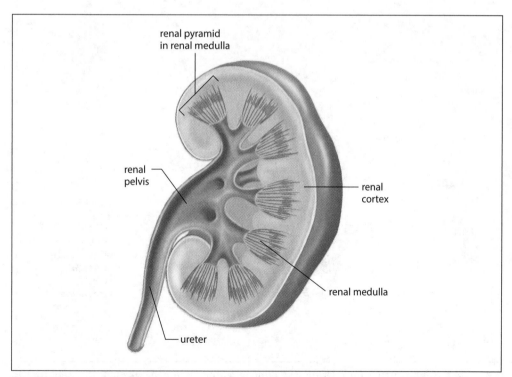

FIGURE 9-16 Kidney structure. Urine is produced in the nephrons of the kidney, which are found within the renal cortex and renal medulla. *Source:* From Sylvia S. Mader, *Biology*, 8th ed., McGraw-Hill, 2004; reproduced with permission of The McGraw-Hill Companies.

The kidneys are responsible for filtering blood, so they have an excellent blood supply. Renal arteries, which branch off the aorta, carry blood into the kidneys, whereas the renal veins carry blood away from the kidneys toward the inferior vena cava. The indentation where the ureter, renal artery, and renal vein attach to each kidney is the **renal hilus**.

NEPHRON

Within the renal medulla of each kidney, there are triangular chunks of tissue called renal pyramids. Within these renal pyramids and extending into the renal cortex are about one million nephrons per kidney. The nephrons, seen in Figure 9-17, are microscopic tubules that are the basic functional units of the kidney and actually produce urine.

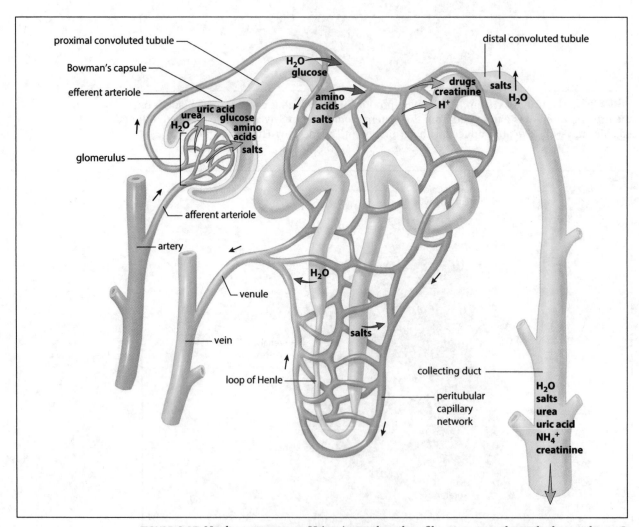

FIGURE 9-17 Nephron structure. Urine is produced as filtrate moves through the nephron. In reality, a nephron is twisted along itself, but for ease of viewing, the nephron shown here has been untwisted. *Source:* From Sylvia S. Mader, *Biology*, 8th ed., McGraw-Hill, 2004; reproduced with permission of The McGraw-Hill Companies.

205

**CHAPTER 9:
Structure and
Integrative Functions
of the Main
Organ Systems**

Each nephron is surrounded by a network of capillaries. Any items leaving the nephron are picked up by the capillaries and returned to the bloodstream. The regions of the nephron and their roles in the filtration of blood and production of urine are as follows:

➤ The renal corpuscle has two parts. The first is the **glomerulus**, which is a network of capillaries, and the second is the **Bowman's capsule**, which surrounds the glomerulus. There is no direct connection between the glomerulus and the Bowman's capsule; rather, there is a space between the two. **Afferent arterioles** carry blood into the glomerulus, where blood pressure pushes certain components of the blood into the Bowman's capsule. **Efferent arterioles** carry blood out of the glomerulus. Only blood components that are small in size enter the Bowman's capsule. This means that blood cells and plasma proteins should not enter the Bowman's capsule, whereas plasma components such as water, ions, small nutrients, nitrogenous wastes, gases, and others should enter the Bowman's capsule. The materials that enter the Bowman's capsule are referred to as **filtrate** and have approximately the same osmotic concentration as the plasma. Approximately 99% of filtrate that enters the nephron should be reabsorbed back into circulation. Any components remaining in the nephron once filtration and reabsorption are complete will be lost as urine and are much more concentrated than the plasma.

➤ The **proximal convoluted tubule** allows for the reabsorption of nutrients such as glucose and amino acids, water, salt, and ions. The majority of reabsorption occurs here.

➤ The **loop of Henle** also allows for reabsorption, primarily of salt (NaCl) and water by osmosis. A fairly complex countercurrent multiplier system is in effect in the loop of Henle. This area is a loop with a descending side and an ascending side that are located in close proximity to each other. Each limb of the loop has a different osmotic concentration. As salt is actively pumped out of the ascending limb, it creates a high osmotic pressure that draws water out of the descending limb via osmosis. Fresh filtrate then enters the loop of Henle, pushing the existing filtrate from the descending limb into the ascending limb. The process of pumping salt out of the ascending limb and the osmotic movement of water out of the descending limb is repeated several times.

➤ The **distal convoluted tubule** is where the fine-tuning of filtrate concentration begins. The activity of the distal convoluted tubule is regulated by hormones. The more water this section of the nephron reabsorbs, the more concentrated the urine becomes. The lower the urine volume, the higher the blood volume becomes.

➤ The **collecting duct** can be shared by several nephrons. The remaining urine empties into the collecting duct, where it moves toward the renal pelvis and ultimately into the ureters to be carried to the bladder. Hormones can be used in the collecting duct to allow for the reabsorption of more water, making the urine even more concentrated.

Regulation of Blood Volume and Pressure. Specific hormones regulate the fine-tuning of filtrate concentration and reabsorption of water, which, in turn, affect blood volume and pressure and the acid–base balance of the blood.

If **antidiuretic hormone (ADH)** is present, more water is reabsorbed in the distal convoluted tubule and the collecting duct of the nephrons. This increases the concentration of urine and decreases urine volume. If aldosterone is present, more salt is reabsorbed from the distal convoluted tubule and collecting ducts. Water follows the movement of salt by osmosis. This results in an increased concentration of filtrate and a decrease in urine volume. Both ADH and aldosterone have the same effects on filtrate concentration. By increasing water reabsorption, blood volume has been increased. The increase in blood volume is one way to increase blood pressure.

The secretion of ADH and aldosterone is regulated by renin produced by the kidneys. **Renin** secretion is triggered by low blood pressure in the afferent arterioles. Renin converts a protein made by the liver called angiotensin I into angiotensin II. Angiotensin II then triggers release of ADH by the posterior pituitary gland and aldosterone by the adrenal cortex.

Diuretics are substances that increase urine volume. Alcohol qualifies as a diuretic because it interferes with the activity of ADH. Caffeine is also a diuretic because it interferes with salt reabsorption and aldosterone's function. Large amounts of alcohol or caffeine have a noticeable effect by increasing urine volume. This in turn decreases blood volume and pressure.

One last hormone that alters nephron function is **ANP (atrial natiuretic peptide)**, which is secreted by the heart. When the heart stretches due to elevated blood pressure, ANP is released. ANP decreases water and salt reabsorption by the nephrons. This results in less concentrated urine, a higher urine volume, and a lower blood volume. The reduced blood volume means a decrease in blood pressure.

MAINTENANCE OF ACID–BASE BALANCE

As the kidneys filter blood, they also balance the pH of blood. Even a relatively minor change to blood pH can have drastic consequences, which is one of the reasons that kidney failure can be deadly. Luckily, dialysis methods are available to mimic normal kidney functions for patients whose kidneys do not work properly.

Recall that CO_2 interacts with water to produce **carbonic acid**. Carbonic acid can then dissociate into hydrogen ions and bicarbonate ions, both of which influence pH. The pH of blood can be adjusted by changing the amount of bicarbonate ions being reabsorbed and altering the amount of hydrogen ions being retained in the nephron. When the blood pH drops and becomes acidic, more bicarbonate ions return to circulation and hydrogen ions are released in urine, which gives urine an acidic pH.

PROPERTIES OF URINE

The substances remaining at the end of the collecting duct of the nephron constitute **urine**. Urine always contains water, ions (such as Ca^{++}, Cl^-, Na^+, and K^+), and

207

CHAPTER 9:
Structure and
Integrative Functions
of the Main
Organ Systems

nitrogenous wastes. Depending on the diet and function of other organs in the body, other components might be present in the urine. Because it was filtered directly from blood, the urine should be sterile. The presence of proteins, blood cells, or nutrients within the urine is considered abnormal.

The three primary nitrogenous wastes, all produced by cells, are as follows:

➤ **Urea.** As cells deaminate amino acids during protein metabolism, the resulting product is ammonia, which is highly toxic. The liver converts ammonia to a less toxic waste called urea. The kidneys will concentrate urea and release it via urine. Urea is the most abundant of nitrogenous waste products.

➤ **Uric acid.** During nucleic acid metabolism in the cell, uric acid is produced as a waste product.

➤ **Creatinine.** As muscle cells use creatine phosphate to produce ATP needed to fuel muscular contraction, creatinine is produced as a waste product.

Additional Functions of the Kidneys

In addition to their role in blood filtration and urine production, the kidneys have two additional jobs. First, the kidneys act to convert vitamin D from the diet into its active form that can be used by the cells. The kidneys are able to convert vitamin D to calcitriol, which helps the body absorb calcium and phosphorus. Second, the kidneys secrete the hormone erythropoietin (EPO), which is used to stimulate red blood cell production in the red bone marrow.

LYMPHATIC SYSTEM

The **lymphatic system** consists of a series of vessels running throughout the body, lymph, and lymphoid tissue as seen in Figure 9-18. The system serves to return fluids that were unclaimed at the capillary beds to the circulatory system, picks up chylomicrons from the digestive tract and returns them to circulation, transports proteins and large glycerides, and fights infection via leukocytes.

The vessels of the lymphatic system carry the fluid **lymph**, which is the same composition as plasma and interstitial fluid. Lymph moves through the vessels primarily due to the influence of muscular contractions that push lymph and valves that prevent the backflow of lymph.

The lymphoid tissues within the system are as follows:

➤ **Lymph nodes** are swellings along lymphatic vessels that contain macrophages for phagocytosis of pathogens and cancer cells and lymphocytes for immune defenses. The lymph is filtered through the nodes before moving on in the system. Clusters of lymph nodes exist in the neck, under the arms, and in the groin. Swelling of the lymph nodes is a sign of infection.

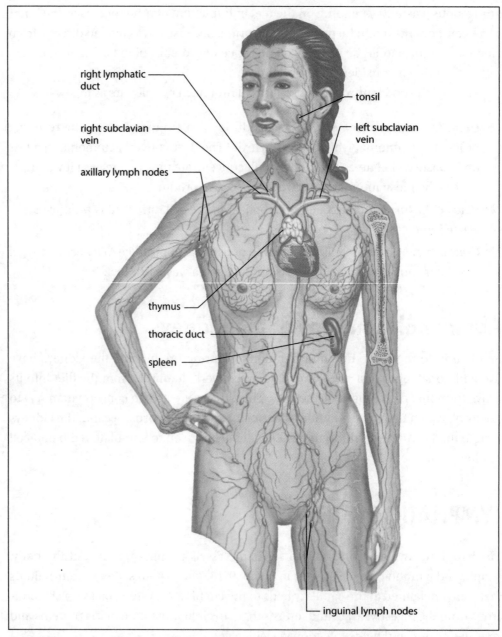

FIGURE 9-18 The lymphatic system is composed of vessels, lymph nodes, the tonsils, spleen, and thymus gland. *Source:* From Sylvia S. Mader, *Biology,* 8th ed., McGraw-Hill, 2004; reproduced with permission of The McGraw-Hill Companies.

➤ **Tonsils** resemble a lymph node in their ability to prevent infection by pathogenic organisms in the throat.

➤ **Peyer's patches** in the small intestine are clusters of lymphatic tissues that serve to prevent infectious organisms from crossing the intestinal wall into the abdomen.

➤ The **thymus gland** allows for the maturation of T cells, which are a form of lymphocytes needed for adaptive immune defenses.

209

CHAPTER 9:
Structure and
Integrative Functions
of the Main
Organ Systems

➤ The **spleen** is located on the left side of the body and acts as a blood filter. In addition, the spleen has an excellent blood supply and acts to destroy old red blood cells and platelets.

IMMUNE SYSTEM

The **immune system** exists anywhere white blood cells are found. This includes the blood, lymph, and within tissues of the body. The job of the immune system is to differentiate "self" cells from "non-self" (foreign cells) and to eliminate both foreign cells and abnormal self cells.

Immune defenses begin with nonspecific, or innate, responses that attempt to prevent foreign cells from entering the body and attack them if they do enter, and later, if needed, to move to specific, or adaptive, responses. An innate immune defense always works the same way, no matter what the offending invader, while adaptive immune defenses are activated and tailor-made to a specific invader.

Innate Defenses

Innate defenses come in several varieties. They are as follows:

➤ Physical and chemical barriers prevent foreign cells from entering the body. The skin is an example of a barrier that generally prevents infection. Mucous membranes provide another good barrier. Chemicals such as sweat, stomach acid, and lysozyme also generally prevent infection.

➤ Defensive leukocytes include macrophages (mature monocytes), polymorphonuclear neutrophils (PMNs), and dendritic cells, and are all capable of phagocytosis to destroy pathogens that may have entered the body. Eosinophils enzymatically destroy large pathogens such as parasitic worms that cannot be phagocytized. Finally, natural killer (NK) cells find self cells that have unusual membrane properties and destroy them. Cancerous cells are notorious for having altered cell membranes and are usually destroyed by NK cells.

➤ Defensive proteins are another category of innate defense. In the case of viral invaders, infected cells can secrete proteins called **interferons**. A virally infected cell releases these proteins as messengers to other cells that are yet to be infected. This limits the spread of the virus within the body. Interferons are not specific; they work against all types of viruses. The **complement system** is a series of multiple plasma proteins that are effective at killing bacteria by causing lysis of their cell membrane. The complement system also enhances phagocytosis within the area of invasion.

➤ When there is damage to tissues, the **inflammatory response** will initiate. It is characterized by redness (due to increased blood flow), heat (due to increased blood flow), swelling, and pain. Increased blood flow to the area is caused by the chemical histamine, which is secreted by basophils. This increased blood flow brings in other white blood cells, proteins, and other components needed to fight infection. Histamine makes capillaries more permeable than normal, and this, in turn, results in increased fluid in the area, which causes swelling. This swelling can put pressure on pain receptors, which causes the sensation of pain.

➤ When the body temperature is reset to a higher level by chemicals called pyrogens, **fever** is the result. Controlled fevers are beneficial as they increase metabolism and stimulate other immune defenses. When fevers get too high, they are dangerous and can cause the denaturing of critical enzymes needed to sustain life.

Adaptive Defenses

When innate defenses fail to control infection, adaptive defenses must be used. Because these are customized to the specific invader, they take at least a week to respond strongly to a new antigen. An antigen is a substance that elicits an immune response.

There are two types of adaptive defenses: **humoral immunity**, involving B lymphocytes, and **cellular immunity**, involving T lymphocytes. Lymphocytes are derived from stem cells in the red bone marrow. B cells complete their maturation in the bone marrow, while T cells mature in the thymus gland. Both types of cells are designed to ultimately destroy antigens, either directly or indirectly.

In humoral immunity, the B cells ultimately secrete antibodies to destroy foreign antigens. In cellular (or cell-mediated) immunity, T cells are used to directly destroy infected or cancerous cells. A specific variety of T cell known as the helper T cell is the key coordinator of both humoral and cellular responses.

HUMORAL IMMUNITY

Humoral immunity involves the production of specific antibody proteins from B cells that have been activated. Each B cell displays an antibody on its cell membrane, and each of the million or more B cells in the body has a different antibody on its membrane. The activation of a particular B cell by a specific antigen is based on shape recognition between the antibody on the B cell membrane and the antigen. The activation process is also dependent on cytokines from a helper T cell, specifically a T_H2 cell, which will be discussed in the next section.

The activation of a particular B cell causes proliferation of that B cell, leading to a population of plasma cells that actively secrete antibodies, and memory B cells that produce the same type of antibody. This is referred to as **clonal selection**, and it is the key event of the primary immune response, which leads to active immunity. It takes at least a week for this response to reach peak levels. Once antibodies are produced in

211

CHAPTER 9:
Structure and
Integrative Functions
of the Main
Organ Systems

large quantities by plasma cells, they circulate through blood, lymph, and tissues where they seek out their antigen and bind to it, forming a complex. Once an antibody binds to an antigen, the complex either is phagocytized or agglutinates and is later removed by phagocytic cells.

The primary immune response and active immunity can be achieved by natural exposure to an antigen or by vaccination. On secondary and subsequent exposures to the same antigen, the memory B cells that were created during the primary exposure can proliferate into plasma cells that produce antibodies, which provides a much faster response to the antigen. Although antibodies don't circulate for long once an antigen has been destroyed, memory B cells can last for years, if not forever.

Sometimes antibodies are passed from one person to another, which leads to passive immunity. This occurs during pregnancy, when maternal antibodies cross the placenta, and during breast-feeding. Breast milk contains antibodies that are transmitted to the newborn. Passive immunity can be induced by the injection of antibodies from one individual to another. Passive immunity is short-lived and declines within a few months.

Antibody Structure. An **antibody** consists of four protein chains bonded together. Two chains are identical heavy chains, and two chains are identical light chains. The structure of an antibody can be seen in Figure 9-19. Variable regions on the chains bind to the antigen, while constant regions on the chains assist in the destruction of the antigen.

There are five types of organizations of constant regions, which result in five different classes of antibodies (also called immunoglobulins): IgG, IgM, IgA, IgD, and IgE. The incredible diversity of antibodies produced by the immune system is based on a genetic recombination system that produces countless variable regions. The genes that produce the variable regions of antibodies are broken into segments that can be

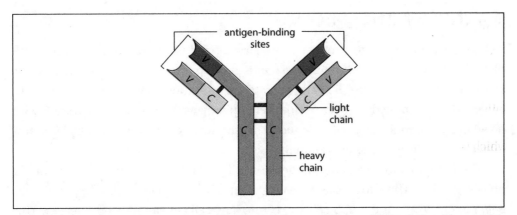

FIGURE 9-19 Antibody structure. Antibodies contain heavy chains and light chains. The variable regions of the antibody allow for antigen binding. *Source:* From Sylvia S. Mader, *Biology*, 8th ed., McGraw-Hill, 2004; reproduced with permission of The McGraw-Hill Companies.

arranged in variable orders during RNA splicing, which produce many variations of the variable region.

CELLULAR IMMUNITY

Cellular immunity is based on the actions of T cells, which come in several varieties. T cells have a cell membrane receptor that, like antibodies on the surface of B cells, recognizes the shape of one particular antigen. However, T cells cannot be directly activated by contact with the antigen.

T cells come in several varieties, two critical ones being $CD4^+$ helper T cells (T_H0) and $CD8^+$ cytotoxic T cells (T_C). The T_H0 cells are ultimately responsible for the activation of humoral and cellular immunity, but they must be presented with an antigen and appropriate cytokine signals in order to activate. Once activated, two populations are produced: T_H1 and T_H2. The T_H1 cells primarily interact with macrophages or dendritic cells when the body is dealing with cancer, viral infection, or intracellular bacterial infections (which are rare). The T_H1 population secretes pro-inflammatory cytokines and activates cell-mediated immunity by producing a population of T_C cells and natural killer (NK) cells that have the ability to seek and destroy cells bearing the foreign antigen. As with plasma cell activation, this primary response takes at least a week to occur. Memory T cells are also produced. Once all cells bearing the foreign antigen have been completely destroyed, regulatory T cells are used to stop the response. Only memory T cells remain, which can be quickly activated to T_C cells on secondary and subsequent exposures to the same antigen.

T_H2 cells primarily interact with B cells and involve the activation of humoral immunity when the body is dealing with extracellular issues such as bacterial infection. T_H2 cells produce anti-inflammatory cytokines and activate plasma cells, which will eventually produce antibodies as described in the previous section.

IMMUNODEFICIENCY DISORDERS

A variety of immune system problems are characterized as **immunodeficiencies**. These disorders occur when the immune system is lacking one or more component of its adaptive defenses. For example, severe combined immunodeficiency syndrome (SCID) occurs when an individual is born without lymphocytes. This renders the person with no adaptive immune defenses and quickly causes death unless the individual is maintained in a sterile, isolated environment.

The HIV virus induces immunodeficiency in an individual. It selectively infects helper T cells. When the virus activates after a latent period, the helper T cells begin to die. Without them, B cell and cytotoxic T cell activation is not present. This leads to an inability to mount humoral and cellular responses to antigens. This leads to acquired immunodeficiency syndrome (AIDS), which can eventually cause death due to an overwhelmed immune system.

213

CHAPTER 9:
Structure and
Integrative Functions
of the Main
Organ Systems

REPRODUCTIVE SYSTEMS

The female and male **reproductive systems** have a common function of producing gametes for sexual reproduction in the form of egg cells in females and sperm cells in males, both of which are produced by the gonads. The process of gamete production via meiosis has already been discussed in Chapter 7. In addition to producing gametes, the female reproductive system has the additional need to be structured to accept sperm from the male system and allow for embryonic and fetal development.

Female Reproductive System

The functions of the female reproductive system are carried out in special structures under the influence of a complex system of hormones that regulate the development of egg cells (oogenesis), their release from the ovary (ovarian cycle), and the preparation of the woman's body for embryo implantation and development (menstrual cycle).

STRUCTURE

The female reproductive system is enclosed within the abdominal cavity and is open to the external environment. Although having an opening to the outside environment is necessary for reproduction and childbirth, it presents some unique challenges in terms of the ability of pathogens to enter the system.

The structures of the female reproductive system consist of two **ovaries**, where egg production occurs, and supporting structures, as shown in Figure 9-20. After an egg is released from an ovary, it is swept into the **fallopian tube** (oviduct) that is associated with that ovary. If sperm are present and they meet with the egg in the fallopian tube, fertilization occurs. The fallopian tubes merge into the **uterus**, which is composed of a muscular myometrium and a vascularized lining called the **endometrium**. If the egg has been fertilized, the embryo implants into the endometrium, where development will continue. If fertilization has not occurred, the egg is lost with the shedding of the endometrium, which occurs about every 28 days during menstruation. The **vagina** serves as an entry point for sperm to enter the system, an exit point for menstrual fluids, and the birth canal during childbirth. The pH of the vagina is acidic, which can discourage the growth of certain pathogens. The **cervix** regulates the opening of the uterus into the vagina and is normally very narrow.

The external genitalia of the female system are known as the **vulva**. The **labia** are folds of skin that surround the opening to the vagina and occur as an outer and inner pair. The **clitoris** is located under the anterior portion of the inner labia. The clitoris has multiple nerve endings and is associated with female sexual arousal.

The breast tissue contains **mammary glands**, which serve the primary purpose of producing milk for a newborn. The tissue that surrounds the glands is fibrous connective tissue. The mammary glands are under the control of several hormones, including **estrogen**, **progesterone**, **oxytocin**, and **prolactin**.

MENSTRUAL CYCLE

The female reproductive cycle lasts about 28 days on average. Characteristic changes occur within the uterus that occur during this time. These changes are referred to as the menstrual (or uterine) cycle.

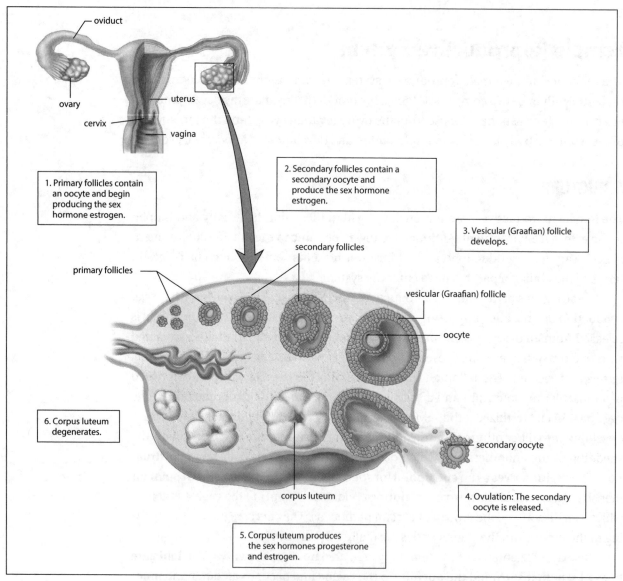

FIGURE 9-20 The female reproductive system. The ovaries release an egg into the fallopian tube during each reproductive cycle. Should the egg be fertilized, the resulting embryo implants in the uterus. *Source:* From Sylvia S. Mader, *Biology*, 8th ed., McGraw-Hill, 2004; reproduced with permission of The McGraw-Hill Companies.

215

CHAPTER 9:
Structure and
Integrative Functions
of the Main
Organ Systems

The menstrual cycle, which has three phases, is as follows:

➤ **Menses.** During the first 5 or so days of the cycle, the existing endometrium is lost via menstrual fluid as arteries serving the endometrium constrict, restricting the cells from O_2 and nutrient, resulting in tissue death.

➤ **The proliferative phase.** During the second week of the cycle, the primary event in the uterus is the proliferation of cells to replace the endometrium that was lost during menstruation.

➤ **The secretory phase.** During the last 2 weeks of the cycle, hormones are secreted to prepare the endometrium for implantation, if an embryo is present. As the 28th day of the cycle approaches, the endometrium deteriorates and menses will soon begin as the cycle restarts.

OVARIAN CYCLE

Eggs are produced through the ovarian cycle, whose timing must be carefully choreographed to the menstrual cycle, both of which can be seen in Figure 9-21. Like the menstrual cycle, the ovarian cycle also typically lasts 28 days.

The ovarian cycle consists of the following phases:

➤ **The pre-ovulatory phase.** This phase consists of the events prior to ovulation and lasts from days 1 to 13 of the cycle. This timing corresponds to menses and the proliferative phase of the menstrual cycle.

➤ **Ovulation.** The rupture of a follicle in the ovary and subsequent release of an egg to a fallopian tube constitutes ovulation. It typically occurs on day 14 of the cycle, although there is considerable individual variation.

➤ **The post-ovulatory phase.** During this phase, the egg may be fertilized. This part of the cycle typically lasts from days 15 to 28 and corresponds with the secretory phase of the menstrual cycle. Should fertilization occur, the embryo implants into the endometrium. If fertilization has not occurred, the menstrual cycle restarts, causing the egg to be lost.

Oogenesis. The events that lead to the maturation of an egg are termed **oogenesis** and are regulated through the ovarian cycle. Within the ovaries of a female, the process of meiosis has begun before she was ever born. This process results in the creation of primary follicles within the ovaries. A **follicle** consists of a potential egg cell surrounded by a shell of follicular cells to support the egg. The number of primary follicles is set at birth and is usually around 700,000. As the female is born and ages, many of these follicles die. By the time a female reaches puberty between ages 12 and 14, as few as 200,000 follicles remain. Although the number has drastically declined and continues to decline with age, there are still more than enough follicles to support the

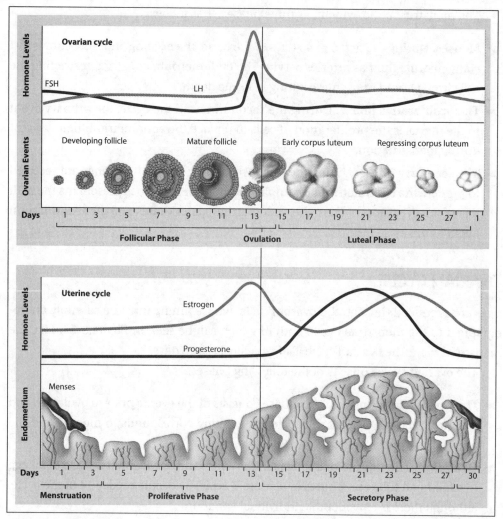

FIGURE 9-21 The female reproductive cycle. The control of the uterine cycle is achieved by estrogen and progesterone. The ovarian cycle is regulated primarily by follicle-stimulating hormone (FSH) and luteinizing hormone (LH). *Source:* From Sylvia S. Mader, *Biology*, 8th ed., McGraw-Hill, 2004; reproduced with permission of The McGraw-Hill Companies.

reproductive needs of a female, because only one egg is released every 28 days. Until puberty begins, these follicles stay in an arresting phase of meiosis.

After puberty, the **ovarian cycle** begins. During the pre-ovulatory phase, a few primary follicles resume meiosis and begin growing as primary oocytes. Starting at day 1 of the cycle, the anterior pituitary gland secretes **follicle-stimulating hormone (FSH)** and **luteinizing hormone (LH)**. Recall that the anterior pituitary is under the control of the hypothalamus. The hypothalamus produces **gonadotropin-releasing hormone (GnRH)**, which stimulates the release of FSH and LH. FSH causes the growth of several follicles, which begin to produce estrogen. The more the follicles grow, the more estrogen is produced. Estrogen levels are at their highest during the second week

217

CHAPTER 9:
Structure and
Integrative Functions
of the Main
Organ Systems

of the cycle, which corresponds to the rebuilding of the endometrium following menstruation.

During the second week of the cycle, the high levels of estrogen actually inhibit FSH such that no more follicles begin to grow on this cycle. As estrogen from the growing follicles continues to rise, there is a massive surge in LH. This surge causes the completion of the first round of meiosis, leading to the formation of a secondary oocyte and the rupture of the follicle within the ovary. This is ovulation, and it happens on day 14 of the cycle. The oocyte is released to the fallopian tubes, and the remnants of the follicle remain in the ovary.

If the oocyte is fertilized, meiosis II occurs, which results in a mature egg (ovum). Only one mature egg is needed during ovulation, so the remaining cells produced during meiosis are termed **polar bodies**. They are much smaller than the egg and are degraded. If more than one egg is released on a given cycle, the potential exists for multiple fertilizations and multiple embryos, resulting in fraternal twins or triplets.

The remains of the follicle in the ovary continue secreting estrogen and become the **corpus luteum**, which also secretes progesterone. The estrogen and progesterone suppress FSH and LH so that no more eggs are released in this cycle. These hormones also keep the endometrium prepared to receive an embryo during the secretory phase (third and fourth weeks) of the menstrual cycle.

At the end of the fourth week of the cycle, if an embryo has not implanted into the endometrium, the cycle restarts. At this point, the corpus luteum degrades. Without the corpus luteum, the levels of estrogen and progesterone decline. The lack of these hormones, particularly the lack of progesterone, is the cause of menstruation, which can occur only when these levels are low. Furthermore, the lack of estrogen and progesterone allows the pituitary gland to begin secreting FSH and LH again to initiate a new cycle.

The ability to perform the ovarian cycle ends at menopause, when the ovaries are no longer sensitive to FSH and LH. The levels of estrogen and progesterone in the body decrease and the ovaries atrophy. This typically occurs between the ages of 45 and 55.

Because estrogen and progesterone have the ability to suppress the actions of FSH and LH, they are the hormones of choice for use in birth control methods such as pills, patches, injections, rings, or implants. The use of synthetic estrogen and/or synthetic progesterone can be used to manipulate the ovaries into bypassing ovulating since FSH and LH are suppressed.

Male Reproductive System

In contrast to the female system, the male reproductive system is not housed completely within the abdominal cavity and is a closed system, which can be seen in

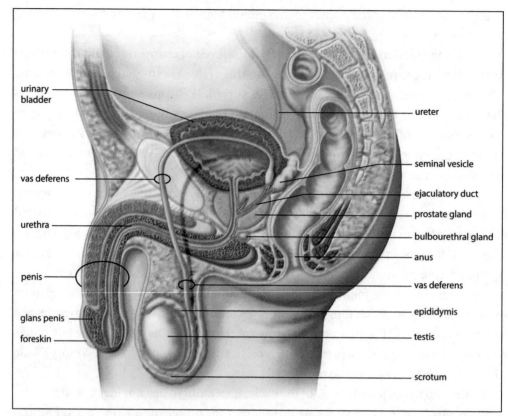

FIGURE 9-22 Sperm are produced in the testes of the male reproductive system. As sperm are released from the male system, secretions from a variety of glands are added to produce semen. *Source:* From Sylvia S. Mader, *Biology*, 8th ed., McGraw-Hill, 2004; reproduced with permission of The McGraw-Hill Companies.

Figure 9-22. The male gonads, or **testes**, produce **sperm**. The remaining reproductive structures serve as a means to transport sperm out of the body and into the female system.

Sperm begin their development in the **seminiferous tubules** of the testes, where they are nourished by **Sertoli cells**. The testes are housed in the scrotum outside of the abdominal cavity, where the temperature is a few degrees cooler than body temperature. Oddly enough, sperm require a temperature cooler than normal body temperature to become functional. As sperm develop in the testes, they move into the **epididymis** associated with each testis. Once in the epididymis, the sperm acquire motility and are stored.

When ejaculation occurs, the sperm must be moved toward the male urethra. The sperm enter the **vas deferens**, which are tubes that move up into the abdominal cavity. From there, the two vas deferens merge into the ejaculatory duct and into the urethra. Recall that the **urethra** is also used for urine passage. When sperm are moving through, the urethra is unavailable to the bladder. The urethra progresses through the length of the penis.

219

CHAPTER 9:
Structure and
Integrative Functions
of the Main
Organ Systems

Once in the urethra, three types of glands add their secretions to the sperm as they pass by. This creates **semen**, which is a mixture of sperm and secretions. The glands of the male reproductive system that provide secretions to semen are as follows:

➤ The **seminal vesicles** provide a fluid rich in nutrients to serve as an energy source for the sperm.

➤ The **prostate gland** wraps around the urethra and deposits a secretion that is alkaline to balance the acidic environment of the vagina.

➤ The **bulbourethral glands** secrete a fluid prior to ejaculation, which may serve to lubricate the urethra for sperm passage.

SPERMATOGENESIS

The process of **spermatogenesis** produces sperm through meiosis. Unlike meiosis in females that produces one egg and three polar bodies, meiosis in men results in the production of four sperm cells. While women need to release only one egg per reproductive cycle, men need millions of sperm per fertilization attempt. While the one egg produced in oogenesis is quite large, the sperm produced in spermatogenesis are quite small. This is because the egg cell must contain additional components needed to support embryonic development. Additional differences between spermatogenesis and oogenesis were presented in Chapter 7.

Spermatogenesis requires the hormonal influence of testosterone and begins at puberty. Testosterone is secreted during development to cause the development of male reproductive structures, but it is then halted until puberty. Diploid cells in the testes called **spermatogonia** differentiate into primary spermatocytes, which undergo meiosis I, producing two haploid secondary spermatocytes. The secondary spermatocytes undergo meiosis II to produce four mature sperm (spermatozoa). The spermatozoa then move to the epididymis to mature. The process takes between 2 and 3 months to complete.

Mature sperm structure can be seen in Figure 9-23. The acrosome contains digestive enzymes that are used to penetrate the egg, the head contains the nucleus that the sperm will contribute to the egg, and the tail is a flagellum that is propelled by ATP, which is produced by large numbers of mitochondria present in the sperm.

Some of the same hormones that are used in the female reproductive system are also used to regulate spermatogenesis. GnRH from the hypothalamus allows for the secretion of LH from the anterior pituitary. LH causes the production of testosterone by cells in the testes. The secretion of GnRH from the hypothalamus also results in the release of FSH from the anterior pituitary. While **testosterone** is needed to stimulate spermatogenesis, FSH is also needed to make the potential sperm cells sensitive to testosterone. The levels of testosterone regulate sperm production in a manner that resembles a thermostat.

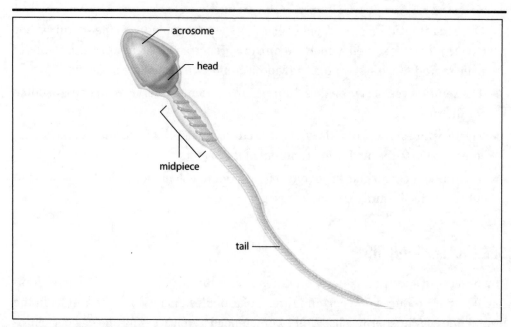

FIGURE 9-23 Sperm structure. The head of the sperm contains the nucleus, which is needed to fertilize an egg. *Source:* From Sylvia S. Mader, *Biology*, 8th ed., McGraw-Hill, 2004; reproduced with permission of The McGraw-Hill Companies.

Unit III Minitest

20 Questions   **30 Minutes**

This minitest is designed to assess your mastery of the content in Chapters 8 and 9 of this volume. The questions have been designed to simulate actual MCAT questions in terms of format and degree of difficulty. They are based on the content categories associated with Foundational Concept 3, which is the theme of this unit. They are also designed to test the scientific inquiry and reasoning skills that the test makers have identified as essential for success in medical school.

In this test, most of the questions are based on short passages that typically describe a laboratory experiment, a research study, or some similar process. There are also some questions that are not based on passages.

Use this test to measure your readiness for the actual MCAT. Try to answer all of the questions within the specified time limit. If you run out of time, you will know that you need to work on improving your pacing.

Complete answer explanations are provided at the end of the minitest. Pay particular attention to the answers for questions you got wrong or skipped. If necessary, go back and review the corresponding chapters or text sections in this unit.

Now turn the page and begin the Unit III Minitest.

Directions: *Choose the best answer to each of the following questions. Questions 1–4 are not based on a passage.*

1. Which of the following drugs might cause muscle spasms (uncontrolled contractions)?
    A. one that elevates calcium levels
    B. one that prevents the use of ATP
    C. one that elongates the sarcomere
    D. one that prevents attachment of myosin heads to actin

2. Diabetes insipidus is an inherited endocrine disorder that causes the kidneys to produce extreme amounts of urine per day that can severely dehydrate the individual with this condition. Management of this disorder involves hormone therapy. Which of the following is the missing hormone in a person with this disorder?
    A. antidiuretic hormone
    B. thyroid-stimulating hormone
    C. glucagon
    D. calcitonin

3. During pulmonary gas exchange, oxygen and carbon dioxide always move
    A. into the alveoli
    B. into the blood
    C. from high to low concentration
    D. out of the blood

4. The hypothalamus is part of the
    A. cerebrum
    B. brain stem
    C. diencephalon
    D. spinal cord

Questions 5–8 are based on the following passage.

Passage I

Guillain-Barré syndrome (GBS) is a rare condition characterized by destruction of the insulating myelin sheath on neurons located in the peripheral nervous system. Many people who develop GBS usually have it happen within days or weeks following recovery from a respiratory or gastrointestinal infection, but the reason GBS develops is uncertain. Others develop GBS following routine surgeries or vaccinations. GBS has been seen in people of all ages, and it affects men and women equally. The symptoms of GBS typically begin as tingling or weakness in the feet that can lead to paralysis that often ascends through the body. Most of the time, GBS is acute and lasts for a relatively brief period of time until remyelination of the peripheral nerves can occur. However, for some people, relapses are common and the condition can be chronic. Rarely, GBS can cause permanent paralysis and respiratory failure.

During GBS, the immune system produces antibodies to the surface antigens of peripheral myelin. These antibodies facilitate the destruction of the myelin, which leads to the neurological symptoms. While GBS does not have a treatment, procedures such as plasmapheresis, also known as plasma exchange, can be used as a means to alleviate the symptoms of GBS. During plasmapheresis, the blood is removed from the body and separated into cells and plasma. The plasma is discarded so that only the blood cells are returned to the body in donated or synthetic plasma. Another treatment option is the intravenous delivery of immunoglobulin. The antibodies present in the immunoglobulin may block the antibodies produced to the surface antigens of peripheral myelin. Typically, the symptoms of GBS subside within months of their onset when treatments such as plasmapheresis or immunoglobulin are used.

5. GBS affects the myelin of the peripheral nervous system. Which neurons in the body should NOT be affected by GBS?
    A. those in the arms and legs
    B. those in the abdominal cavity
    C. those that innervate the heart
    D. those in the spinal cord

6. GBS can eventually lead to muscle paralysis due to demyelination of peripheral nerves. The BEST explanation for this would be that
    A. the peripheral nerves can no longer conduct action potentials due to a lack of myelin
    B. the muscle cells no longer respond to acetylcholine at the neuromuscular junction
    C. the sodium-potassium pumps in the neurons are not functioning properly
    D. the brain is failing to send the appropriate signals to the peripheral nerves

7. Based on the information provided in the passage, GBS could BEST be described as
    A. a dominant genetic disorder
    B. a sex-linked genetic disorder
    C. an autoimmune disorder
    D. an infectious disease

8. Plasmapheresis seems to help many patients with GBS. The MOST reasonable explanation for why plasmapheresis would alleviate the symptoms of GBS would be that
    A. replacing the plasma would decrease the number of lymphocytes attacking myelin of the peripheral nerves
    B. there would be less of an attack on peripheral myelin when the antibodies against myelin are removed with the plasma
    C. replacing the plasma makes the immune system more capable of fighting the infections that are characteristic of GBS
    D. replacing the plasma would remove any toxins responsible for the symptoms

Questions 9–12 are based on the following passage.

Passage II

The thyroid gland is best known for its role in the regulation of metabolism via triiodothyronine (T3) and thyroxine (T4). Thyroid-stimulating hormone (TSH) is secreted by the pituitary gland in response to declining levels of T3 and T4. TSH activates the thyroid gland to release T3 and T4, which are stored as thyroglobulin (bound to protein). T3 is about five times more physiologically potent than T4. Thyroglobulin is enzymatically converted to T3, T4, and globulin, and T3 and T4 are released. T4 is converted in the liver to T3 and reverse T3 (RT3). About 80% of T3 comes from T4 conversion and the other 20% comes directly from the thyroid gland. Reverse T3 blocks the action of T3 and T4 by occupying T3 and T4 cell receptor sites.

A symptom of a thyroid hormone abnormality is the swelling of the thyroid that is referred to as a goiter, which can necessitate a portion or even all of the thyroid gland being surgically removed. After the surgery, synthetic hormones are given in an attempt to regulate the metabolism. Because the thyroid also deals with calcium homeostasis, complete removal of the thyroid can cause calcium levels to become extremely low.

The following data was collected from blood drawn to complete a thyroid panel on a patient suffering from a goiter:

	Patient Values	Expected Normal Values
Triiodothyronine (T3)	6.5 pg/mL	2.3–4.2 pg/mL
Thyroxine (T4)	14.2 μg/dL	4.5–12 μg/dL
Thyroid-stimulating hormone (TSH)	0.10 μIU/mL	0.35–2.5 μIU/L

9. Which conclusion is BEST supported by the data?
    A. This individual has hypothyroidism, which is caused by low levels of TSH.
    B. This individual has hypothyroidism, which is caused by abnormally low levels of thyroglobulin.
    C. This individual has hyperthyroidism, which is due to decreased levels of T3.
    D. This individual has hyperthyroidism, which is caused by elevated levels of T3.

10. After complete thyroid removal (which includes removal of the parathyroids), a patient's blood calcium becomes very low. Which of the following responses could potentially help increase calcium levels?
    A. activation of osteoclasts to degrade bone tissue
    B. activation of osteoblasts to build bone tissue
    C. taking synthetic calcitonin
    D. taking synthetic calcitonin in combination with parathyroid hormone

11. Hyperthyroidism can have multiple causes. All of the following endocrine structures could produce hormones that could potentially be involved with hyperthyroidism EXCEPT
    A. the hypothalamus
    B. the anterior pituitary gland
    C. the thyroid gland
    D. the adrenal glands

12. An individual is producing normal levels of T3 and T4, but they do not seem to be functioning properly. The MOST likely problem is a deficiency of
    A. calcium
    B. sodium
    C. potassium
    D. iodine

Questions 13–16 are based on the following passage.

Passage III

The process of induced erythrocythemia, or blood doping, has become common among certain circles of athletes such as cyclists. The purpose of blood doping is to provide an endurance advantage to the athlete. There are several ways to induce erythrocythemia, including the injection of synthetic oxygen carriers, blood transfusions, and the injection of hormones.

Synthetic oxygen carriers are modified proteins that have a relatively high affinity for oxygen. These can provide short-term increases in the oxygen-carrying ability of blood, but they are quickly degraded. Blood transfusions can be used right before an athletic event. The transfused erythrocytes can be homologous in nature, meaning that they are harvested from a donor's blood, or they can be autologous, meaning they are removed from the athlete 5 to 10 weeks before the event and stored. The cells are then reinfused right before an athletic event. Another approach to blood doping involves injections of the hormone erythropoietin (EPO). The EPO used for this purpose is a recombinant molecule. It is available by prescription for certain medical conditions, but it has been widely abused by some athletes.

Testing for blood doping is not always conclusive. For autologous or homologous transfusions, the only indicator of doping is an elevated hematocrit or hemoglobin count, which is not conclusive evidence of doping. If EPO is being used, it can be detected in the urine but only for short periods of time. Further, the recombinant version of EPO is hard to distinguish from the natural version, and certain other proteins present in the urine may resemble EPO.

13. What sort of benefit would blood doping provide an athlete?
    A. It would increase the number of white blood cells, making the athlete less likely to develop infections.
    B. It would increase the clotting ability of the athlete's blood, making the athlete less likely to lose large volumes of blood in the event of an injury.
    C. It would increase the number of red blood cells that can provide more oxygen to produce more ATP during aerobic cellular respiration.
    D. It would decrease the viscosity of the blood, making it easier for the heart to pump.

14. Some athletes prefer the use of autologous transfusions as compared to homologous transfusions. What would be a potential benefit of an autologous transfusion?
    A. It would provide more erythrocytes, since some of the ones from a homologous transfusion will die while the blood is in storage waiting to be infused.
    B. It would require longer-term advantages in athletic performance as compared to a homologous transfusion.
    C. It would make it easier to train more vigorously right after the blood was removed from the athlete.
    D. It would provide less risk of the transmission of diseases or transfusion reactions as compared to a homologous transfusion.

15. Erythropoietin can be a life-saving drug for patients with certain medical conditions. Which of the following conditions could MOST likely be helped by the injection of EPO?
    A. coronary artery disease
    B. hypotension
    C. renal failure
    D. anemia

16. If the autologous doping procedure requires the removal of cells from the athlete and later those cells are reinfused into that same person, how can this provide an advantage?
    A. The athlete has become used to functioning with fewer red blood cells after the removal, so the reinfusion provides an extra boost before a performance.
    B. The erythrocytes removed from the individual have been naturally replaced after the procedure, so the number of erythrocytes in circulation after the reinfusion is greatly increased.
    C. The reinfusion increases the ability for the cells to tolerate anaerobic respiration and lactic acid production for longer periods of time.
    D. The autologous procedure really does not provide any measurable benefits to the athlete.

Questions 17–20 are not based on a passage.

17. The hormone that is NOT released by the anterior pituitary gland is
    A. growth hormone
    B. antidiuretic hormone
    C. thyroid-stimulating hormone
    D. follicle-stimulating hormone

18. Curare is an arrow poison that binds to ACh (acetylcholine) receptors and prevents this neurotransmitter from exerting its usual physiological action. The likely effect of curare is
    A. diminished heart rate
    B. an increase in nerve conduction
    C. paralysis
    D. rapid breathing

19. Oxygen tensions in the alveoli (AL), the pulmonary artery (PA), and the pulmonary vein (PV) are all different. Given the dynamics of gas exchange in the lungs, the appropriate values of partial pressures for each of these three sites are
    A. AL: 40 mm Hg; PA: 160 mm Hg; PV: 100 mm Hg
    B. AL: 40 mm Hg; PA: 100 mm Hg; PV: 160 mm Hg
    C. AL: 100 mm Hg; PA: 40 mm Hg; PV: 160 mm Hg
    D. AL: 160 mm Hg, PA: 40 mm Hg; PV: 100 mm Hg

20. Venous blood coming from the head area in humans returns to the heart through the
    A. subclavian vein
    B. vein of Galen
    C. jugular vein
    D. superior vena cava

This is the end of the Unit III Minitest.

Unit III Minitest Answers and Explanations

1. **The correct answer is A.** During a muscle contraction, the sarcomeres contract as the result of myosin heads attaching to actin and pulling the fibers inward. In order for this to occur, ATP and calcium are required. If there were excessive amounts of calcium, you would expect more contractions to occur.

2. **The correct answer is A.** Of the hormones listed, the only one that is involved with water levels and the kidneys is antidiuretic hormone. The hormone increases water reabsorption in the nephrons, increasing blood volume and pressure, and decreasing urine volume. Thyroid-stimulating hormone acts on the thyroid gland to regulate metabolism. Glucagon stimulates the breakdown of glycogen to increase blood sugar levels. Calcitonin is used to decrease blood calcium levels and stimulate osteoblasts to build new bone matrix.

3. **The correct answer is C.** Pulmonary gas exchange is always based on simple diffusion. Diffusion allows for the movement of a substance from an area of high concentration of the substance to an area of low concentration of the substance. Depending on the concentrations, oxygen and carbon dioxide will move in variable directions. Choices A, B, and D indicate that the movement of gases always occurs in a fixed direction, which is incorrect.

4. **The correct answer is C.** The hypothalamus is located in the brain, which allows choice D to be eliminated immediately. The cerebrum is the largest portion of the brain that is divided into right and left hemispheres, which are connected by the corpus callosum. The processing of conscious thought and sensory information occurs in the cerebrum. The brain stem consists of the pons (connects the spinal cord to the cerebellum), medulla oblongata (reflex centers for vital functions), and reticular activating system (the activating system for the cerebrum). The hypothalamus and thalamus are both located in the diencephalon. The hypothalamus is involved in endocrine regulation as well as regulating conditions such as thirst and hunger.

5. **The correct answer is D.** This question is asking for a simple understanding of the structures of the peripheral nervous system as compared to the central nervous system. The central nervous system is composed of the brain and spinal cord, while the peripheral nervous system is composed of nerves outside of the brain and cord. Because GBS affects only the peripheral nervous system, the neurons in the central nervous system should be unaffected. Of the choices listed, the neurons of the arms and legs, abdominal cavity, and heart are all part of the peripheral nervous system and subject to GBS. The neurons of the spinal cord are part of the central nervous system and should be unaffected by GBS.

6. **The correct answer is** A. The myelin sheath is used to insulate the axons of neurons. Within the myelin sheath there are gaps, known as nodes of Ranvier, where the myelin is absent. Action potentials move down the axon and jump from one node to the next. When the myelin is removed, the gap from one node to the next becomes so large that the action potentials can no longer jump the gap. This means that the action potential never reaches the end of the neuron, and the message is not passed to other neurons. Choice A is most indicative of this problem. Choice B suggests that the problem is with the response of muscle cells to the neurotransmitter acetylcholine. If the action potential never reaches the end of the neuron, acetylcholine will not be released to the neuromuscular junction; therefore, the issue is not with the muscle cells' response. The sodium-potassium pumps are used to maintain resting potential in neurons, and there is nothing in the passage or question that would indicate that there is a problem with this. Because GBS is not a problem with the central nervous system, there would be no logical reason to assume that the problem is with the brain.

7. **The correct answer is** C. The passage described GBS as a disorder with unknown causes that leads to the production of antibodies from the immune system that attack the peripheral myelin. Because there was no pattern of inheritance stated and the disease is unpredictable in terms of who it strikes, there would be no reason to think this is a genetic condition. This allows choices A and B to be eliminated. The passage mentions that GBS can follow an infection in some but not all cases. No other evidence was provided to suggest that GBS is an infection. This leaves choice C as the best answer. Autoimmune diseases are characterized by an immune response to self-structures. Because the immune system is producing antibodies against the peripheral myelin, this would count as an autoimmune condition.

8. **The correct answer is** B. The passage described plasmapheresis as the separation of blood and plasma where the plasma is discarded and the blood cells are returned to the patient as donated or synthetic plasma. If this helps with the symptoms of GBS, this would indicate that something in the plasma is causing the problem. The passage indicated that antibodies against myelin cause the demyelination characteristic of GBS. Plasma cells secrete antibodies into fluids of the body, including plasma. By removing the plasma, the antibody concentration is decreased, leading to a reduced level of attack on peripheral myelin.

9. **The correct answer is D.** According to the data, TSH levels are low and T3 and T4 levels are elevated. Choice B suggests that the problem is related to thyroglobulin levels. Because this is not mentioned in the data, choice B can be eliminated. Choice C directly contradicts the data. The data show increased levels of T3 (when compared to expected values) and the choice indicates that T3 levels are decreased. The passage indicates an inverse relationship between TSH and T3/T4. When TSH is high, this is in response to low T3 and T4. When TSH is low, this is in response to high levels of T3 and T4. T3 and T4 directly regulate metabolism, so it makes sense that if their levels are elevated, metabolism increases. This is characteristic of hyperthyroidism. If T3 and T4 levels were decreased, metabolism should slow, indicating hypothyroidism. As a response to this condition, TSH levels would rise. Based on the data given, choice A should be eliminated because hypothyroidism would cause an increase in TSH levels. This leaves choice D as the only option. The elevated levels of T3 would be characteristic of hyperthyroidism.

10. **The correct answer is A.** To answer this question, you need to be familiar with mechanisms used in the body to maintain calcium homeostasis and bone cell action. The hormones calcitonin and parathyroid hormone both regulate blood calcium levels. Calcitonin, secreted by the thyroid gland, decreases blood calcium by storing excess calcium in bone matrix due to the activity of osteoblasts. Parathyroid hormone, secreted by the parathyroid glands located on top of the thyroid, is antagonistic to calcitonin and increases blood calcium levels. Osteoblasts are bone cells that build bone tissue when there is excess calcium. Their activity is regulated by calcitonin. When active, osteoblasts reduce blood calcium levels. Osteoclasts break down bone tissue and are regulated by parathyroid hormone. When active, osteoclasts increase blood calcium levels. If a patient has had his or her thyroid and parathyroids removed, it would be safe to assume that calcitonin and parathyroid levels would be decreased, making it difficult to regulate blood calcium levels. Choice B suggests that activating osteoblasts would help increase calcium levels. Because osteoblasts build bone and decrease blood calcium, this would actually further decrease the calcium levels in the blood. Taking synthetic calcitonin as suggested by choices C and D would only decrease calcium levels further as calcitonin activates osteoblasts. One potential solution to increase blood calcium levels would be to increase bone matrix breakdown as suggested by choice A. Osteoclasts are the bone cells responsible for this response.

11. **The correct answer is** D. This question relies on your knowledge of the endocrine system. The thyroid gland itself produces T3 and T4 that could be involved with hyperthyroidism, thus eliminating choice C. The thyroid is regulated by thyroid-stimulating hormone (TSH) secreted by the anterior pituitary gland, which eliminates choice B. The anterior pituitary gland is regulated by hormones from the hypothalamus, eliminating choice A. Therefore, the hypothalamus, anterior pituitary, and thyroid gland all could potentially have a role in a thyroid problem. The adrenal glands do not secrete any hormones related to thyroid function, making choice D the correct answer.

12. **The correct answer is** D. This question requires an understanding of the requirements of T3 and T4. Without a certain mineral, neither hormone can function properly. Both T3 and T4 require iodine from the diet to function.

13. **The correct answer is** C. The passage explains that blood doping is used to increase erythrocyte counts in the athlete. Since the function of erythrocytes and hemoglobin is to carry oxygen, it would be expected that an increase in red blood cell count would allow for more oxygen to be transported. This oxygen would be used for electron transport in aerobic cellular respiration, which produces ATP to be used by the athlete.

14. **The correct answer is** D. You know that autologous transfusions come from the athlete's own blood and homologous transfusions come from someone else's blood. Just as is the case with any type of transfusion, there can be problems with incompatibilities or with infectious agents that can be transmitted by infected tissues. Whether the blood transfusion is homologous or autologous, there would be no difference in the ability to carry oxygen by the erythrocytes that would provide an athletic advantage. Autologous transfusions would provide no more erythrocytes than a homologous transfusion. In fact, autologous transfusions often contain fewer cells.

15. **The correct answer is** D. EPO stimulates the cells of the bone marrow to differentiate into new red blood cells. Of the conditions listed, anemia is characterized by a low erythrocyte or hemoglobin count. In this case, additional EPO could stimulate the production of more erythrocytes to correct the condition. Coronary artery disease, hypotension, and renal failure are not associated with erythrocyte deficiencies.

16. **The correct answer is** B. Once the erythrocytes have been collected, the athlete has a low erythrocyte count. His or her own EPO is released to stimulate the production of new cells and return the erythrocyte count to normal within a few weeks (similar to what happens to anyone who donates blood). When the erythrocytes are reinfused in the athlete who already has a normal count, they now have extra erythrocytes that can carry more oxygen in the body and perhaps provide an athletic advantage.

17. **The correct answer is B.** The hormones released by the anterior pituitary gland include: growth hormone, prolactin, melanocyte-stimulating hormone, endorphins, enkephalins, thyroid-stimulating hormone, adrenocorticotropic hormone, follicle-stimulating hormone, and luteininzing hormone. The hormones released by the posterior pituitary gland include oxytocin and antidiuretic hormone.

18. **The correct answer is C.** Acetylcholine is a neurotransmitter found in both the central nervous system (CNS) and the peripheral nervous system (PNS). Because of its presence and function in the CNS and PNS, the impairment of acetylcholine as a direct result of curare exerts a devastating effect on the human body, that is, paralysis.

19. **The correct answer is D.** The pulmonary artery carries deoxygenated blood to the lungs. One would therefore expect it to have the lowest oxygen tension. Blood entering the capillaries around the alveoli from the pulmonary artery does, in fact, have a pO_2 of around 40 mm Hg. Not surprisingly, since it is the source of the O_2 used by the body, inspired air in the alveoli has the highest of the partial pressures, 160 mm Hg. By the time the blood has passed through the capillary beds around the alveoli and into the pulmonary vein, its pO_2 has been raised from 40 mm Hg to 100 mm Hg, which is also the average pO_2 of the air in the alveoli. So the correct values of partial pressures with the corresponding sites are AL: 160 mm Hg, PA: 40 mm Hg; PV: 100 mm Hg.

20. **The correct answer is D.** Veins are vessels that carry deoxygenated blood (with the exception of the pulmonary vein) from the systemic circulation to the heart. The subclavian veins, found underneath the clavicle or collarbone return blood from the arms to the heart. The jugular veins, found in the neck, drain blood from the head into the subclavian veins. The superior vena cava is the vein that directly returns blood into the right atrium of the heart. The vein of Galen drains blood from the deep parts of the brain.